Douglass and Lincoln

By the same authors

Sarah's Long Walk: The Free Blacks of Boston and How Their Struggle for Equality Changed America

By Stephen Kendrick

Night Watch: A Novel
Holy Clues

Douglass and Lincoln

*How a Revolutionary Black Leader
and a Reluctant Liberator
Struggled to End Slavery
and Save the Union*

PAUL KENDRICK AND
STEPHEN KENDRICK

WALKER & COMPANY
NEW YORK

Published by Walker Publishing Company, Inc., New York
Distributed to the trade by Macmillan

All papers used by Walker & Company are natural, recyclable products made from wood grown in well-managed forests. The manufacturing processes conform to the environmental regulations of the country of origin.

LIBRARY OF CONGRESS CATALOGING-IN-PUBLICATION DATA HAS BEEN APPLIED FOR.

ISBN-10: 0-8027-1523-0
ISBN-13: 978-0-8027-1523-4

Visit Walker & Company's Web site at www.walkerbooks.com

First U.S. edition 2008

1 3 5 7 9 10 8 6 4 2

Typeset by Westchester Book Group
Printed in the United States of America by Quebecor World Fairfield

For Moormans, Kendricks, and Gotliebs,
from Virginia to Ohio to California,
the Civil War until today.
To our family.

"I am to speak to you tonight of the civil war, by which this vast country—this continent is convulsed. The fate of the greatest of all Republics trembles in the balance...The lesson of the hour is written down in characters of blood and fire."

—Frederick Douglass

Contents

1865

The Mission

In the early April dusk of 1866, nearing the first anniversary of Abraham Lincoln's assassination, a large Springfield crowd filed into Representatives Hall of the imposing Illinois State Capitol building. In this great gallery a year earlier the president's rapidly blackening body had lain in state, with thousands of his fellow townspeople filing by to say goodbye. A few could still recall the day twenty-eight years earlier that the gangly young lawyer had ridden into town.

They were gathering on the anniversary to hear a lecture titled "The Assassination and Its Consequences," and it brought back more than just memories of Lincoln's funeral. In this vast room Lincoln had accepted the 1858 Republican Senate nomination, delivering his controversial "House Divided" speech; though losing that contest to his longtime rival Stephen Douglas, the obscure lawyer found himself unexpectedly propelled to the presidency. In this stately stone building, Lincoln had appeared over two hundred times before the state supreme court; had meticulously researched in the law library his Cooper Union speech; and had gone each evening to a relaxed men's club for political talk, tales, and conviviality.

Governor Richard Oglesby, an old friend of the late president, escorted the evening's presenter up to the speaker's desk. By coincidence, Oglesby had been in Washington on the last day of the president's life, dropping by the White House to chat with his exhausted but cheerful friend, who was clearly savoring the end of the brutal war. This night, before "a large audience, composed of the most intelligent, refined and cultured of our citizens," the governor introduced the speaker, renowned abolitionist orator Frederick Douglass. The Republican-leaning *Illinois State Journal* noted that in his introduction Oglesby "paid a well deserved need of praise to the colored race, whose devotion to our country in its hour of peril assisted in ridding our land of rebellion . . ."[1] The less enthused *Springfield Register* described the evening in different terms: "The radical negro party of this city are reduced to the desperate straights [sic] of importing the negro Douglass to bolster up their tottering party organization . . . This won't save you, gentlemen. Such men as Fred. Douglass . . . have ruined the country already."[2]

Douglass stepped forward and was "greeted with prolonged applause—a fitting tribute to a worthy man." Though he had been presenting his talk on Lincoln's assassination throughout the country for several months, standing where Lincoln spoke gave grave emphasis to his opening point that only great figures truly educated this world. "Prior to the Civil War there was apparently no danger menacing our country, but a few far seeing men foresaw the calamities that have come upon us, and their warnings were treated as idle talk . . . The few listen and the many pass on, unheeding the precipice over which they are being hurled." The speaker soon thundered in full flow, the packed crowd captivated in his spell. A highly experienced public orator, Frederick Douglass, by force of words fused to the impressive personal dignity in his majestic bearing, had transformed himself from the slave child Frederick Bailey into an internationally known figure who calmly claimed his place in the world. In his time, only fellow abolitionist Wendell Phillips equaled him as a speaker, but no other orator could compare to the redemptive power of the life story he embodied. His narrative was compelling for more than just his daring escape from slavery on the eastern shore of Maryland. Through years of dogged and at times extremely dangerous touring from town to town, by writing a bestselling personal testimony of his struggle to freedom, by editing one of the nation's most notable black newspapers, and finally, through his service as a recruiting agent for black soldiers, Frederick Douglass had become the voice of his people.

With his splendid mane of graying hair swept back from his broad forehead, blazing brown eyes, deep regal voice, and overwhelmingly powerful physical presence, Douglass awed white and black listeners alike. He had been a slave, yet in this commanding personal appeal, audiences had no trouble believing President Lincoln had invited this man to the White House. The personal meetings of Douglass and President Lincoln in Washington during the Civil War had represented a racial revolution in themselves, and Douglass reminded his audience of the stunning social impact of the conflict. He forcefully recalled, "Mr. Lincoln was a tall man—morally and intellectually, as well as physically—and like the high peak of a mountain, he caught the light of the coming dispensation . . . At the time of his death, slavery was abolished, and liberty established; and he who today argues in behalf of slavery or any of its

Frederick Douglass

horrid pretensions, stamps upon the grave of Abraham Lincoln." Douglass then added words more revealing than his listeners would ever know about the president he had dealt with: "He did not profess to be a Moses, and turn Pharaoh."[3]

While the president in his essential decency had never expressed the slightest temptation to "turn Pharaoh," the uncertain tides of war and the nation's deep reservoir of hatred toward Douglass's people threatened at every crisis to turn this unparalleled opportunity for a great Exodus into disaster. Lincoln had spoken truly of his personal convictions when he wrote: "If Slavery is not wrong, nothing is wrong."[4] But Lincoln had been born in the slave state of Kentucky and had married into the slave-owning Todd family of Lexington. His only truly intimate friend, Joshua Speed, had returned to Kentucky after his Springfield days to oversee a slave plantation. Further, Lincoln had been nurtured in "Free Soil" Illinois with its fervent antiblack laws and had long been an open and steadfast opponent to radical abolitionism. It was not surprising that this man had been a reluctant liberator.

The intent of Douglass's talk was not to dwell in that past, but to confront new realities facing a victorious North and a world without Lincoln, struck down by "the crime of all crimes, the sum of all villainies." This speech was not marked by triumph, but rather by a looming menace that all the gains of the Civil War might be surrendered. "The danger impending over us is the cold, cruel wanton surrender and betrayal of our friends and allies,"[5] cried Douglass, referring to the many thousands of slaves who streamed into Union lines as "contraband," the men and women who had picked the crops, cooked the food, and fed valuable information to the army, and most of all, the 180,000 black soldiers at last granted the right to carry a musket. One in ten Union soldiers who had served was black, and Lincoln, before his death, rightly noted that these men had provided the deciding edge of victory.

Though he did not say so that night, Douglass had spent the last four years engaged in a long and public contest with a president who was slow to emancipate, reluctant to put black soldiers into battle, and at his death had made no firm commitment to give the vote to the black man, except possibly perhaps for "the very intelligent, and . . . those who serve our cause as soldiers."[6] All these struggles between the two men were set aside by Douglass this night.

When it had counted, at critical twists and turns of the war, Lincoln, in fact, had become an effective collaborator in Douglass's decades-long pursuit of the total and irrevocable destruction of slavery. The odds of this black abolitionist agitator and a cautious prairie lawyer ever meeting—much less profoundly influencing each other as allies—seemed unlikely. Yet the violent lessons of the war had drawn them together in what Douglass in 1862 called "characters of blood and fire."[7] A strange partnership even in their own time, in the midst of deep and weighty disagreements, they managed to forge a strong mutual understanding and respect. In the end, Douglass's understanding of the meaning of this war and his personal mission—the liberation of black Americans—was to be inescapably bound up in the life, and the death, of the paradoxical and enigmatic President Lincoln.

Lincoln's mission was to save the Union, while Douglass's mission was different and two-pronged: emancipation through this conflict and then equality in the future. The latter quest speaks with particular power and relevance through the years. At the heart of Douglass's message was the belief that the nation must confront the interconnectedness of black and white. Many, including Lincoln, had tried to evade this reality. Douglass understood that the Union itself would not survive without the monumental contribution of African-Americans, though their rightful place in the country would not be secured until white Americans respected their rights and allowed them opportunities within the lifeblood of the nation. Douglass prophesied that for a nation to be redeemed, we would need each other, then and now. Lincoln needed the black soldier to win his war; Douglass needed Lincoln to win his people's freedom; and in the end, they needed each other to move the nation forward. Their relationship, their struggle, tells us much about ourselves as a people and about why the failure to fully achieve Douglass's vision of equality means our Civil War is not yet over.

It is a remarkable fact that by 1950 Frederick Douglass was a nearly forgotten man, except perhaps for schoolchildren still encouraged to read his first and briefest autobiography. When the historian Philip Foner transcribed hundreds of pages of forgotten speeches and long-scattered letters in the late 1940s, certain that Douglass was a missing key figure in our history, to his astonishment, "No commercial publisher or even university press displayed the slightest interest in making available the letters, editorials, and speeches of this man of towering dimensions."[8] Finally, a small radical press consented to publish them. The power of Douglass's voice, once again in circulation, served to spark a considerable reevaluation and renewal of interest in Douglass and his world of radical abolitionism.

The Civil War has often been called America's *Iliad*, but it has not been noted enough that we are still engaged in writing it. Frederick Douglass is a relatively new player in the Lincoln saga, and the reason for this is relatively simple: Lincoln, as the Great Emancipator, has always been portrayed as the sole wise and benevolent actor in the great drama of the Civil War. With cumulative force, early Lincoln biographers presented a man bedeviled by fierce and unrelenting Radical Republicans and obsessive abolitionists, whose fanaticism helped push the nation into an "unnecessary war." As the new president came to power, the nation stumbled almost heedlessly into a needless sectional war over slavery. Both sides of this great and tragic conflict fought nobly and with great courage, "brother against brother." It was a simple narrative, and since it possessed so many reassuring elements, it long constituted a compelling and comfortable story that stood the test of many generations.

The silence in those earlier biographies about the role of Douglass in the Civil War era reflected an oddity that historians of the last forty years have had to struggle with: how could one accurately tell the story of the Civil War without referring to 180,000 black troops in the Union army, or to the tidal wave of black people who freed themselves by crossing Union lines, forcing Lincoln's hand to face the challenge of emancipation (a reality that was not Lincoln's so much to give as to recognize); or to the radical abolitionists, including the overlooked Frederick Douglass, who were perhaps more the tale's heroes than its villains? And that perhaps Lincoln, still undeniably great, might not have been the only actor on the stage—that the war was a complex, messy, and complicated tale, and that its hero was, in fact, flawed in ways that the old story would not allow.

The Civil Rights era made these historical questions not merely valid but socially inescapable. In Memphis the night before he was killed, Martin Luther King Jr. evoked a panorama of scenes in history he would be tempted to see: "I would come on up even to 1863, and watch a vacillating president by the name of Abraham Lincoln finally come up to the conclusion that he had to sign the Emancipation Proclamation."[9] The old vision of Lincoln as the secular savior of the black people was becoming tarnished, fairly or unfairly, with a new narrative, exemplified by *Ebony* magazine's editor Lerone Bennett's searing and angry *Forced into Glory: Abraham Lincoln's White Dream*, a book that pointed out, quite accurately, that Lincoln had been a white supremacist sharing the racial prejudices of his times. This disenchantment with Lincoln had in truth started with W. E. B. Du Bois, who as early as 1922 had been compelled to recant harsh words about Lincoln.

In this climate, a figure such as Frederick Douglass reemerged in his old power. Because of the way we have largely ignored the role of African-Americans in the epic of the Civil War, and in the muted and almost amnesiac manner in which the story of the resulting failure of the Reconstruction era has been told, Americans have been largely blind to a startling truth: that the epic of the emancipation of four million slaves remains one of the greatest stories in world history. In that magnificent story, Douglass had been a national hero. He was a fighter, facing down death from early slave breakers many times in his youth and facing down rioting mobs throughout his travels. The writing of three autobiographies had well suited him for stepping into this ennobling heroic role, for he understood that his life had always been the story of his people redeemed, that somehow his personal odyssey to fame and worldwide attention was both a vindication and a symbol for what it was possible for a black man to achieve—in a nation that refused to offer manhood, equality, even the right to vote.

One reason he emerges as a figure second only to Lincoln is that he spoke the truth, spoke it to powerful figures who did not wish to hear it, accurately predicted the path the war would take, and offered everything he had, including the lives of his children, to gain freedom for others. In a talk he gave all across the North in 1864 entitled "The Mission of the War," this greatness and clarity of vision still speak. Calling the conflict "a solitary and ghastly horror," he asked, "Now, for what is all this desolation, ruin, shame, suffering and sorrow? Can anybody want the answer? . . . We all know it is Slavery." Yet in the midst of the numbing loss, he dared to face the larger meaning of this violence. "But even from the length of this struggle, we who mourn over it may well enough draw some consolation when we reflect upon the vastness and grandeur of its mission . . . The blow we strike is not merely to free a country or a continent—but the whole world from slavery—for when slavery fails here—it will fall everywhere." He added, "We have no business to mourn our mission."

He forcefully reminded his hundreds of listeners, and thousands more through the reprinting of his words—for no black man in America had ever reached so many Americans—that four things must happen in order that this daunting yet grand mission be accomplished: that this war "at untold cost of blood and treasure, shall be and of right ought to be, an Abolition War"; and that the peace to come must be "an Abolition peace." That every black man and woman be "entitled to all the rights, protections and opportunities for achieving distinction" as all other citizens; and lastly, that the black man must have the vote.[10]

Though he had sat and talked with Lincoln in the White House only five months earlier, and had been impressed with the president's personal qualities of honesty, earnestness, and above all, a refreshing and unusual mutuality, man to man, without any evident racial overtones, he now boldly addressed a president who was, he felt, incapable of seeing the mission of the war in this way. "Our chief danger lies in the absence of all moral feeling in the utterances of our rulers . . . the President told the country virtually that the abolition or non-abolition of Slavery was a matter of indifference to him. He would save the Union with Slavery or without Slavery."[11]

Not even the Emancipation Proclamation, issued under the banner of military necessity twelve months before, could possibly fulfill the pressing mission of destroying slavery once and for all. The president had made clear for three years that saving the Union was his goal, and from that first shot at Fort Sumter, Douglass had been equally clear that this goal was not enough. The hope of reunion with the South was doomed unless the higher mission of eradicating slavery was brought to the fore. "What business, then, have we to be pouring out our treasure and shedding our best blood like water for that worn-out, dead and buried Union, which had already become a calamity and a curse?"[12] This direct challenge to Lincoln was only part of a larger story of Lincoln and Douglass's dispute over the meaning of the war, and thus, the truth of America.

Their first face-to-face conversation remains one of the pivotal moments in American history—when a former slave could enter the office of the president

for conversation and consultation upon significant issues and festering problems, and more remarkable still, when Lincoln could seem to enjoy Douglass's
opinions and views, no matter how contrary to his own. And it is true that
Douglass freely recalled, "Lincoln is the first white man I ever spent an hour
with who did not remind me I was a Negro."[13]

Yet these admirable sentiments do not come close to encompassing the
true nature of the contest between them, as when after the first inaugural address Douglass contemptuously noted of the new president, "What an excellent slave hound he is . . ."[14] Or as he wrote in 1862, ". . . Mr. Lincoln
assumes the language and arguments of an itinerant Colonization lecturer,
showing all the inconsistencies, his pride of race and blood, his contempt for
Negroes and his canting hypocrisy."[15] Douglass wrote in a letter to New York
editor Theodore Tilton, just after his second meeting in 1864 with Lincoln in
the White House, "When there was any shadow of a hope that a man of a
more decided anti-slavery conviction and policy could be elected, I was not
for Mr. Lincoln."[16]

Lincoln possessed an unusual ability to absorb criticism and rise above
political abuse that beggars our imagination today. Douglass himself certainly came to understand that this cautious and measured politician had indeed been the essential man in this national crisis, perhaps the only national
leader in his time who could have won union and emancipation both. Douglass saw Lincoln in all his imperfections and perceived "slowness" in response
to the black cry for freedom, yet he stated in the dedication of the Freedmen's monument of Lincoln in 1876 that blacks were correct to revere him:
"We came to the conclusion that the hour and the man of our redemption
had somehow met in the person of Abraham Lincoln."[17]

Some readers will find Lincoln the reluctant liberator disturbing. No
matter how many times the "real" Lincoln is presented, there seems to be a
collective cultural reassertion of his mythic persona, a figure whose larger-
than-life mystique places him almost beyond the reach of ordinary historical
inquiry. Taking a fresh and direct look at the records of what Lincoln and
Douglass said and did, and at how their relationship affected the "fiery trial"
of the Civil War, is to respect the vast challenges they faced and mastered.
The secret of Lincoln's instinctive bonding to one of his most severe critics is
that the president sensed that he and Douglass shared common ground, as
was evident in Lincoln's Gettysburg Address, where for all time Lincoln
calmly and simply evoked a vision of America's "new birth of freedom."

Americans have always moved instinctively to a self-understanding of
themselves as being a people with a special, almost sacred, national mission,
ever since John Winthrop's 1630 "Shining City on a Hill" sermon noting

"the eyes of all people are upon us."[18] All across the American saga, poet, preacher, and politician alike have noted this powerful mission of being, as Whitman put it, "custodians of the future of humanity."[19] For Lincoln, the crisis of slavery had to be faced not solely for the Civil War generation but "for a vast future also." Jefferson, not Lincoln, had been the first to use the evocative phrase of America being "the last best hope of mankind."[20] This was a tall order in 1861, for a society in which four million men and women were slaves and in which the author of those very words had been a slave owner on the bucolic, peaceful crest of Monticello.

Both Lincoln and Douglass instinctively knew that the fate of America was irrevocably bound up in the "peculiar institution" of slavery, and that the war was nothing less than a violent rebirth that would either ratify or would forever nullify this destiny. Neither victory for the North nor the abolition of slavery was ever preordained. Any compromise before the guns of Fort Sumter would have left those four million slaves trapped. If Bull Run had gone the North's way, then the North's widely held vision of a quick resolution of the war would also have left slavery in place.

If General George B. McClellan had possessed the courage to drive home the Peninsula campaign in 1862, or had the Grant-like willingness to fully risk his men on the line in order to destroy Robert E. Lee at Antietam, the South might have collapsed—but well before emancipation. Victory would have been won by a powerful general who adamantly, and publicly, wished slavery to continue undisturbed.

If Lee had not possessed the headstrong will to send Longstreet's men on Pickett's Charge, but instead had maneuvered his army toward Harrisburg and Philadelphia, then Europe might well have decisively moved into the conflict and stymied any further prosecution of the war by the Lincoln administration. Had Atlanta not fallen when it did, Lincoln would likely have lost the 1864 election to McClellan, effectively leaving slavery alive.

During the war, Douglass warily assessed all of these dire possibilities and knew exactly how thin the line of success truly was. The cause of abolitionism was largely upheld by people for whom slavery was an abstraction. Bearing its scars across his back, Douglass knew slavery's realities in a way they never could, infusing him with a sense of desperation and danger at every twist and turn of the war. The price of saving the Union at several points looked to be nothing less than the sacrifice of his people. Above all, he understood that Lincoln was fighting a different war than he was.

Fearful that the Emancipation Proclamation, presented and released only as a desperate military necessity, would itself become null upon any early cessation of the war, whether in Union victory or in its defeat, Douglass viewed the conflict as far more than the progress of the Union army. For him, the war was a complicated and dangerous psychological maneuvering to produce an emerging sense that the Confederacy and the "peculiar institution" of slavery must be fully defeated *at one and the same time*. This realization among Northerners was achingly slow to grow and, even until the last year of the war, was never assured. The truth of the war was that there were many plausible scenarios of victory for Lincoln that could have spelled disaster for Douglass's mission. Moreover, there were no assurances that the North could subdue the South before its own political will exhausted itself.

To 1860

CHAPTER I

Black Republicans

T he vast throng milled excitedly about the town square, almost twelve thousand people filling the normally quiet little town of Ottawa, Illinois, on a steamy late summer day in 1858. It seemed the whole populace of the state had turned out for this first of seven debates, with a fevered anticipation born of the expectation that this senatorial election would dramatically affect the nation's future and would be razor close. In the seventy years of the young republic, there had never been a political race quite like this one. Reporters were anxious to cover the novel debate format, with one eastern scribe proclaiming, "The Prairies are on fire."[1]

The two candidates had known each other for more than twenty-two years, rivals from the first. The wary antagonists had come to the burgeoning free state of Illinois as settlers from other states, Abraham Lincoln from Kentucky by way of Indiana, Stephen Douglas from Vermont by way of upstate New York. As poor and nearly itinerant young men, they had located in adjacent central counties, one to Sangamon, the other to Morgan. Lincoln, the Springfield Whig who idealized Henry Clay, soon found himself embroiled in constant battle with Douglas, the "Young America" Democrat who envisioned himself the next Andrew Jackson. Though each had mastered the law, both clearly thrived on the slashing pell-mell of politics, which drove their rivalry even more fiercely. Both worked hard to turn themselves into prosperous and self-styled western men—straight-talking, confident, humorous, effective speakers who felt no need to follow the strictures of classic oratory as practiced back east.

Senator Stephen A. Douglas, nicknamed "the Little Giant" by some, was a small rotund man, barely over five feet tall. Stephen Douglas (who dropped the second "s" from his name when he went west) was running for the Senate

Abraham Lincoln, 1859. Photograph by Samuel M. Fassett.

for the third time, a nationally prominent figure perennially mentioned as a Democratic candidate for president. If he could defeat his long-time but obscure challenger now, the presidential nomination for 1860 would be his. But the senator, unlike his supporters, did not underestimate his rival. Upon learning of his opponent's nomination, he said, "I shall have my hands full. He is the strong man of the party—full of wit, facts, dates—and the best stump speaker, with his droll ways and dry jokes, in the West. He is as honest as he is shrewd, and if I beat him my victory will be hardly won."[2]

Douglas's adversary was a well-respected leader in the rapidly developing Republican party in the state, but in truth, Lincoln had virtually dropped out of politics after a brief and not very successful two-year stint in Congress twelve years earlier, and he was now a successful railroad lawyer. Abraham Lincoln did not have as high an estimation of his opponent as Douglas had of him, despite Stephen Douglas's manifest success. He resented Douglas's agile ability to twist his opponent's words in debate, and, he confided to a friend, the senator's ability to tell a lie to ten thousand listeners one day and to deny it to five thousand the next.[3] Most of all, Lincoln bristled at the way their political fortunes had so dramatically diverged. Lincoln was never a man to reveal much about his inner state, feelings, hopes, resentments, but many years later, an undated fragment written before this period of frustrated self-analysis was discovered in Lincoln's writings, and the lawyer did not spare himself in a raw comparison: "We were both young men then, he a trifle younger than I. Even then, we were both ambitious; I, perhaps, quite as much as he. With *me*, the race of ambition has been a failure—a flat failure; with *him* it has been one of splendid success."[4]

The election was likely to be Lincoln's last chance to reverse that course of fortune, and unexpectedly, his prospects were increasingly promising. The senator was now in severe trouble in his home state, and Lincoln's new Republican party was clearly on the rise. The two men had been shadow-boxing in speeches for four years over the one issue that compelled the nation's fierce interest, the spread of slavery into western territories soon to become states. Before the agreement for these debates, dueling speeches in Springfield and Chicago had already well prepared the ground of battle and future lines of attack, and the seven debates up and down the state were now attracting strong interest from all over a country convulsed over the fate of slavery.

Why was the whole nation riveted to this one senatorial race? Lincoln was not exaggerating the fame and importance of the Little Giant when he had said the previous month "that *he* is a *very great man*, and that the largest of *us* are very small ones."[5] After all, Stephen Douglas was the man who had helped pass the Compromise of 1850 that averted civil war, the man who also, almost inexplicably, four years later single-handedly smashed the 1820 Missouri Compromise with stunning legislation that allowed the vast territories of Kansas and Nebraska to enter the Union as either slave *or* free states. Instead of all the old painfully worked out compromises of decades past, Stephen Douglas trumpeted the doctrine of popular sovereignty, letting the people vote! What could be more reasonable, more democratic, than to put the whole issue of slavery to the test of the people in each territory as they formed these new states?

His northern supporters were, however, unnerved by the recent *Dred Scott* Supreme Court decision that clearly undermined Douglas's dream of letting the territories simply vote slavery up or down (Douglas famously claimed "not to care"). Chief Justice Roger B. Taney, a Maryland slave owner, had shocked many northerners with this notorious decision proclaiming that blacks were "beings of an inferior order, and altogether unfit to associate with the white race . . . and so far inferior, that they had no rights which the white man was bound to respect."[6] Further, the decision effectively claimed no state, whether it claimed to be free or not, could legally exclude slavery.

Senator Stephen Douglas

Still, Douglas was such a dominating national figure that he felt his notion of popular sovereignty could still put an end to the endless disputes and rising crises over slavery—that he could save the Union and claim the presidency.

As Lincoln was now anxious to remind the voters of the free state of Illinois, the problem was that Douglas's popular sovereignty dramatically increased these tensions and the mutual distrust between North and South. Each incoming state, particularly "Bloody Kansas," was now an open battle zone, and the prospects for peace among the states lessened with every fiery speech, every insult, every exchange of bullets, every election. The senator might still be a giant in national politics, but the voters of his state were angry and restive, and he was in danger of losing all.

If there is any cardinal rule in politics, particularly when an incumbent is in trouble, it is this: Move to the offensive, hard. On August 21 on the great platform in Ottawa, Douglas was slated to speak first. Outfitted in a white broad-brimmed plantation hat, a bright blue coat with great brass buttons that contrasted with his cream vest and pants, he was hard to miss. Engaging, compelling, he gesticulated in strong slashing motions, strode the stage with utter confidence. Barely ten minutes into his remarks, he struck: "Lincoln was to bring into the Abolition camp the old line Whigs, and transfer them over to Giddings, Chase, Fred Douglass, and Parson Lovejoy, who were ready to receive them and christen them to their new faith."[7] He claimed the faith was called the "Black Republicans." He hit hard again five minutes later, invoking Frederick Douglass's name a second and then a third time.

Lincoln might be in favor of equal rights for blacks, asserted the senator, but not he: "I believe this Government was made on the white basis. I believe it was made by the white man, for the benefit of white men and their posterity for ever . . . I do not question Mr. Lincoln's conscientious belief that the negro was made his equal, and hence is his brother; but for my own part, I do not regard the negro as my equal, and positively deny that he is my brother or any kin to me whatsoever." Then a fourth time, he claimed his old friend deserved a medal from "Fred Douglass for his Abolitionism."[8]

When his turn at last came, Lincoln replied that the senator's claimed indifference to whether slavery was to be voted up or down was really a covert method of threatening even free states with the acceptance of slavery. And Lincoln truly despised slavery: "I hate it because of the monstrous injustice of slavery itself. I hate it because it deprives our republican example of its just influence in the world—enables the enemies of free institutions, with plausibility, to taunt us as hypocrites . . ."[9] Yet Douglas's blows had found their mark, because Lincoln then tried to blunt the effectiveness of the senator's accusation.

If millions of slaves could not all be shipped to Liberia, then what? "Free them, and make them politically and socially our equals? My own feelings will not admit of this," Lincoln said, "and if mine would, we well know that those of the great mass of white people would not . . . We cannot, then, make them equals."[10]

Without a strong answer to Douglas now, Lincoln's victory would be an impossibility. After all, he was attempting to win the Senate seat of a state that, though free, had strong and effective Black Laws that refused any black resident the right to vote, join the state militia, testify against a white person in court, or serve on a jury. Interracial marriage was illegal. The Black Laws had long imposed steep fines and local injunctions against blacks living in Illinois but just five years earlier the state had passed a law making any further black settlement illegal. In his long political career, Lincoln had not spoken against these laws—nor did he do so now: "I have no purpose to introduce political and social equality between the white and the black races. There is a physical difference between the two, which, in my judgment, will probably forever forbid their living together upon the footing of perfect equality, and inasmuch as it becomes a necessity that there must be a difference, I, as well as Judge Douglas, am in favor of the race to which I belong having the superior position."[11]

From the vast historical record of Lincoln's recorded words, from those written by his hand, transcribed by reporters, or comments remembered later by friend and foe alike, Lincoln sincerely believed this controversial passage, even though certainly forced by political necessity to speak these words. Yet, he added these lines: ". . . there is no reason in the world why the negro is not entitled to all the natural rights enumerated in the Declaration of Independence, the right to life, liberty and the pursuit of happiness." While he might agree with Douglas that no black was his equal "in moral or intellectual endowment," Lincoln chose, when he edited the debates for publication, to put these words in italic so they would not be missed: "But in the right to eat the bread, without the leave of anybody else, which his own hand earns, *he is my equal and the equal of Judge Douglas, and the equal of every living man.*"[12]

Most observers, and perhaps Lincoln himself, thought that Douglas got the better of him in that first debate in Ottawa. However, Lincoln recovered and found his stride at the next debate stop of Freeport. He started out more aggressively, posing an important question to Douglas, forcing the senator to explicitly state that northern voters had the clear right to outlaw slavery, despite the recent *Dred Scott* decision. The Freeport Doctrine that Douglas endorsed that afternoon would later heighten southern Democratic voters' distrust of him, but it is unlikely Lincoln was thinking that far ahead. More immediately, Lincoln wanted voters to severely doubt the truthfulness of their senator, as he made the point repeatedly that the Little Giant was part of a great conspiracy along with President James Buchanan, former president Franklin Pierce, and Chief Justice Roger B. Taney to make slavery "perpetual and national."[13] This effort to make Illinois citizens conclude that their senator wanted slavery in every state, north or south, was an audacious one, hardly grounded in truth. Douglas bitterly resented the charge, which made Lincoln only more eager to repeat the taunt throughout the debates.

Yet this explosive charge was not actually indicative of Lincoln's usual style, as he generally treated political opponents with cool, reasoned disagreement laced with a sly humor. One observer of the debates, Carl Schurz, who later became a friend and political advisor, remembered Lincoln's "tone of earnest truthfulness, of elevated, noble sentiment, and of kindly sympathy."[14] Lincoln's clear, high-pitched almost falsetto western twang rang out to the edges of the crowd, and to the nation beyond. Though even his greatest admirers could see what a long gawky figure Abraham Lincoln struck, there was also something strangely compelling in his speaking that made people quickly forget the rumpled clothes, the awkward flatfooted walk, the tousled wild hair, the thin, scrawny neck. His longtime law partner, William Herndon, acknowledged that when Lincoln began speaking, his voice was "shrill-squeaking-piping, unpleasant," but that as he warmed up and eased into the flow of his address, then it became "harmonious, melodious—musical, if you please."[15]

At six foot four, Lincoln appeared oddly elongated, with his considerable strength masked by narrow shoulders, huge hands, and long legs out of proportion with his frame. His complexion was rough and heavily wrinkled, his nose massive and jutting, his thin mouth expansive, his cheeks sunken. Most strange of all, his deep-set gray eyes, pensive and somber, did not match—his heavy-lidded and hooded right eye gave him a cold, off-center stare. Some described him as ugly, others were almost spellbound by his singular demeanor, as if these extreme features formed a visage distinctly majestic. He did not seem at all sensitive about his looks, and in fact delighted in making fun of himself.

Stephen Douglas was not so innocent in his humor. Over and over again, Douglas would declare Abraham Lincoln to be in secret league with the fiery black speaker and editor Frederick Douglass. In some sense, it is odd that the Lincoln-Douglas debates have such an exalted reputation, for they are full of abuse, racial insults, extraneous diversions and sallies, exemplified by Douglas's most devastating story: "I have reason to recollect that some people in this country think that Fred Douglass is a very good man. The last time I came here to make a speech . . . I saw a carriage, and a magnificent one it was, drive up and take a position on the outside of the crowd; a beautiful young lady was sitting on the box seat, whilst Fred. Douglass and her mother reclined inside, and the owner of the carriage acted as driver." The crowd laughed and jeered, as Douglas made it clear that Lincoln's politics meant they would soon be driving the despised Douglass around with their wives and daughters. And why had the abolitionist Douglass been in town? Why, to speak "for his friend Lincoln as the champion of the black man."[16]

In all, Stephen Douglas goaded Lincoln in the debates by mentioning Frederick Douglass by name fifteen times, even repeating the carriage story to the crowd's delight at the next debate in Jonesboro, Illinois. Lincoln made no direct reply to either the carriage tale or to the continuing taunts of his supposed Black Republican identity. When he had the next chance to speak first, at Charlestown (the town in the debates closest to the Mason-Dixon line, and most sympathetic to the South), Lincoln tried a new tactic to fend off this poisonous and very effective attack, and also to indirectly address the anxious sexual subtext of what having a man like Fred Douglass seated next to a white wife and daughter might mean for the good voters of Illinois. Lincoln used the old politician's trick of pretending he had not planned to discuss the topic in that day's debate, but that, providentially, an "elderly gentleman"

had just earnestly asked him to discuss black and white equality—so he
thought he might just repeat he did not believe in any such thing, "that I am
not nor ever have been in favor of making voters or jurors of negroes, nor of
qualifying them to hold office, nor to intermarry with white people."

He continued, articulating beliefs widely held by voters from both political parties and, truth be known, many abolitionists themselves, that these
bars to equality were due to "a physical difference between the white and
black races which I believe will forever prevent the races living together on
terms of social and political equality." If they were to be forced to coexist,
there must be a superior race, "and I as much as any other man am in favor
of having the superior position assigned to the white race." Then he struck a
particularly Lincolnian note, bemused, ironic, amusing—and a devastatingly
effective political reply. In believing whites were above the black race, he still
did not "perceive that because the white man is to have the superior position
the negro should be denied everything. I do not understand that because I do
not want a negro woman for a slave I must necessarily want her for a wife."[17]

Still, Douglas made one more attempt at Charlestown to evoke the dark
shadow of Frederick Douglass and his cohorts, before dropping the abolitionist's name in the remaining three debates. Reminding his listeners that
Lincoln's Black Republican party had been chasing him around the state for
years, he made an interesting rhetorical twist in this age of the Fugitive Slave
Act: "They had the same negro hunting me down, and they now have a negro
traversing the northern counties of the state and speaking in behalf of Lincoln . . . in order to show how much interest the colored brethren felt in the
success of their brother Abe." Adding that it would take too much of his remaining time to read selections from it, the senator noted a recent address by
Frederick Douglass in Poughkeepsie, New York, in which this nemesis "con-
jures all the friends of negro equality and negro citizenship to rally as one
man around Abraham Lincoln, the perfect embodiment of their principles,
and by all means to defeat Stephen A. Douglas."[18]

Frederick Douglass's Poughkeepsie address appears to contain his first
mention of Lincoln, though the emerging Republican candidate's name was
offered (a common mistake until the election of 1860) as "Abram." The
grand platform collapsed just before his speech, sending all "in one conglom-
erate mass of pine, hemlock and humanity."[19] Falling down with the throng,
his head was struck by a splintering board, yet Douglass still managed to rise
and speak for well over an hour.

Delivered in early August of 1858 just before the debates, Frederick Douglass's speech was among the first to comment on the battle between Lincoln
and Douglas. Noting that the nation had existed only eighty-two years and

thirty-one days, Douglass honed in on the fact that this senatorial campaign was about the nature of the Declaration of Independence itself. "The contest going on just now in the state of Illinois is worthy of attention. Stephen A. Douglas, author of the Kansas-Nebraska bill, is energetically endeavoring to hold his seat in the United States Senate, and Mr. Abram Lincoln is endeavoring as energetically to get that seat for himself." He added quickly that this was only "a partial view of the subject. The truth is, that Slavery and Anti-Slavery are at the bottom of the contest."[20]

Senator Douglas was correct in noting that Frederick Douglass was keenly gunning for him. In the abolitionist's view, the senator's troubles placed him in "an extravagance of political profligacy which can be neither forgiven or forgotten . . ." Still, Douglass knew there was no counting the Little Giant out, for he had money, influence, and great talent. In the end, he was "one of the most restless, ambitious, boldest and most unscrupulous enemies with whom the cause of the colored man has had to contend." With a mocking reference to their sharing a name, Frederick Douglass added, "It seems to me that the white Douglas should occasionally meet his desserts at the hands of a black one. Once I thought he was about to make the name respectable, but now I despair of him, and must do the best I can for it myself."

Concluding, he added, "I now leave him in the hands of Mr. Lincoln . . ." In this prescient speech, Douglass not only accurately predicted the great importance of the Senate race, but admiringly quoted at length Lincoln's recent oration at the beginning of the campaign, forever known as the House Divided speech. Though Lincoln was clearly not in the abolitionist camp, Douglass admired the lawyer's tough-minded vision of a nation that could not "endure permanently half Slave and half Free." He called Lincoln's bold and closely reasoned address "a great speech."[21]

The remaining debates ground on along the same well-trod themes, with little more rhetorical fireworks or inspirational tropes. The contestants were growing tired, and there were only so many ways to lay out their themes— Senator Douglas contended that Lincoln was somehow a radical abolitionist, despite all he said and what was in his (admittedly spare) political record; and Lincoln claimed that Douglas, despite his proclaimed neutrality toward slavery, was in a secret cabal to extend "the peculiar institution" not only into the western territories but into the free states. Neither candidate's attempt to sway the voters of Illinois was based entirely on fact.

Only in the closing words of the last debate in Alton, on October 15, 1858, were words said that somehow elevated the entire exercise and indicated what the future course of the nation might hold. Lincoln stated how odd, and troubling, it was for his rival to put himself before the people by refusing to state a position on slavery, to run on a platform "upon the basis of caring nothing about *the very thing that every body does care the most about*." Lincoln finally, with only minutes more remaining to him, stated in stark and moving terms what was beyond the surface discussion over the western expansion of slavery: "It is the eternal struggle between the two principles—right and wrong—throughout the world. They are the two principles that have stood face to face from the beginning of time; and will ever continue to struggle. The one is the common right of humanity and the other the divine right of kings. It is the same principle in whatever shape it develops itself. It is the same spirit that says, 'You work and toil and earn bread, and I'll eat it.' "[22]

So the great debates ended, and the combatants, in exhaustion, awaited the people's verdict—though not by their direct vote, as in this time each county elected state legislators, who then in turn voted for the new senator by their party affiliation. Despite Lincoln's long-held optimism that he would win the popular vote, the senator had strong advantages in enough individual counties, the only vote that really mattered. The Republicans did indeed poll a slight majority, but on Election Day 1858, Stephen Douglas was returned to the Senate by the state legislature's vote, 54 to 46. While Lincoln had the satisfaction of being able to claim he had indeed defeated his rival in sheer votes, the disheartening reality was that he was not going to the Senate.

Personally devastated, Lincoln, who by this time in his life had become adept at handling painful disappointment and thwarted ambition, reflected, rightly, that he had made a powerful contribution to the national debate on the future of slavery, one that would likely affect future campaigns. If he slid back into his accustomed obscurity, at least he had pressed the Little Giant as no one else had done before.

There are three reasons Lincoln did not return to anonymity after losing: his cool, logically compelling arguments against his forceful rival gave the newly emerging Republican party great hopes in the upcoming presidential contest; his personal realization that law was no longer consuming enough for his great vaunting inner ambition; and a singular and unusual political move for a losing candidate. In 1859, he helped arrange for the publishing of his personal scrapbook of the transcripts of the debates, and when they sold over thirty thousand copies, suddenly Lincoln was obscure no more.

The debates were not the first time the names of Abraham Lincoln and Frederick Douglass had been linked. Two years before, the *Illinois State Register* said of Lincoln, "his niggerism has as dark a hue as that of Garrison or Fred Douglass."[23] Douglass's fame was such that there were hundreds of references to the reformer all through the 1850s, especially when Lincoln was sharing a law practice with a fervent abolitionist, William Herndon. The innately conservative and cautious Lincoln was well served by his junior partner, whose reforming enthusiasms and attraction to New England Transcendental thought would have alerted him to the latest moves and innovations of the growing abolitionist parties, whether Free Soil, Liberty, Radical Abolitionist, and the extreme uncompromising edges of the new Republican movement.

Douglass and Senator Douglas had their own fascinating history. Frederick Douglass had long been determined to debate the senator himself, long before Lincoln's candidacy, saying of the Little Giant that no one had done more to intensify hatred of black people. Douglass spoke in several Illinois frontier towns long before the 1858 campaign. After seeing him in Chicago, the *Illinois Daily Journal* conceded in 1853 that Douglass was "the ablest and most accomplished speaker of the African race."[24]

The idea of a Douglass-Douglas debate would not die easily. In 1857, the same newspaper reported that a group of black Chicagoans passed resolutions "daring Senator Douglas to measure intellectual strength in debate with 'black Fred Douglass.' "[25] The group had decried the senator's epithets against their people, and they wanted to see their senator in debate with the foremost black orator in America. The white newspaper was excited at the prospect of a leader of the nation taking on Douglass.

As he had mentioned in the Lincoln debates, Stephen Douglas did indeed feel haunted by the former slave, who set up a speaking tour that closely followed his movements. The *Illinois Daily Journal* commented, "It has been quite common for white men to hunt negros, but we now find a negro hunting a white man!" One debate was even arranged but canceled by the senator, and he managed to evade his black political stalker in the next four years—daring only to evoke him in order to goad Lincoln.[26]

Frederick Douglass managed to convince many that a debate between him and Senator Douglas would be worthwhile. Douglass's hometown newspaper, the *Rochester Democrat and American*, wrote in 1859 that it would be interesting if friends of "the little giant in Illinois arrange for a joint debate between the two Douglases." But in a testament to the respect Lincoln was gaining across the country, they thought that it would "not be fair seeing how hard a task the Senator has in his contests with 'Long Abe.' "[27]

Almost as a consolation for not getting the chance to face the Little Giant, in the winter of 1858, Frederick Douglass embarked on a long Midwest tour through the prairies, making sure he spoke in many of the sites of the Lincoln-Douglas debates, with appearances in Freeport, Galesburg, and Ottawa.

Beginning with Freeport on February 15 and 16, Douglass called for immediate national emancipation. The *Freeport Journal* described him as "fluent and ready-willed," and said he "has a knack of saying impudent things about American institutions." The institution they referred to was slavery. The next night he was in Dixon, where the newspaper found this "Anglo-Ethiopian" to have "*all* the attributes of a great orator." In Mendota the following day, the *Mendota Press Observer* cited his rise from slavery without formal education and doubted whether "all history can furnish any instance more remarkable." Douglass won over the reporter with his wit, which he found to be a vindication of the black man's claims to humanity. Recognition of the fundamental humanity of black people was a major theme during the tour. Douglass would trace the achievements of the Egyptians and those of African descent all over the world, arguing that racial differences came from climates and geography instead of distinct inequalities. The *Belvidere Standard* dismissed such assertions, writing, "The lecture was a very good one, and interesting, but science is rather out of Fred's line."[28]

The pace of a lecture a day continued. At Dunn's Hall in Galesburg, Douglass found a larger receptive audience; they often interrupted him with applause, especially for his satirical impressions of self-deluded and self-serving slaveholders. Coming off this success, Douglass had a smaller crowd in Peoria, then a larger one, and finally an invitation to come back a week later for two more special lectures. Tickets were quickly made available at local bookstores, selling for fifteen cents for one and twenty-five cents for a pair. The local newspaper reported that even those who attended for the purpose of heckling came away "astonished and interested." Douglass, simply by standing before them, was nothing less than "a living example of what the negro can attain to." They found his very presence an effective antislavery argument. Douglass's final engagement was one of the largest audiences ever fit into Rouse's Hall.[29]

Perhaps the most moving episode of the tour came after Douglass's engagement in Belvidere. An older white man approached him, warmly touching his hand. Douglass was puzzled at first glance, but then remembered that this man had helped him when he had finally reached New Bedford, Massachusetts, as a fugitive from slavery. Mr. Cobb had not only employed Douglass sweeping chimneys, but had protected him from a white workman from Baltimore who was about to strike him with a shovel. Much had changed in twenty years. The fugitive chimney sweep was now a nationally known figure, speaking to thousands.[30]

By 1859, so too had the life of Abraham Lincoln changed, with his mounting presidential ambitions propelling him to travel widely, speaking to Republican groups from Kansas to Wisconsin to Ohio and all the New England states. Many wanted to hear the man who had battled the Little Giant so effectively. If his rival Stephen Douglas was indeed going to be the presidential nominee for the Democrats, the new and fledgling Republican party wanted to hear the powerful arguments that had so daunted him. Slowly, Lincoln's constant stream of speaking appearances made the lawyer admit of the approaching 1860 election, "The taste *is* in my mouth a little."[31]

In editing the senatorial debates for publication, Lincoln painstakingly pasted down the long yellowing newspaper columns he had so carefully collected and clipped, including those repeating the senator's wholesale fabrication of Lincoln's supposed tie to "Fred Douglass." Still, Lincoln made no further recorded reference then or later during the presidential campaign to having been falsely associated with the radical Douglass.

Indeed, it was precisely because Lincoln was so far from being a Black Republican that this unlikely Illinois politician slowly rose to national prominence, to gain widespread acceptance among the broad middle ground of his party. Still, to be an acceptable and passably agreeable compromise candidate was not likely to be enough to supplant the leading Republican, New York's wily, urbane Senator William Henry Seward.

CHAPTER 2

A Self-Made Man

For Douglass, escaping from slavery was a necessity rather than a choice. Slave masters stole more than a lifetime of one's labor, they stole the core of one's self. To resist was a revolutionary act, a political statement.

Yet the experience of freedom was more than escape from bondage. The talk Frederick Douglass delivered most frequently was not one on the abolitionist cause, but rather one about "Self-Made Men." In hundreds of speeches and articles, and most especially in his three published autobiographies, he asserted that his rise from slavery was more than merely living out the American economic dream; it was a radical inner transformation, a revolutionary redefinition of what being an American actually meant. Douglass was intent on being an equal citizen in a society that, in the 1857 Dred Scott decision of the United States Supreme Court, declared this to be impossible.

During his lifetime, Douglass never knew the month or year of his birth. He shared this melancholy fact of slave life in his first autobiography: "By far the larger part of the slaves know as little of their ages as horses know of theirs, and it is the wish of most masters within my knowledge to keep their slaves thus ignorant."[1] Records show he was born in February of 1818 in Talbot County, on the Eastern Shore of Maryland. His age was just one piece of knowledge that he longed for all his life. He also did not know who his father was. In his first autobiography, he wrote that his father was a white man, and he hinted that it was Capt. Aaron Anthony, his first owner. Anthony was remembered as a drunkard, tortured by the moral disparity between tender moments when he would call Douglass his "little Indian boy" and jealous rages when he would mercilessly whip slave women. By Douglass's last autobiography, *Life and Times*, he concluded his paternal search with a simple sentence, "Of my father I know nothing."[2]

Douglass remembered his mother, Harriet Bailey, though he only saw her a precious few times and always at night. Anthony separated mother and child by sending her to another family twelve miles away, yet despite the exertion of being a field hand, on some nights she took the long walk to let her son fall asleep on her shoulder. He remembered her as saying little and carrying a burdened and sad presence. By the time he awakened, she was always gone. Douglass was cared for some years by his maternal grandparents. When he turned seven, he learned his mother was dead. His reaction to her death was muted, for he hardly knew this woman who was a mother and a near stranger both. It was only in the years to come that he felt a lingering sadness and longing for her.

This pain and a need to search for something firm to stand on marked his lifelong relationship with the land and seascape of eastern Maryland, as well as the people who had claimed him as property. He once told Maryland lawyer James Hall what it felt like to be "separated from all the dear ones of my youth as if by the shadow of death," and he implored Hall to discover anything he could as to the circumstances of his early life. Few freed slaves ever had the money or the favorable circumstances to reach back into their past, but Douglass did, and he added that these "tidings from the place, the people, the friends, and the objects associated with my youthful days have for me an interest which you can better imagine than I can express."[3] In 1854 he wrote that the search for some kind of definite past was a powerful reason to hate slavery's cruelty: "The thought of only being a creature of the *present* and the *past*, troubled me, and I longed to have a *future*—a future with hope in it."[4]

Douglass's first owner lived on an Eastern Shore plantation owned by the distinguished Lloyd family. Young Frederick was selected to be the playmate of Lloyd's son, Daniel. Being around an educated and privileged boy broadened Douglass's earliest horizons. After Anthony died in 1826, his estate, including his slaves, was divided among his three children. Before the estate could be settled, his daughter, Lucretia Anthony Auld, died and her widower husband, Thomas Auld, became Douglass's second owner. A few years before Anthony's death, the Aulds had arranged for Douglass to spend his crucial early adolescent years with Thomas's brother and sister-in-law, Hugh and Sophia Auld, in Baltimore. There he rubbed shoulders with free blacks and sensed a wider world beyond servitude. Douglass believed that just the opportunity to leave behind plantation life, even for a few years, had ensured his spirit was not broken at a young age. During his time in Baltimore, his new master's wife, Sophia Auld, showed him kindness that revealed to him that white people were varied and capable of something beyond cruelty.

The motherless Douglass felt tenderness toward the woman who began to teach him to read. When Sophia Auld offered to teach him the ABCs, this brief kindness was harshly interrupted by her husband, Hugh, who claimed "Learning . . . would forever unfit him to be a slave." These words were to the young boy "a new and special revelation," enlightening him in a moment that the true path to freedom lay in the power of expression. "What he dreaded, I most desired," Douglass later wrote.[5] In his brief years near the docks of Baltimore, he befriended local white boys and bribed them to help him learn to read.

Being in Baltimore also allowed Douglass to purchase a book, the most important fifty cents he ever spent. Caleb Bingham, a Massachusetts educator with abolitionist sympathies, had edited and collected in 1797 a wide variety of great and patriotic oratory in a profoundly influential book called *The Columbian Orator*. The boy not only read and absorbed its messages of personal liberty, but used *The Columbian Orator* to train himself as a public speaker, reading its speeches aloud and practicing them "with Rules calculated to Improve Youth and Others in the Ornamental and Useful Art of Eloquence."[6] Douglass's self-understanding radically shifted when he read a passage titled "Dialogue Between a Master and Slave," in which the slave is able to so masterfully refute his owner's argument for bondage that he is in the end emancipated. At the age of twelve, Douglass became obsessed with the passage. Never had he heard such impressive and subversive abolitionist ideas articulated. He tried to forget the power of what he had read, but everywhere he turned, he was reminded of the condition in which he was trapped, one he now understood to be unnatural. *The Columbian Orator* showed eloquence and oratory as the most crucial weapon against injustice.

He felt from a very young age that he was somehow special, marked for some great purpose. This inner belief of greatness did not minimize the obstacles and crushing oppression he was forced to overcome, but his charismatic personality combined with certain special circumstances allowed this belief to survive savage beatings, periods of depression, and repeated failures to escape to freedom. His glowering handsome features and forceful physical presence, even in the condition of slavery, made him an impressive figure. Yet, something else distinguished him: that hunger to read and write which he accomplished through his own wiles and through the focused application of his strong intelligence. Above all, he learned to speak eloquently before crowds, where his special talent for weaving a compelling story in a powerful conversational style reinforced this inner conviction of a special destiny.

While Douglass was a slave in Baltimore, a black preacher named Charles Lawson told him that he saw the young man going on to do a mighty work for the Lord. Despite all that was moving against him, Douglass felt God had chosen him for a great mission.

At age fifteen, however, he was sent back to the Eastern Shore to the town of St. Michaels, to return to intensive field labor. He later wrote that the years back in farm work almost destroyed his sense of self, much less his hope of freedom. To be an obedient slave, one must live without thought. After the Baltimore years and his tantalizing taste of the power of reading, Douglass was a hard man to render numb. In Douglass's *Narrative,* he described the tough contest between keeping alive an inner sense of self and a kind of blankness, a numbed "beast-like stupor" of ceaseless labor.[7] As he was the only slave in the region who could read, his owners distrusted him and strove to break him. This long vicious battle over his will and sense of self only served in the end to reinforce his self-image as separate, special, and eager for release.

The land around St. Michaels is a narrow geographic area where the Chesapeake Bay is never very far from sight, with its rich salt smell and blue vistas. Working in these fields offered Douglass continual views of the sea, just as the harbor of Baltimore had done. He wrote movingly of standing before the Chesapeake waters, watching the freedom of vessels moving with the wind, spending hours staring at them "with saddened heart and tearful eye." He saw mighty ships sail off to places that he could not go.[8] Such views also were a constant reminder that it was possible to somehow, someday, leave this place, to escape the confines of his master's fields and this narrow near-life.

During this time, young Frederick Bailey, as he was named then, encountered Edward Covey. Slave owners sent insubordinate slaves to Covey so that he could destroy any resolve or resistance left in their constitution. For months, the fifteen-year-old endured the slave breaker's presence, leading to a whipping a week upon his already-scarred back, and the young man was close to cracking.

Finally, Covey thrashed a hickory slat against Frederick's head, causing a wound so painful that Frederick ran to his master to beg for help, to no avail. An older slave named Sandy encountered Frederick during his dejected walk back to Covey and did his best to treat his wound. As Frederick climbed down the ladder in the barn, Covey rushed from behind to bind the boy's strong legs with a rope. As he resisted, Covey grabbed on hard, sending them both falling to the barn floor. At this moment, something odd happened inside of the young man. A sudden, desperate spirit of resistance filled him and without regards to the consequences, he resolved never to be beaten again, even if it meant his death. He rose to his feet and grabbed the shocked white man by his throat. This was the last thing the slave breaker expected. Covey broke free and yelled, *"Are you going to resist*, you scoundrel?" The overseer and his prey battled in the searing August sun for two long hours to a standstill. Valuing his infamous reputation, Covey told no one about the fight and never whipped Frederick again.[9]

After a failed attempt to escape in 1836, the eighteen-year-old Frederick Bailey found himself waiting to learn his fate in a local jail cell. He faced the worst jeopardy yet as he was liable to be severely punished and resold to slave traders who would send him deeper into the South, where eventual escape might be all but impossible. At the last moment, Thomas Auld decided instead to send Frederick back to Baltimore.

Though life back in Baltimore allowed considerably more comfort and safety, and even with discussions with Auld on how he might someday be able to buy his freedom, Frederick continued to chafe under his straitened life. Then he met Anna Murray, a young woman who would be a catalyst for realizing his dream of freedom. Five years older than Douglass, she was a native of Maryland. Her parents had been slaves, but she was born unbound. Feeling the need to be self-sufficient, she had moved to Baltimore at seventeen to work for a white family.

While there was a powerful social division in antebellum black Baltimore between being free and enslaved, the enterprising Douglass won her trust and heart. The ambitious young man's dream of freedom enthralled her, and she contributed her hard-earned savings to his plan. With a train ticket, a disguise as a sailor, seaman's papers that would not bear too much close examination, and the great good fortune of not being betrayed along the way, Douglass took four boats and three trains to arrive in bustling New York with a sensation he had never before felt: freedom.

After Anna joined him in New York, they were married and eventually settled in New Bedford, Massachusetts. As a fugitive, though, he was not safe. This was the new reality of Douglass's life, even in the free states of the North. Douglass did hard, low-paying menial work as a ship's caulker—but at least he now earned for himself, struggling for enough money to support a new and quickly growing family. Moreover, as he eked out a strenuous new life, the process of self-creation continued, especially in one crucial way. In talking with a man who was harboring him in his first weeks of freedom, it was suggested that he take the name of a romantic Scottish hero named Douglas, from Walter Scott's novel *The Lady of the Lake*. There was no more Frederick Bailey. He freely chose a new name from a fictional protagonist who bravely fought to reclaim his rightful inheritance.

Though he believed his future lay in physically demanding jobs, Douglass still hankered after learning, especially in regard to the alluring world of abolitionism. He attended an antislavery conference on Nantucket in August 1841. William Coffin, one of the white organizers, recognized him in the audience from a church where Douglass sometimes spoke and asked him to share his story with the crowd. His listeners found him to be a commanding and persuasive speaker. William Lloyd Garrison, who witnessed the moment, was stunned and called the young man a prodigy. His natural talent was so apparent that these organizers immediately offered him a job as a traveling antislavery agent.

Woman's suffrage pioneer Elizabeth Cady Stanton described first hearing Douglass in these early days, saying that he stood "like an African prince, conscious of his dignity and power, grand wit, satire and indignation." She looked around at the greatest abolitionist orators utterly fixated on Douglass's magnetic stage presence, "laughing and crying by turns with his rapid flights from pathos to humor." For the rest of that day, "All other speakers seemed tame after Douglass."[10] Seemingly overnight he became an abolitionist luminary, a man telling the story of his escape into freedom so compellingly, so vividly, that he quickly claimed the attention of first the freedom circuit and then the nation.

There was only one problem with this success. He related his staggering story of rising up from slavery with such sophistication, such sudden and inspiring eloquence that many refused to believe that he was only three years out of bondage. Traveling across the country speaking with reformers, Douglass gained access to more and more books, newspapers, and conversations with his fellow abolitionist agitators—and these all served to stimulate his eager and retentive mind. John Collins, a white abolitionist who often traveled with him, reminded him to "Give us the facts . . . we will take care of the philosophy." They were uncomfortable not just with his opinions, but also with the increasingly polished and fluent way he expressed them. George Foster told him, "People won't believe you ever was a slave, Frederick, if you keep on this way." Collins patronizingly added, "Better to have a *little* of the plantation manner of speech than not; 'tis not best that you seem too learned."[11]

From that first moment when Douglass walked to the front of that Nantucket room and unleashed his rhetorical fire, his chief mentor and early protector was William Lloyd Garrison. The mild-looking, bespectacled man hid behind his gentle countenance an inner fire, a radicalism that, tied to the powerful authenticity of Douglass's own story, made the two a persuasive and effective team for many years. With Garrison's encouragement, he and Anna settled in Lynn, Massachusetts, with Douglass completely giving his heart to the small and publicly shunned abolitionist movement.

William Lloyd Garrison

Douglass's personal charisma and renowned eloquence made him an important public figure, though in antebellum America it was astonishing that any black man could claim such status. He spoke mostly from rough manuscripts, and from surviving multiple newspaper transcriptions of certain speeches he gave repeatedly, we know that they differed according to the venue and the feeling of the moment. He departed freely from his notes, such was his sure confidence as an orator. This element of his fame, the accomplished manner in which he varied his tone from thunderous rousing calls to sly mimicry, then moments of earthy humor, all these things galvanized his listeners. One observer remembered seeing Douglass stalk from one edge of the platform to another, "all roused up like a Numidian Lion," concluding he was seeing something more than an eloquent address: "He was an insurgent slave taking hold on the right of speech."[12]

From 1841 on, his life was one of incessant, grueling travel. Each year was punctuated by these long speaking circuits across all of the northern states, though he felt increasingly nervous whenever speaking engagements came within striking distance of the South. What made him interesting, exotic, and controversial in the free states made him a marked man whenever he neared the border state of Kentucky, his old home state of Maryland, and even southern Pennsylvania, where kidnapping was commonplace. His was a difficult and lonely life. It was not simply the dusty travel, the wear of three-hour lectures on

Frederick Douglass, circa 1850, after 1847
daguerreotype by an unidentified artist

his throat, the poor food along the way, but the debilitating sense of danger and degradation at every stop. Though a famous orator, and increasingly well-paid, he was still a black man. The difficulties of arranging travel, managing to find a place to stay the night, wondering what kind of mob might greet him at the site of each night's speech—none of these things ever subsided before the Civil War.

Then, in 1845, he made one of the most audacious moves of his life. The publication of his memoir of his early years in slavery, *Narrative of the Life of Frederick Douglass, an American Slave,* was a provocation in itself, but Douglass also dared to reveal personal information about his life as a free man. These facts were enticing to those who wanted the young abolitionist speaker snatched back into the slavery out of which he had come. He almost taunted his former owner Thomas Auld to recapture him by not only revealing the name his owner had known him by, Frederick Augustus Washington Bailey, but by actually mailing the slaveholder a copy of the book. When the book became an unexpected best-seller, worried friends realized that he was now in some danger and arranged for him to go to England to represent the American abolitionist movement. At the time, this escape to England was a disheartening reminder that no matter with what confidence and dexterity Douglass comported himself on abolitionism platforms of the North, he was still someone's property back in Maryland. More southern men than just Auld wanted him back and silenced.

The 1845 visit to England made Douglass an international figure and without question the most prominent black abolitionist on either side of the Atlantic. At speeches all over the north of England and Scotland, thousands came to hear him. In the midst of such interest bordering on adulation, he was reminded that in Britain he was perceived as a different category of person. "Why, sir, the Americans do not know that I am a man. They talk of me as a box of goods; they speak of me in connection with sheep, horses and cattle. But here, how different! Why, sir, the very dogs of old England know that I am a man!"[13] Then, he had written to his abolitionist mentor, William Lloyd Garrison, that the English experience was a powerful one, with "the entire absence of anything that looked like racial prejudice against me, on account of the colour of my skin—contrasted so strongly with my long and bitter experience in the United States, that I look with wonder and amazement at the transition."[14]

The trip was extremely successful; generous British admirers had gathered enough money to pay off his old owner. At last he was a free man. Upon his return from his sojourn in England, Douglass celebrated his newfound freedom by forging a new life in many directions. He moved Anna and their young children into a new home in Rochester, New York, and decided to offer a strong voice by editing *The North Star*, a rival newspaper to Garrison's *Liberator*. He did this, he admitted, "without a day's schooling . . . I could hardly spell two words correctly . . ."[15] This decision to create a black-owned and edited newspaper was to become a painful wedge in his old partnership with Garrison. In the end, Douglass's inner need to make his own way, to express his own brand of abolitionism, could not be denied or repressed, no matter how much he owed to the man who had first urged him to greatness. There was a destiny for him that Garrison could not support. Garrison had needed a former slave to tell a tale of salvation; Douglass wanted something more, to push himself to the very limit of his abilities and talents. Not even Garrison's sincere and radical abolitionism could accept such independence and personal autonomy on the part of a black man.

In the mid-nineteenth century, Rochester, the City of Flowers, was known to have few rivals for beauty among American cities. Blossoming tulips, roses, and fruit trees adorned the city. A resident wrote to a friend in 1827, "Rochester is the best place we have yet seen for giving strangers an idea of the newness of this country."[16] For Douglass, looking to begin anew, it had seemed the perfect place for a self-made man, one intent on being a writer, editor, and publisher, not only an abolitionist circuit speaker.

Though it looked like an old New England town, Rochester was first founded in 1817. The city grew quickly, gaining 8,000 residents in ten years. It went from forest to boomtown overnight. Much of its success came from the opening of the Erie Canal and, later, being on the route of the New York Central railroad. The awe-inspiring power and beauty of the waterfalls of the Genesee River helped Rochester earn its place in early America's folklore in 1829, when a daring man named Sam Patch jumped 120 feet into the main falls. Widely publicized beforehand, a mesmerized crowd watched the inebriated Patch's arms flailing all the way down, a leap from which he would never emerge.[17]

Rochester's black population was small, numbering less than 3 percent of the population in 1834. Yet, Douglass found abolitionist allies—white and black—that proved especially useful for conducting the Underground Railroad. Rochester was the last stop for thousands of frantic flights to freedom ending in Canada, across Lake Ontario. It was not uncommon for Douglass to arrive at work at the *North Star* press offices with tired and hungry fugitives waiting on the steps for his aid. As "superintendent" of the Rochester station, Douglass knew the obscure places to hide: barns, lofts, woodsheds, attics, anywhere a fugitive could be safe for a time. His newspaper office even had a trap door leading to a clandestine stairway. Douglass and his wife, Anna, fed them and gave them train fare to complete their journey, or placed them in boats heading across the lake. One evening Douglass realized he had eleven fugitives staying with his family. Despite the danger, he would later say, "I never did more congenial, attractive, fascinating and satisfactory work." Although he was realistic about the overall effectiveness of the Underground Railroad, he admitted that ". . . as a means of destroying slavery, it was like an attempt to bail out the ocean with a teaspoon . . ."[18] Having been a slave, however, even one less soul in bondage brought him great joy. The southern shore of Lake Ontario was a vista of freedom for his soul and the route to freedom for many fugitives.[19]

The *North Star* debuted in 1847 with the slogan, "Right is of no Sex—Truth is of no Color—God is Father of us all, and we are all Brethren." Writing for this antislavery periodical day after day, week after week, forced Douglass to refine and further articulate his ideas. Years later he felt that the clarity with which he spoke during the Civil War had come from the long nights of work and developing his thinking in the newspaper years of the 1850s. The pressure of constant deadlines meant this life "was the best school possible for me." Often Douglass would write all day and then hop on a train for a town hosting his evening speaking engagement. If the engagement finished in time, he would catch a train back to Rochester, otherwise he stayed the night in whatever hamlet he found himself, still managing to be back in his office as early as possible. The office was not elaborate—simply a small single room with an old printing press, cases of type all along the wall, a desk for Douglass to write, and a fireplace to warm him through long Rochester winters.[20]

Douglass was a very careful man in dealing out the details of his personal life. Matters of the heart, especially, were kept carefully hidden, even as he seemed to fully share his redemptive journey from slave to citizen. In hundreds of pages of autobiography, he related what he felt he needed to in order to accomplish his life's mission of ending slavery—and not a whit more. Each slave, every black soul, was meant to be redeemed in Douglass's *Pilgrim's Progress* to freedom; inner confusions, the toll of constant racial belittlements, and struggles within his own immediate family had no part in the tale he wished to tell. Above all, he wished to portray himself as someone whose potential not even slavery could destroy.

In essentially raising himself—without the ordinary supports of family or sustained childhood friendships—he was slavery's child, growing up in emotionally barren and harsh circumstances, a desert devoid of love and simple protection. That the damage done was so hidden and carefully managed is a remarkable sign of powerful internal strength. In an era that celebrated the doctrine of self-creation, he was after all truly the self-created man par excellence.

Dating back to Tom Paine's vision that in America "we have it in our power to begin the world over again,"[21] self-creation is the American ideal. The intensity and fervor of Douglass's oft-delivered addresses on this theme reflect something more arduous than simply the ideology of the economically rising man. In his *Collected Papers*, three versions of the talk—often revised and refreshed to reflect further ruminations upon his own life—are preserved, from 1859 to a final draft in 1893. (In this final draft, he calls Abraham Lincoln: "the King of American self-made men; the man who rose highest and will be remembered as the most popular and beloved President since Washington. This man came to us, not from the schools or from the mansions of eases and luxury, but from the backwoods.")[22]

Douglass championed hard work, industry, and well-tempered zeal as qualities crucial for greatness that is earned, not given. He defined such souls as "men, who under peculiar difficulties and without ordinary helps of favoring circumstances, have attained knowledge, usefulness, power and position . . ." In clear reference to his own "peculiar difficulties," he further defined the obstacles to selfhood: "not only without the voluntary assistance or friendly co-operation of society, but often in open and derisive defiance of all the efforts of society . . . to repress, retard and keep them down." In the end, these men were "indebted to themselves for themselves." From poverty and from "hunger, rags, and destitution, they have come; motherless and fatherless, they have come, and may come."

Douglass used these extraordinarily personal references as instructive themes in his frequent "self-made" discourses. The extreme impoverishment, both emotional and economic, of his early years was displayed for more than personal vindication or self-aggrandizement—it was transformed into an extremely eloquent and persuasive argument for the vast unrealized potential of his people. He pointed to "genuine heroism" of anyone who could triumph against such imposing odds, but that was not really the point of the lecture: "Every instance of such success is an example and a help to humanity."[23]

The most revealing aspect of his "self-made" talk, however, is a little noted coda at its conclusion. Despite the admiration such men deserved, Douglass confessed, "I am far from considering them the best made men. Their symmetry is often marred by the effects of their extra exertion . . . the long and rugged road over which they have been compelled to travel, have left their marks, sometimes quite visibly and unpleasantly, upon them." (He then alluded to editor Horace Greeley, who was said to be a self-made man who "worshipped his maker.") He added, "A self-made man is also likely to be full of contrarieties. He may be large, but at the same time, awkward; swift, but ungraceful; a man of power, but deficient in the polish and amiable proportions of the affluent and regularly educated man."[24]

Douglass clearly felt these "contrarieties," though few would have witnessed outer awkwardness in his own regal and refined demeanor—but the description applied extraordinarily well to Abraham Lincoln, whose awkwardness and lack of urbane polish was legendary.

CHAPTER 3

To the Brink

All night long in dense fog, Frederick Douglass's ship, the *Nova Scotian*, lay just outside of Liverpool, the great English port promising both freedom and a long exile from his homeland, wife, five children, and a vocation. Sending up rockets, blowing whistles, burning blue lights, and firing cannon into the murk did nothing to part the disorienting haze. It was late November 1859 and Douglass found himself once again cast into the role of fugitive with no way of envisaging his future course.

As he waited for the crowded docks of bustling Liverpool to at last come into view, Douglass faced a different kind of danger. Although Douglass was now technically a free man, this present threat was as perilous to his freedom as his first anxious escape to England twelve years before. As he prepared to give his "Self-Made Men" lecture at Philadelphia's National Hall, word reached him that in the aftermath of the Harpers Ferry raid, letters from him had been found in Captain John Brown's belongings, which put him in grave danger. Governor Henry Wise of Virginia wanted Douglass indicted for abetting Brown's recent bloody attempt to seize a federal arsenal. He even sent a private detective to track him down beyond the continental United States. If any boat intercepted a British ship carrying Douglass, Wise announced, he wanted the "privilege of seeing him well hung."[1] Worse, President James Buchanan, clearly anxious to appease the governor, had ordered federal marshals to arrest Douglass. They had been only steps behind him for weeks. Douglass had been extraordinarily lucky so far to have evaded them. After the daring raid electrified the country, a terrified South wanted vengeance. Strangely, through either a sense of wounded innocence or bravado, Douglass wasted valuable time in Philadelphia by casually going about his previous plans. With word of Governor Wise's declaration spreading, every minute was imperative.

At this point, someone Douglass did not even know likely saved his life. Officials in Washington, D.C., sent a telegraph to the sheriff of Philadelphia County to apprehend Douglass. The telegraph came in to a local operator named James Hern, who happened to be an avowed abolitionist. Hern managed to delay the delivery of the telegraph three vital hours, just long enough for a warning of its content to reach Douglass. By the time the telegraph arrived on the sheriff's desk, Douglass had left Philadelphia and was on his way home to Rochester.

Douglass had allowed himself to think his home city would be safer, but he had been home only a matter of minutes when he learned that law enforcement agents were closing in on him. The choice was now clear: he needed a way out of the country. His long experience as a trusted conductor on the Underground Railroad now came into play, as he was spirited from Rochester across Lake Ontario to momentary safety in Clifton, Canada, then to Hamilton, Toronto, and finally a hasty all-night train trip to Montreal. Yet even there, rumors of capture swirled about him, so he moved on to Quebec, with "the snow eight inches deep, cracking under one's feet with the sharp cover-your-ears sound . . . The sleigh bells are ringing, and the Frenchmen and their ponies are dashing through the streets . . ." He enjoyed the sights of the Old Town for only a day, and on November 12, he set sail for England.[2] Boarding the ship, he wondered if he might be going into exile for the rest of his life.

All this had come from Douglass having listened over the years, sometimes with admiration and sometimes with severe misgiving, to his friend Captain Brown's audacious schemes for a southern slave insurrection. There had been so many conversations, hushed late night consultations, expectant discussions of invasion over unrolled maps. Most recently, Douglass and Brown had shared an anguished farewell in an isolated stone quarry in Chambersburg, Pennsylvania, after Douglass finally refused to join in the doomed crusade.

Although Brown had shown in Kansas that he was not afraid of a little blood on his hands (or pools of it from five broadsword-hacked men on the creeks of Osawatomie, Kansas), the long years of frustrated planning, fundraising, delays, and perplexing changes of direction had made it seem as if Brown's violent scheme would go unfulfilled forever. But then, less than a month after their last conversation in Chambersburg, the old man had suddenly struck, at last making good on his long-nurtured plan of slave revolution.

Though every aspect of the ill-thought-out plan had gone disastrously wrong, proving to be exactly the fiasco Douglass had feared it would

John Brown

be, it was strange how little this had mattered to Brown's desired hope of terrorizing the slaveholders he so abhorred. While nearly the whole raiding party had been quickly and effectively killed or captured, Brown, as he awaited hanging, had a martyr's satisfaction in suddenly finding himself a hated specter of insurrection to the South and, as well, an unexpected hero to many in the North. Abraham Lincoln, invited to speak at the prestigious Cooper Union Institute in New York in 1860, took the opportunity to reflect another common reaction among the free states: "John Brown's effort was peculiar. It was not a slave insurrection. It was an attempt by white men to get up a revolt among slaves, in which the slaves refused to participate. In fact, it was so absurd that the slaves, with all their ignorance, saw plainly enough that it could not succeed."[3]

Whether a failure or not, the Harpers Ferry attack revealed in southern hearts a deep-rooted and growing fear of slave rebellion, especially one abetted by perceived northern fanatics. Even a plainly incompetent company of twenty-two men quickly became a looming threat intent on destroying their whole way of life. When letters from Frederick Douglass were found in

Brown's captured baggage, Douglass had been quickly and dangerously drawn into the net of retribution.

Ironically, he had never wished to know any of the specifics of John Brown's planned attack on the vulnerable federal arsenal at Harpers Ferry. Still, more than twelve years ago Brown had shared with Douglass at their very first meeting in 1847 an overarching hope of someday stirring slaves to rebellion. Fresh from his return from his first trip to England, after giving a speech, Douglass was invited into the Brown home in Springfield, Massachusetts, where the antislavery Brown was then living. After a plain meal of beef soup, Brown took the opportunity to try out his revolutionary ideas on the prominent black leader. By his fireside, Brown cautiously shared with Douglass his initial vision, which was not so much a general slave uprising as the creation of a small army operating in a series of quick incursions in the very heart of the South, using the shelter of the Allegheny Mountains for protection. Douglass remembered the captain as "lean, strong, and sinewy, of the best New England mold, built for times of trouble . . ." He found the white man impressive, his mouth "strong and square," with blue-gray eyes "full of light and fire."[4]

Their friendship continued over the next decade, and slowly, as Douglass drew away from the nonviolent moral suasion policy of the Garrisonians, he became more sympathetic to Brown's willingness to employ violence to attack slavery, especially after the passage of the 1850 Fugitive Slave Law. Still, something held him back, despite his respect and fondness for Brown.

To Douglass's relief, he at last found himself safe on British soil, in the clear now. The trip to Europe had been long planned, but his need to escape quickly through Canada had hastened his departure. He courageously used his many speeches and appearances in Scotland and England over the next five months to make clear his admiration for his now-infamous friend, freely admitting he had not been as bold, as dedicated unto death as John Brown. In years to come, he had to endure the taunts of those who claimed he was a coward, unwilling to dare all at Harpers Ferry.

Douglass, who faced down death many times in his career, was clearly not a coward, but he freely admitted he was intent on staying alive to pursue his own goals, so that he could follow his own way to defeat slavery. He had been beaten on a Massachusetts railway car in protest over segregated travel and had endured savage beatings while enslaved. But Douglass claimed that the closest he had ever come to death was on an 1843 speaking tour in the small town of Pendleton, Indiana. As Douglass began their program, William White, a white abolitionist friend, observed a menacing group of men gathering at the edges of the crowd. Suddenly, the scene descended into violence, and Douglass saw White trapped in the midst of the mob. Seizing a club, Douglass swung wildly as he rushed into the ferocious crowd. As Douglass's weapon was knocked out of his hands, he tried to run, but he was hurled to the ground. An assailant clubbed Douglass's hand, shattering it. White saw the club raised again for a second blow to the prostrate Douglass, and sprinting toward his wounded comrade, he threw his body against the rioter. The blow averted, Douglass stumbled up, and he and his companion managed to dash away from their attackers. Years after the narrow escape, that violent morning still haunted his dreams. He often found himself going to sleep troubled, "thinking about Pendleton." For a reminder, he only had to look down at a hand that had never healed correctly, paining him the rest of his life.[5]

Frederick Douglass was well acquainted with danger; whenever critics maintained that he should have joined Brown at Harpers Ferry, he had no trouble rejecting the idea. His gifts were dramatically different from Brown's. For the rest of his days, his praise for Brown's sacrificial spirit would be unstinted and sincere, yet in the end, he had decided that he must live for his cause, not be a martyr to it.

In a letter written on the ship for readers of his newspaper (now renamed *Frederick Douglass' Paper*) and mailed upon his arrival in England, he reminded his countrymen, "John Brown has not failed. He has dropped an *idea*, equal to a thousand bombshells into the very Bastille of slavery. That idea will live and grow, and one day will, unless slavery is otherwise abolished, cover Virginia with sorrow and blood."[6]

While in England, Douglass's warm memories and familiar sights from his earlier sojourn comforted him in his exile, and he quickly took up his accustomed task of swaying as many listeners as he could reach. The crowds in the British Isles were ready once again to flock to his lectures, anxious to see the man so closely associated with John Brown. On the platform, Douglass's eyes burned with cool intensity. His voice was rich and sonorous, easily filling vast halls with the practiced dramatic pauses and cadences of a preacher. He was now forty-two and his body still had the powerful bearing of youth, broad shoulders and powerful arms imbuing him with an even greater presence. It was not hard to imagine that this man had once relied on his body for grueling physical labor. Francis Grimké, a fellow abolitionist and black clergyman, thought "Michelangelo would have delighted to chisel in marble, or cast in bronze that noble form and figure!" Spiritualist Margaret Fox remarked that his lectures "would set the people Crazy," adding she thought that he was "as fine looking as Ever."[7]

He held his impressive six-foot frame so firmly upright that he gave the impression of being taller than he was. When he spoke in public, his fluid and graceful movements conveyed a natural dignity and self-confident air. As

Unitarian minister and abolitionist Thomas Wentworth Higginson once strolled with Douglass, he thought to himself, "Make the most of this opportunity. You never before have walked the streets with so distinguished-looking a man, and you never will again."[8]

On December 7, 1859, Douglass's youngest child, twelve-year-old Annie, wrote him news from home:

My Dear Father,

I am proceeding in my gramar very well for my teacher says so. I am in the first reader and I can read. I expect that you will have a german letter from me in a very short time. I have learned another piece and it is a Anti Slavery. I am going to speak it in school. My piece is this.

<blockquote>
He is not the man for me
Who buys or sells a slave
Not he who will not set him free
But send him to his grave
But he whose noble heart beats warm
For all men's life and liberty
Who loves alike each human form
That's the man for me.
</blockquote>

It is in the Garland of Freedom and four verses of it. My letter will not be very long. Poor Mr. Brown is dead. That hard hearted man said he must die, and they took him in an open field and about a half mile from the jail and hung him . . .

From your affectionate Daughter,
Annie Douglass."[9]

The Douglass of 1859 was indeed a much more confident and accomplished man than the fugitive speaker of 1845. There was no escaping the exhilaration of this experience of freedom, abundantly displayed in Glasgow, Scotland, on March 26, 1860, in "American Constitution and the Slave," one of the most impressive speeches of his life. The address marked the end of his long and painful process of pulling away from his Garrisonian abolitionist roots and summation of his journey to independent thinking. Douglass's shift from Garrison's view (along with his having had the audacity to start his own newspaper) had made his old friend an implacable enemy.

To fully break from Garrison and his philosophies was wrenching, but Douglass had tired of conceding to the South their argument that the United States Constitution was a proslavery document. Further, he now resisted William Lloyd Garrison's often expressed notion that seceding from the Union was a viable option for northern states. Instead, Douglass came to view the Declaration of Independence's proclamation that "all men are created equal" as the proper lens through which to understand the essential meaning of the Constitution. The Declaration spelled out America's ideals, leaving a firm hope for the redemption of the nation under the subsequent Constitution with the additions of the Bill of Rights.

To Garrison, however, Douglass's changing ideas were nothing less than "base and selfish."[10] Garrison was never one to tolerate such dissent, and their political differences turned personal and messy, to the point that Garrison's *Liberator* newspaper published allegations of an adulterous liaison between Douglass and his generous supporter and close ally Julia Griffiths, a white Englishwoman, who for some years had actually lived in the Douglass home.

The startling allegation was quickly and fervently denied, but with so many personal letters from that period lost or destroyed, it is today impossible to know if Garrison's audacious condemnation of his old friend was in fact true. Douglass published a calm, reassuring letter from his wife, Anna (though Anna had for years stoutly refused to learn to read or write), denying any strain or trouble from Julia Griffiths's presence in their lives. Eventually, the dispute settled into banked coals of simmering resentment, leaving real damage done to the abolitionist movement and untold personal anguish to Douglass himself. In the aftermath of the embarrassing imbroglio, Julia returned to England in 1855. Long after her marriage to an English clergyman named Crofts she continued to write Douglass and advise him with warmth and concern. The relationship was so sustaining and vital to Douglass that in 1859 he went directly from Liverpool to her new home in Halifax, from which he began his extensive speaking tour in England.

After years of self-taught legal and political study, he now felt fully prepared to repudiate Garrison's rejection of the Constitution. In the end, the nation's founding document "leans to freedom, not to slavery," and this could save the country. With a presidential contest impending back home, Douglass believed such truths made abolitionist hopes realistic, though the leading Republican candidate, New York senator William H. Seward, was hardly a raving abolitionist and Stephen Douglas loomed in the background as a viable Democratic candidate. Still, Douglass firmly staked his ground, believing "the way to abolish slavery in America is to vote such men into power as will use their power for the Abolition of slavery." It is hard to miss in this speech a wistful note that with great events on the horizon, he was achingly far from being able to influence such an outcome.

The background of this major address was his answering the taunts of Garrison abolitionists about changing his mind on these important ideas. His answer to them was direct and affecting, a rare personal opening for a man who seldom opened his heart. "When I escaped from slavery, twenty-two years ago, the world was all new to me, and if I had been in a hogshead with the bung in, I could not have been much more ignorant of many things than I was then. All I knew was that I had two elbows and a good appetite, and that I was a human being—a sort of non-descript creature, but still struggling for life." In this state of unfolding development, he had fallen under the spell of Garrison and his allies, and in his rapid and fervent efforts of creating himself as a speaker and as a man, he had naturally accepted their views and perspectives. "They were my friends, the friends of my people, and nothing was more natural than that I should receive as gospel all they told me."[11]

During his five months in exile, Douglass had moved on from the well-intentioned influences of past mentors to confront the meaning—the mission—of his life. Though he had planned to spend more time in England and was about to embark for the continent for further travel, to France and perhaps Germany, fate seized him in early 1860 with a cruel and shocking turn that propelled him home. He returned in time to witness the election of a new president and the long-foretold shattering of his country into warring factions.

On March 13, 1860, Douglass received a letter from home saying his youngest child was dead. In shock and guilt, he resolved to return home, immediately. Annie's death changed everything, and the England idyll was over in a bitter instant. No matter what possible dangers awaited him, he felt he had no choice as a father and husband but to return home to Rochester without delay.

A family friend described the little girl as "the gentle, darling little Annie, with her winning, modest shyness, but happy to trust to the friendly face of the lady who held her small, soft, velvety hand kindly while talking to her father and mother." Her sister called her "blithe and lively." In Douglass's own newspaper, Annie was affectionately called the "pet of her father." She possessed a carefree cheerfulness unmatched in the family.[12]

Yet even at her young age, she had developed a passion for the work of her father. In fact, it was a belief within the family that shock from the death of John Brown had somehow contributed to her death. To Annie, "poor

Mr. Brown" was not an abstract martyr; he had stayed with the Douglass family for a long stretch in 1858 and insisted on paying three dollars a week in board. During this time, the stern old man occasionally showed a more tender side, captivating the imagination of young Annie when she sat on his knee.[13] In front of Douglass's children, Brown used planed boards and dividers to depict a chain of fortification in the mountains for his abolitionist guerillas. Douglass often did not quite know what to make of the wild designs, commenting that "I was less interested in these drawings than my children were." Annie obviously had had great difficulty processing Brown's death—perhaps Douglass could have helped her deal with this grief had he not been in England during that highly sensitive time.[14]

Douglass's oldest daughter, Rosetta, reported in a family letter that they had heard from their father, and "his grief was great." But it is her next sentence that is particularly powerful: "I trust that the next letter will evince more composure of mind." Such anguished sadness was to be expected from a father who has lost a child. (Later, in Douglass's narrative, he quickly passes over Annie's death. In their brevity and simplicity, however, these few sentences capture Douglass's heart: calling her the "light and life of my house," he was "deeply distressed by this bereavement.")[15] Letters from those close to him suggest that Douglass grieved many years over his daughter's death. Friends continued to show concern for Douglass's sorrow throughout the Civil War.

For a girl with ardent attachments to her father combined with an "excitable temperament," her father's self-exile with no immediate prospect of return apparently caused her great anxiety for his safety. Hearing adults talk of Brown's death and her father's possible future punishment, Annie retreated from the world, losing her power to speak or hear. The medical cause of her death was never clear, and it seems odd to have Douglass's interpretation of her death in a letter he wrote "To My British Anti-Slavery Friends," as "resulting, no doubt, from over-anxiety for the safety of her father, and deep sorrow for the death of dear old John Brown, upon whose knee she had often sat only a few months before."[16] In that letter, he promised to return to finish his speaking tour, but it was not to be. Claims of America pressed in on every side.[17]

Acting upon a quick impulse without careful thought, he took the first outgoing ship headed to America. Determined to be with his family, he now displayed as much courage as he had ever summoned in a long career. The prospect of being a free man in Europe was a heady prospect, especially if circumstances forced such an exile upon him. Had Annie not died, it is impossible to know when Douglass might have returned to the United States. He knew well that he might be risking his life when he boarded to return to his homeland. A fall and a severe injury to his shoulder only worsened the misery of the return trip.[18]

The city of Rochester that Douglass returned to after Annie's death had been his home for more than ten years. His homecoming from England in 1860 proved to be quiet and subdued. He prudently laid low upon rejoining his grieving family because for weeks, he still feared extradition to Virginia. Yet, luck was with him in that the congressional committee appointed to track down John Brown's allies and supporters had dissolved into a largely fruitless effort and in the end found no evidence tying Douglass to the plotting of the raid. In addition, with the nation absorbed with the upcoming presidential contest, even southern congressmen had seemed to lose their bloodlust for revenge over Harpers Ferry. With the whole country facing potential disaster, Brown's raid had receded, a precursor to an infinitely larger looming cataclysm. Douglass, having feared the worst, found himself pleasantly amazed that the danger to him seemed to be fading. The congressional committee eventually gave up its work, and within three months Douglass returned to the high visibility he had previously enjoyed. As the presidential campaign year of 1860 proceeded, Douglass stood ready to influence its outcome as effectively as he could by a new grueling, nearly frantic speaking tour.

It was his newspaper, *Frederick Douglass' Paper,* that made his life difficult. He wondered if he should end the effort. Upon his return from England, there is disappointment and exhaustion in his words, describing "nearly thirteen years of effort . . . I am now very sorry to give up the effort." The temptation to give up his life as an editor and publisher was not a pose, but a symptom of the dismal state Douglass was feeling in 1860. These difficulties had a long story, and Douglass well understood why so many black-edited newspapers failed. In 1848, he had mortgaged his home to keep the paper from collapsing. At one point, he was fifteen hundred dollars in debt, no trifling sum in 1855. Finding subscribers was a constant struggle throughout this period, though he averaged around 3,000 subscribers. Overhead costs always seemed to mount. When Douglass returned from England, he found the paper running at around a $30 deficit per week. He decided at once to cease publication, but the pleas of readers convinced him to continue. Soon he was losing $50 a week.[19]

From month to month, his speaking engagements kept the enterprise afloat. As much as the paper meant to him, Douglass wearily confided to a friend, "I see nothing for me but to let the paper go down."[20] Yet time and time again, generous gifts from abolitionist and philanthropist Gerrit Smith had kept the newspaper alive in an era when Douglass's voice was a powerful national influence. The best he could do was to keep the paper alive as a monthly publication, with reduced pages and paper size.

The home he retreated to after his exhausting daily pace was a half-hour walk from the pressroom situated in the center of downtown Rochester. Sitting on a hill, surrounded by gardens, fruit trees and farmland, it seemed to be an island away from the world for Douglass. This rural retreat, their second home in Rochester, was far enough from the city to allow Douglass to rest from his intense busy public life and into a private world, one shrouded in secrecy that no amount of research is likely to fully pierce.[21]

His marriage to Anna was both a comfort as well as a hidden source of pain and unfulfillment over the years. She was dutiful, loyal, supportive, and clearly valued her husband as a great man, worthy of her total focus. They were both devoted to their children, and the home they created was filled with children growing with encouragement from him and firm discipline and care from her. Rosetta, whose short biography of her mother is the fullest account of Anna that survives, was the oldest, born in 1839; Lewis followed the next year. Two more boys, Frederick, Jr. and Charles, were born before Douglass went to England in 1845, and Annie was born in 1849 after his return as a free man.

Yet, despite his devotion to his children, in 1848 Douglass had described himself as a "most unhappy man." Moreover, three years before the Civil War, Douglass wrote to a friend that, "if I should write down all her complaints there would be no room even to put my name at the bottom."[22]

Douglass and Anna had profoundly different approaches to the world of ideas. He constantly pressured her to absorb new ideas, but she never shared his intellectual interests. She never learned to read, although he set up numerous opportunities for her to do so. Douglass's feelings on their differences were never clearer than when he was commenting on a letter, noting someone had to read it "over and over again until Dear Anna shall fully understand their contents."[23]

Anna provided her husband a firm foundation, a clean home, food and comforts, clean linens, smoothly ironed suits. All these practical things were the work of her own hands, as was caring for the fugitive slaves that came into the Douglass household. When Douglass was ill during his frequent bouts with bronchitis, she sat by his bedside and cared for him. Yet, her dedication to these tasks in lieu of mental stimulation was problematic for a man with a restless mind like Douglass. The relationship also suffered from their frequent separations, as he traveled incessantly, including two long stays in Europe. Rosetta wrote that when he was home, "Father was mother's honored guest."[24]

Anna Douglass

Regardless of the state of their marriage, Douglass was extraordinarily proud of his family, perhaps especially so because as a boy he had suffered having all family supports stripped away. Anna raised their five children, and he was devoted to them even if he was the epitome of the absentee father. She was frugal and stern with the children, and they realized they would have a more successful chance pleading their case with their father after transgressions. Her criticisms could be blunt and harsh, whether she directed them at family members or guests.

Anna had friends in New Bedford and Lynn, but she never grew close with anyone in Rochester, retreating into her home and into herself. Douglass wanted her to travel more with him, but Anna simply felt more comfortable tending to matters in the home and in her garden. Mostly, she felt unease around the plethora of white visitors her husband brought to the house. After preparing and serving the meal, she was content to retire to the back porch and her rocking chair. Rosetta, however, recalled her mother talking with her father about certain current events, especially in the anti-slavery movement.[25]

The marriage may have been strained also by Douglass's inviting white female friends and associates to stay in the family home for long stretches of time. His relationship with Julia Griffiths provoked many rumors. When the writer Ottilie Assing entered his life in the early 1850s, she most certainly claimed his bed. Assing spent summers in the Douglass family home over a decade and Douglass often stayed with her in her home in Hoboken, New Jersey. Assing was German-born and raised on European cultural values and liberal revolutions. She had come to America at age thirty-three to work as a journalist and immediately comprehended the promise of the abolitionist movement. When she heard about the strikingly handsome former slave Frederick Douglass, she desired to meet this great man. As emotional as she was intellectual, she excited and captivated Douglass. They would garden, cook, play croquet, and read together. Her letters to her sister describe an idyllic scene of two lovers feeding peaches and cherries to each other, while enjoying the lush, picturesque region around Rochester. They hiked the mountains, explored the countryside, strolled and sailed along the Genesee River.[26]

Douglass's letters over three decades reveal that, outside of his family, those closest to him were European women, especially Julia Griffiths and Rosine Draz (another friend from his English sojourns). Like Assing, they were educated, intellectual women, who shared unwavering devotion and adoration of him.

His twenty-five-year relationship with Assing never caused Douglass to leave his marriage for several reasons. Because of his role as the most prominent black leader in America, divorce in the 1860s was simply not an option. After all, Douglass's career was bound up in a vivid presentation of his own life for the perceived benefit of his people; in an era when divorce was uncommon and disdained, it would have devastated his public persona and influence. Furthermore, Douglass wrote that he believed slavery created a crippling social system with no use for family. Thus, to give up the family he had created in lieu of the one denied to him would be to abandon part of what he had won by becoming free. Regardless of Assing, Douglass did have a profound love for his family, not just in an abstract sense but in the day-to-day reality of his life. He may or may not have felt guilt for a love life that he did not try hard to hide within the family itself, yet his actions throughout the Civil War years show how much his children truly meant to him, and the extent to which he would go to protect and help them.

On the eve of the great presidential race, Douglass felt lost in "months of anxiety, sickness, sorrow and death."[27] Memories from a tortured past, a floundering paper, a fading marriage, a secret interracial affair, and the death of his youngest and most beloved daughter were all part of the mountain of baggage Douglass was carrying. These disappointments and his pressing need

Ottilie Assing

to keep much of himself hidden to the world wore at him, along with the constant fatigue of touring about the country.

Yet, these personal problems were not the only causes of his profound despair. The excitement and firm idealism of the late 1840s had been tested by a long decade of setbacks, and a case could be made that abolitionism was weaker than ever by 1860 in terms of national support, despite the fact that increasing numbers of white northerners identified with the cause. On the political side, the previous decade had begun with the enactment of the Fugitive Slave Law that federally sanctioned taking any black person into slavery with virtually no legal recourse. Even worse, in 1857 the *Dred Scott* decision by Chief Justice Roger B. Taney's Supreme Court acknowledged slavery as an institution with no legal restraints and boundaries, even in the free states, despite those states' laws against the "peculiar institution." After all of Douglass's heartfelt and heartrending speeches, all the meetings and prayers for the cause, it was profoundly dispiriting for those toiling for more than twenty-five years to read the chief justice's words: "The black man had no rights that the white man had any right to respect." The ruling made brutally clear that black people were not, and might never be, citizens of the United States. The decade concluded with John Brown's execution in Virginia.

By April, notwithstanding his despair, Douglass was speaking widely, reclaiming his status as the most prominent black voice in America. The times were indeed discouraging, but events were also arising that were remarkable and potentially fruitful in terms of who might replace the ineffective and dithering President James Buchanan. In that month, at the Democratic national convention, Stephen Douglas's chances for the presidency were dealt a deathblow when his party broke into two sectional factions, with southern delegates distrustful of him and at the last moment deciding to back Kentuckian John C. Breckenridge instead. Then, in early May the newly formed Constitutional Union party nominated John Bell, further splitting the Democratic opposition. For a political organization as young as the Republican party, suddenly its prospects were bright and the nomination highly prized. That candidate would be the next president.

As the Republicans gathered in Chicago in mid-May, Illinois native son candidate Abraham Lincoln (likely angling for an advantageous position to be his state's next senator) seemingly out of nowhere became, on the third ballot, the party's compromise candidate, everyone's favored second choice. Douglass had long thought his New York senator, William Seward, would garner the honor. In his paper, he lamented that Seward, who had been instrumental in shaping Republican antislavery ideology, was "shoved aside to make room for a man whose abilities are untried and whose political history too meager to form a basis on which to judge his future."[28] The first true western candidate, Lincoln was as little harmed by the sudden emergence of his rail-splitter persona as by the shrewd dealing of his campaign managers. In the end, he won because delegates had developed an admiration for his clear, cogent speeches that had so effectively demarcated a winning position against Stephen Douglas.

Wasting not a moment, Douglass assessed his man in positive terms, something fellow abolitionists for the most part resisted, in an editorial headed "The Chicago Nominations." He claimed Lincoln was "a radical Republican, and is fully committed to the doctrine of the 'irrepressible conflict.'" In his debates with Senator Douglas, he came fully up to "the highest mark of Republicanism, and he is a man of will and nerve . . ." Noting that "Illinois will form a sort of pivot," he felt "the old personal rivalry between him [Douglas] and Mr. Lincoln will render the campaign especially spicy."[29] Douglass predicted to a friend that if Lincoln won the election, Seward would be the nominee in 1864.[30]

For the most part, Douglass in his public writings about Lincoln during the election season endeavored to keep a positive tone. Remembering Lincoln's 1858 stern warning that the nation could not endure half-slave, half-free, he realized Lincoln might not be an abolitionist but seemed to be a man of strong character and perceptive insight into the national predicament. Douglass called him "calm, cool, deliberate." He complimented Lincoln's ". . . well balanced head; great firmness of will" and called him "one of the most frank, honest men in political life." Yet, he had to admit even these good qualities hardly qualified him to be a presidential nominee, especially in such a critical hour. He doubted that Lincoln knew anything of literary culture or diplomatic skill. At best, the Republicans nominated him based on their faith in his potential.[31]

In August of 1860 Douglass wrote a doubt-ridden article entitled "The Prospect in the Future." He told his readers that the work of the last twenty-five years had "reached a point of weary hopelessness." A month before, Douglass had told fellow journalist and abolitionist James Redpath that although he had labored to write and speak, it was for people without "ears or hearts for the appeals of justice and humanity." Slaveholders were "beyond the reach of moral and humane consideration," and the only thing that could end slavery was the threat of death to them. He was reduced to "little hope of the freedom of the slave by peaceful means."[32]

As the summer of 1860 faded into autumn, Douglass became more excited about the upcoming presidential contest than any previous election. He decided to throw himself into the race with "former faith and more ardent hope than ever before."[33] He was excited because the choice was extraordinarily clear as to whether an American's vote would hinder or help the slave. He believed that this election would be an opportunity to educate the American people on his emancipation agenda. Whom he would actually vote for was a more complicated question.

There were other facts that gave Douglass serious pause. As the election drew closer, Douglass learned Lincoln had not signed a petition in the Illinois legislature that would give black people the right to give evidence in court against a white person. Lincoln was against black suffrage and showed little aversion to implementation of the Fugitive Slave Law. What worried Douglass more was a lesson from the nation's recent history. The past few presidents had also been relative political unknowns, selected over more substantive candidates based on their having accumulated fewer enemies. They had turned out to be weak, vacillating leaders, of the disastrous ilk of Franklin Pierce and the overwhelmed James Buchanan, then presiding over the impending sundering of the country. What Douglass saw was "one host of incompetent kin folks takes the place of another." Douglass found the thought of this trend continuing deeply distressing, and this nonentity Lincoln promised more of the same. In this crucial election, "the road to the Presidency does not lead through the swamps of compromise and concession any longer."[34]

Douglass was never satisfied with the new Republican party for one simple reason: They were more against slavery's political power and sway than against slavery itself. He thought they opposed slavery in places only where white people did not want to deal with the institution, or for that matter, the actuality of black fellow citizens. Republicans wished to keep the western territories free of slavery under a stirring cry for "free labor," all the while enacting laws to restrict the free blacks living amongst them. Douglass ridiculed this covert racism.

Douglass was realistic enough to know a political party that pushed abolition and equality—as the Liberty party showed all too well in its ineffective appeal—would face electoral disaster. Thus, he developed mixed feelings about the election, knowing a Republican victory could present new possibilities for hurting the proslavery powers and clearing the way for more moral antislavery advocacy—even as he still felt compelled to support explicitly abolitionist candidates. In the end, he believed the significance of this vital election was "The slaveholders know that the day of their power is over when a Republican President is elected." Practically speaking, he desired Lincoln's victory, but could not cast his personal vote, which the state of New York allowed, for anyone not in favor of immediate, unconditional emancipation.[35]

His stance drew criticism. One Republican party member had written to him the year before: "The only difference between us is, that one acts on the practical side of the question, and the other on the theoretic. It is all very fine to talk about the short-comings of the Republican Party, but the question is, *What are you going to do about it?*"[36] The answer was to vote for his friend Gerrit Smith, whose futile candidacy might still send a message about the political power of radical abolitionism. Still, in the back of his mind was the hope that a Lincoln victory would begin a new era of antislavery advocacy, and even better, that the president would come to demonstrate "growth in grace."[37]

As the election drew closer, most of Douglass's energies went toward a campaign to defeat a New York state law necessitating that a black man have at least two hundred and fifty dollars in real property to be able to vote. He spoke throughout the state about this injustice and wrote a pamphlet entitled "The Suffrage Question in Relation to Colored Voters in the State of New York." On November 4, Election Day, Douglass stood at a polling place in Rochester from dawn to dusk. Douglass's cause failed by a two-to-one margin, but there was bigger news from the day.[38]

Abraham Lincoln was elected sixteenth president of the United States, a minority president to be sure with less than 40 percent of the vote, but elected nonetheless with 180 electoral votes. His rival Stephen Douglas received respectable vote totals from both North and South, but ended his national career, getting only 12 electoral votes from Missouri and New Jersey, far fewer than John Breckenridge, 72, and John Bell, 39.

On election day, Lincoln betrayed no nervousness—recent state elections in Pennsylvania and Ohio had already indicated that, with his opponents so divided, his election was almost assured. He spent most of the evening in the telegraph office until past midnight, when news from New York confirmed his election, and then he ambled home to inform his wife, Mary.

Four days later, South Carolina began the process of formal secession from the Union. Lincoln seemed sanguine, writing, "Rest fully assured, that the good people of the South who will put themselves in the same temper and mood towards me which you do, will find no cause to complain of me." In the next four months, the president-elect issued no policy statement or made any effort to quell the rising tide of secession. He maintained a steady silence in public, only occasionally writing letters to his supporters in stalwart and encouraging words with little policy to them.[39]

Lincoln seemed to feel that he understood the southern mind and heart, that his good will would somehow prevail in the crisis, despite each day's further unsettling news. The only firm signal he sent from Springfield was to reinforce a stance he had articulated many times in the last six years, ever since his Peoria speech of 1854, that stopping the extension of slavery was his sole unyielding line of policy. To Illinois senator Lyman Trumbull, a convenient conduit for getting the policy word out, Lincoln wrote, "Let there be no compromise on the question of extending slavery. If there be, all our labor is lost, and, ere long, must be done again . . . Have none of it. Stand firm. The tug has to come, & better now, than any time hereafter."[40]

Douglass assessed that Lincoln still believed in the South's constitutional right to hold slaves, despite his personal opposition to slavery's extension. Yet, there was no denying Lincoln's election signaled the breaking of slavery's effective stranglehold on the country's political workings, what abolitionists labeled "the slave power." A Republican president represented the end of decades of the nation taking "the law from the lips of an exacting, haughty and imperious slave oligarchy." The North had shown strength at last, because they had elected "if not an Abolitionist, at least an anti-slavery reputation to the Presidency of the United States."[41]

Though pleased, Douglass went on to warn that the Republicans would have to be pushed to take action against slavery. Worrying that the abolition movement might in fact lose momentum because of a perception that they at last had an ally in power, Douglass rallied radical abolitionists to "writing, publishing, organizing, lecturing, holding meetings, with the earnest aim not to prevent the extension of slavery, but to abolish the system altogether."[42] They would need newfound energy and a unified voice to pressure Lincoln.

CHAPTER 4

"I Used to Be a Slave . . ."

Abraham Lincoln was essentially secretive in nature, reticent to let others peer too deeply into his inner self. Mary Lincoln wrote that he kept his emotions to himself, always. "Even between ourselves, when our deep and touching sorrows, were one and the same, his expressions were few."[1] The only son of four to survive into maturity, Robert Lincoln, a deeply reticent man himself, could recall only a few close conversations with his father and none that revealed any sense of the inner man. Those who knew Lincoln best did not deceive themselves that they truly understood him, or were in his close confidence, personally or politically. He was mysterious, bewildering to his friends and allies, and part of his sway, his powerfully attractive hold on others, was in this deep silence as to his plans, hopes, intentions, and, especially, his past. Judge David Davis, who probably spent as much time with Lincoln on the legal circuit as any man, called his friend, "the most reticent—Secretive man I ever saw—or Expect to see."[2] William Herndon, his longtime law partner, called Lincoln "the most closed mouth person there ever was," and added in notes to himself of his friend that he was "a profound mystery—an enigma—a sphinx—a riddle . . . incommunicative—silent—reticent—secretive . . ."[3]

Lincoln was reluctant to share much of his early life, even when it was clearly to his advantage as a politician to do so. Responding to requests for his life story, he twice wrote a few paragraphs about his early years, and only in the context of being forced to produce effective campaign literature, for which he was painfully curt and short, stating, "There is not much of it, for the reason, I suppose, that there is not much of me. If any thing be made out of it, I wish it to be modest, and not to go beyond the material."[4] One editor, John Scripps of the *Chicago Press and Tribune*, later described his difficulty in getting Lincoln to relate any of his early life: "He seemed to be painfully impressed with the extreme poverty of his early surroundings—the utter absence of all romantic and heroic elements. 'Why, Scripps,' said he on one occasion, 'it is a great piece of folly to attempt to make anything out of my early life. It can all be condensed into a single sentence, and that sentence you will find in "Gray's Elegy": 'The short and simple annals of the poor.' That's my life, and that's all you or any one else can make of it.'"[5]

Above all, Lincoln resisted revisiting his youth, or dwelling on aspects of his life that he clearly found painful to recall, particularly the extreme deprivations of his past. He said in an early political speech, "we were all slaves one time or another," but that being white, he could free himself while a slave could not. He pointed to a friend, adding, "He used to be a slave, but he has made himself free, and I used to be a slave, but now I am so free that they let me practice law."[6] This whimsical note hardly conveys the extent of Lincoln's deep abhorrence of his childhood's grinding poverty and emotional neglect, particularly from his father Thomas's abusive behavior. In a poem written when he was thirty-seven, Lincoln described the desolate nature of prairie life, and the "loved ones lost / In dreamy shadows . . ." The poem contains the lines:

> I hear the lone survivors tell
> How nought from death could save,
> Til every sound appears a knell,
> And every spot a grave.
>
> I range the fields with pensive tread,
> And pace the hollow rooms;
> And feel (companions of the dead)
> I'm living in the tombs.[7]

He had endured the death of his mother, Nancy, when he was eight years old. His only sister, Sally, died in childbirth when he was nineteen. Young Lincoln had every reason to be left numbed and embittered from the touch of death.

Lincoln took considerable pride in his success in law and his escape from the poverty of his origins. He rarely visited his Coles County relatives though, as a successful lawyer in Springfield, he lived only a few hours' travel from them. There is no record of any member of his family ever being invited to his Springfield home. More intensely, he avoided his father as best he could, and after turning down a request to visit the dying Thomas Lincoln, refused to attend his funeral. Lincoln never made a positive utterance about

his father. There were deep chasms between the two men and Lincoln felt he
knew what it was to be exploited and demoralized. His law partner William
Herndon reported that Lincoln said "his father taught him to work; but he
never taught him to love it." Lincoln wanted nothing to do with his origins,
with the exception of his stepmother, Sarah, to whom he felt fondly grateful.

Lincoln calling himself a slave illustrates a great deal about how he arrived at his concept of freedom. He considered himself to have been in a
state akin to oppression because of the manual labor, poverty, and lack of opportunity. Although he had never put on false airs, with his accent, manners,
and tousled clothing certainly reflecting his western beginnings, he was privately chagrined at having been portrayed as the rail-splitter candidate. What
Abraham Lincoln, Esq., ultimately became—through force of will, a passionate belief in work, and a shrewd and penetrating intelligence—was a
wealthy railroad corporate lawyer, not rail-splitter.

President-elect Lincoln needed a place to plan for his new administration and
to greet the hundreds of guests, reporters, and office seekers clambering for
his attention, so he used the governor's corner office in the Springfield State
House, recently vacant because of the death of Governor William Bissell.
Abraham Lincoln walked each morning from his home on Eighth Street to
climb the great steps to the spacious offices on the second floor.

There was no time to celebrate his unlikely rise to power as he struggled
to keep up with his suddenly burgeoning correspondence, as well as playing
host to a perpetual stream of visitors. Three weeks after the election, Henry
Villard of the *New York Herald* watched Lincoln take a moment to relax with
friends, with the president-elect in an expansive mood. When it was suggested that it was too bad that when he entered office as president, his first
problem would be the question of slavery, Lincoln "told the story of the
Kentucky justice of the peace whose first case was a criminal prosecution for
the abuse of slaves. Unable to find any precedents, he exclaimed at last angrily: 'I will be damned if I don't feel almost sorry for being elected when the
niggers is the first thing I have to attend to.'"[8]

It was ironic that a man who had entered politics thirty years before, absorbed with typical Whig topics such as internal improvements, tariffs, taxes,
and westward expansion, now had chief responsibility for the fate of some
four and a half million people held in slavery. This was the issue that would
define his political life and beyond, his legacy and legend. Still, while Lincoln
was no abolitionist, or even by instinct a reformer, he possessed a deep abhorrence of slavery. Finding slavery distasteful and contradictory to his vision of

"free men, free labor," however, was far from casting his lot with the abolitionists; and working against the spread of slavery into the western territories was a long way from wishing to see it eradicated in the South. Through most of his presidency, Lincoln would be adamant that even if slavery were to finally end, slaveholders should have the right to a gradual (up to the year 1900 in one proposal), voluntary, and fully compensated "emancipation."

Lincoln was born in the slave state of Kentucky in 1809, though his parents attended a church opposed to slavery. When Lincoln was seven, in 1816, his father moved the family to Indiana, to settle in a county with only five black people. This limited number was not surprising because strict laws discouraged free blacks from entering the Northwest Territory.

One of the great quandaries of Lincoln's life was in explaining how he, not by temperament or philosophy in any sense an abolitionist, would still be a politician who disliked slavery in such a steadfast and visceral way. Perhaps the explanation lies in Lincoln's lifelong aversion to cruelty of any kind, and even more importantly, from the manner in which slavery so clearly violated the economic principle that an individual's labor was one's own. No man believed in the surging and hopeful capacity of the "self-made man" ideology more than Lincoln, whose entire political philosophy was firmly based on the notion that to rise, to re-create yourself through labor and hard work, was the essence of the American experiment.

From the beginning of his political career, Lincoln took his own roots in manual labor and near-poverty on the western frontier and fused them with a Whig economic philosophy that he never abandoned. In 1847, he stated that the purpose of politics was to secure "to each laborer the whole product of his labor, or as nearly as possible, is a most worthy object of any good government."[9] There are dozens of such formulations in Lincoln's public statements, but he summed up his belief that the essence of America was not simply upward social and class mobility, but the primacy of labor and the right of all to profit from their work. As he said in the great debates and repeated many times, notably to fellow Kentuckian and abolitionist Cassius M. Clay, "I always thought that the man who made the corn should eat the corn."[10]

Lincoln demonstrated his aversion to slavery while a young state legislator in Illinois. In 1837, Lincoln and Daniel Stone were the only members to sign onto a resolution that affirmed "that the institution of slavery is founded on both injustice and bad policy." However, the two men also noted in the same remonstrance that abolitionism too must be blamed for this dire state of affairs, that those extremists actually tended "to increase than to abate its evils."[11]

During two brief years as a congressman in Washington, Lincoln first voted against ending slavery in the capital city, but later introduced a measure that would have allowed compensated and gradual emancipation in the District of Columbia. However during this time, and in the years he concentrated on his law practice, he came to believe there was no good solution to the problem of slavery.

When his sole term as a congressman ended, Lincoln retreated from politics until slavery brought him back from the lonely roads of the Illinois legal circuit. When Stephen Douglas introduced the Kansas-Nebraska Act in 1854, it nullified the old Missouri Compromise and opened the vast western territories to slavery. A visceral outraged reaction to this proposal, from a man he heartily distrusted, drew Lincoln back into politics. Between 1854 and 1860, Lincoln's addresses held to a central theme of excluding slavery from new territories as the first step toward slavery's decline and eventual extinction.

For many who shared his Free Soil ideology, this aversion to slavery was not out of compassion for the slave's plight, but from a strong desire to exclude black people from the new territories, whether they were slave or free. During his time serving in Washington, Lincoln's home state easily passed a constitutional article forbidding black people from entering the state. Ensuring that this land would be for enterprising white men, not wealthy slaveholders and their hated slaves, gave these ideas appeal. Lincoln did not endorse these laws, but he did not repudiate them either.

Although Lincoln abhorred slavery, some of his friends were slaveholders. In 1855 after visiting Joshua Speed on his Farmington plantation outside of Louisville, Kentucky, the young lawyer wrote to his friend's sister Mary about seeing twelve slaves being transported on a passing boat. The twelve enslaved people were chained in two groups, with the clevises around their left wrists connected back to the main chain. He said they looked "like so many fish upon a trot-line," but Lincoln still saw their humanity, which many in his time did not.

> In this condition they were being separated forever from the scenes of their childhood, their friends, their fathers and mothers, and brothers and sisters, and many of them, from their wives and children, and going into perpetual slavery where the lash of the master is proverbially more ruthless and unrelenting than any other where . . .[12]

This was not the only time Lincoln referred to this incident. Many years later, writing to his slaveholding friend Joshua Speed, Lincoln carefully but honestly confronted their strong differences on the issue of slavery, "I confess I hate to see the poor creatures hunted down, and caught, and carried back to their stripes, and unrewarded toils; but I bite my lip and keep quiet." Then he brought up the long-ago memory of those slaves tied together on that steamboat: ". . . ten or a dozen slaves, shackled together with irons. That sight was a continual torment to me; and I see something like it every time I touch the Ohio, or any other slave border." Still, to Speed, he resisted the label of abolitionist, stating, "I now do no more than oppose the *extension* of slavery."[13]

His abhorrence of slavery was more abstract than personal. He believed the institution betrayed the Declaration of Independence's clear intent, allowing those who hated democracy to effectively deny its true power. In the end, the problem with slavery was that it "enables the enemies of free institutions, with plausibility, to taunt us as hypocrites."[14] Even so, Lincoln could not accept the abolitionist agenda either.

Lincoln did not deal with slavery with moral indifference. He repeatedly called it an evil, describing slavery as cancerous or a dangerous snake, and wished it would be contained in such a way that it would eventually be excised or wither away. However, he did not know if extinction could possibly happen in his lifetime, for he believed the Constitution protected the right of southerners to sustain the practice. As a lawyer, his relations with slavery revealed this ambivalence. In more than one Illinois case, Lincoln and Herndon—his partner was adamantly an abolitionist—defended the rights of newly freed slaves and beleaguered black clients. In 1847, however, Lincoln prosecuted the case of Robert Matson, a Kentucky slave owner trying to recover his runaway slaves in Coles County. The slaves claimed that they were free in a free state, but Lincoln pointed out that Matson deserved to retain them as slaves because of the so-called right of transit. He lost the case.[15]

Still, Lincoln genuinely could never comprehend southern assertions that blacks were "property in the same sense that hogs and horses are." Lincoln could clearly see "mind, feeling, souls, family affections, hopes, joys, sorrows—something that made them more than *hogs* or *horses*."[16] Despite this sensitivity, Lincoln had little familiarity with black people as individuals. After his election, a story began circulating that he had attended a gathering of free black people presenting Governor Salmon Chase of Ohio with a silver pitcher. Lincoln called the story a fiction and curtly wrote, "I never was in a meeting of negroes in my life . . ."[17]

While the black community was one he did not know well, he did befriend William de Fleurville, better known as "Billy the Barber." The Haitian emigrant first made his living cutting hair in Baltimore but headed west for new opportunities. He made it only as far as Illinois, where Lincoln met the hungry, desperate man in a tavern. Luckily for de Fleurville, Lincoln immediately recognized their common wit and resolved to help him set up a business in Springfield. Lincoln assisted him in obtaining a shop and found him his first clients. In time, the barbershop would be a second home for Lincoln, with law books strewn about the room as evidence of Lincoln's affinity for the place. Billy the Barber would go on to be a beloved fixture in an otherwise racist community.[18]

Opposition to slavery's extension did not mean Lincoln believed in social equality between the races. He long labored toward the goal of removing black people from the United States through voluntary colonization. Active in the Illinois State Colonization Society, he served in leadership positions, addressing the membership and donating money. In this, he was following Henry Clay, his ideal of a statesman. As a slave owner, Clay might have been expected to stoutly defend slavery, but he knew the institution well enough to be antislavery in his sentiments. Lincoln loved him for his "devotion to the cause of human liberty—a strong sympathy with the oppressed everywhere, and an ardent wish for their elevation." When Clay died, Lincoln was selected to offer his Springfield eulogy, in which he quoted his hero on colonization: "They must blow out the moral lights around us, and extinguish that greatest torch . . ." Lincoln used Clay's own summation: "There is a moral fitness in the idea of returning to Africa her children . . ." To this, the young politician added a heartfelt, "Every succeeding year has added strength to the hope of its realization. May it indeed be realized!"[19]

Lincoln thought that politicians, such as Stephen Douglas, who accused him of championing black equality were raising a false issue; the real issue that mattered was that one sector of America looked upon the slavery as wrong while another "does not look upon it as a wrong."[20] He tried to present a calm demeanor when confronted with these effective taunts, but he showed his frustration privately, angrily scribbling on an undated piece of paper: "Negro equality! Fudge!! How long, in the government of a God, great enough to make and maintain this Universe, shall there continue knaves to vend, and fools to gulp, so low a piece of demagougeism [sic] as this."[21]

In the end, though so much of his political career was predicated on the slavery controversy, he admitted, "If all the earthly power were given to me, I should not know what to do, as to the existing institution."[22] This frustration was not a political position, but a sincere perplexity as to what must be done. The idea that the nation would tear itself apart over slavery was an agony for him, and something in him resisted the idea that southerners could be sincere in their threat of secession, and beyond that, war. Deep down he trusted, as Jefferson had before him, that the corrosive nature of slavery would eventually cause it to collapse upon itself, that it would die an appropriate death.

Exactly how this might happen was beyond his imagination, and perhaps his perplexity was mixed with equal measures of wishful thinking and denial.

Frederick Douglass saw Lincoln's election as a shift, a change, a potential opening, and people long accustomed to disappointment will happily take even chaos instead of the status quo and the stagnant. At the very least, Douglass believed anything that incensed the South the way the rise of Lincoln seemed to must be a positive development.

Rumors of secession by the South were now spreading. These were bewildering days as an anxious nation felt caught in a whirlwind that threatened a frightening new reality. Had the South truly reached a point where they felt they could no longer remain? Would the nation not endure a full century?

While the thought of conflict between North and South was something Douglass had long dreamed of, such a thought truly horrified most northerners, conjuring a sense of bloody apocalypse, not a time of jubilee. Douglass anticipated new opportunities for abolitionists after Lincoln's election, but he and other prominent radicals soon found fresh anger directed at them with a vitriol they had not encountered before. If the country was falling apart because of slavery, many began to violently blame abolitionists like Douglass for the coming schism. In Knoxville, Tennessee, a ferocious crowd mistook a man for Douglass and attacked him with bludgeons and knives.[23]

He was to learn this more personally in, of all places, Boston. The experience would be another of his close brushes with death.

On the frozen morning of December 3, Douglass walked into the Tremont Temple, the imposing building that stood only feet away from the Park Street Church, where William Lloyd Garrison had made his first antislavery speech in the city thirty years ago. Boston had sheltered Garrison's pioneering antislavery newspaper, the *Liberator*, as well as the equally powerful voices of black radicals such as David Walker and Maria Stewart. The forceful and effective black community had led a civil rights revolution culminating in the first racial integration of an American city's school system in 1855. Douglass assumed he was entering a city venerated as a beacon of antislavery reform; instead, it was a powder keg.

Douglass was prepared to speak at an event organized to commemorate the first anniversary of John Brown's martyrdom. There was an electric air to the proceedings, as hundreds of abolitionist sympathizers filed into the hall. Also entering were conservative Boston residents, some from affluent Beacon Hill town houses across the Boston Common, people whose profits in business ventures had long been linked to southern cotton for the looms of Lawrence and Lowell. Working-class Bostonians entered too, many of them dock workers from Boston's North End, tied to the South through the Democratic politics of the Little Giant and hatred of economic competition from free blacks. Although these two groups did not share financial standing, they had mutual contempt for abolitionists whom they perceived to be splitting the nation in two.

From the moment organizer and journalist John Redpath called the meeting to order, the hissing began. J. Stella Martin, a black minister, tried his best to quiet the crowd and to begin electing officers for the meeting, but he received a similar response from the restive crowd. Martin told the abrasive audience, "I hope this is not South Carolina." Redpath walked off the stage, then down an aisle to where the most heckling seemed to be coming from. He had grown up in Scotland and showed that his literary sophistication did not outweigh his penchant for a fight. He grabbed a critic by the collar and began dragging him to the door. Redpath repeatedly tried to heave him out of the proceedings, but the man's friends surrounded him and successfully freed the startled spectator.

Martin was still on stage attempting to yell over the crowd and bring the assembly to order. Democrats screamed that he would not silence them. Abolitionists in the hall gave three cheers for Frederick Douglass. Franklin Sanborn, a wealthy abolitionist who had been implicated in John Brown's raid, tried to assist Martin, pleading, "This is not the Boston I have known."

The crowd cried "Put him out," and a man broke onto the stage, shaking his fist at the speakers. They shouted "Where's the Union?" and one man shrieked that John Brown was in hell. All Douglass heard was mad laughter and competing cheers in the growing chaos. Martin called for police to restore order, and when they appeared, the superintendent of the theater appealed for the crowd to respect those that had rented the hall. This seemed to work for a few moments.

Then a surprising motion went up for an antiabolitionist named Richard S. Fay, recently failed candidate for Congress and son of a well-known judge, to be chairman. His supporters were the majority in the hall, and the motion passed with deafening support.

Police now swarmed the hall. Dock workers raised their fists and older men lifted their canes as they pushed toward the stage. They sensed they now controlled the meeting. As Fay started to address the fuming crowd, Douglass was ready to make his presence felt. Rising on stage, he asked, "Mr. Chairman, will you allow me one word?"

Tremont Temple

Fay angrily replied, "No! not yet!" A deafening noise rose from the shocked abolitionists, whose celebration was being hijacked. Fay then lamented the possible dissolution of the Union while Douglass kept trying to interrupt him. The crowd cried, "Order! Order! Sit Down! Throttle him." The Reverend Martin told his supporters in the hall, "We do not recognize him as chairman."

Coldly, Fay countered, "If you keep quiet while I speak, you will hear some truths which you do not hear at home." As the police moved through the hall pulling apart those exchanging blows, Fay read resolutions condemning John Brown, determined to reassure the South that Massachusetts did not sympathize with the "martyr."

Douglass forcefully interrupted again, and though Fay's supporters called for him to quickly end the assembly, he told Douglass to speak quickly. Fay's people did not want to hear Douglass, and they stood on their seats to jeer him. Douglass bellowed over the shouts, "This is one of the most impudent . . . barefaced . . . outrageous acts on free speech . . . that I have ever witnessed in Boston or elsewhere . . . I know your masters."

The crowd chanted, "Treason, treason! Police! Police! Put him out! Put him out!"

He continued, "I have served the same master that you are serving." Men screamed as he continued, "You are serving the slaveholders. Sir, there is a law which we are bound to obey, and the Abolitionists are most prompt to obey it. It is the law written in the Constitution of the United States, saying, 'all men are born free and equal.'" Douglass coolly added that this applied even to "the stout, big-fisted fellow down there, who has just insulted me." Douglass's supporters roared with laughter. Fay's men were indignant, demanding "Put a rope round his neck."

The police moved to the front of the stage and Douglass assured them, "I will sit down when my time is out." He fearlessly taunted again, "If I was a slave-driver, and had hold of that man for five minutes, I would let more daylight through his skin than ever got there before." At this taunt, Fay and his men declared that Douglass was finished and began to fling chairs at him. Word of the proceedings now spread around the streets of Boston, and more antiabolitionists came rushing in. Yet Douglass would not stop, howling, "I will not yield the floor." As the level of crowd violence rose higher, the police seized Douglass to carry him away.

Douglass broke free from their hands and ran to the other end of the platform. Three cheers went up for him. Members of the mob gleefully shrieked, "Put *him* out." The chief of police announced, "If you retire, you will stop the police from performing a very unpleasant duty." Douglass still tried to speak, "We will not yield our place on the platform. No, by God!"

Some agitators drew their guns and pointed at the black speakers still on the stage. Women screeched in fear. Police now began to hurl black men out of the hall, and Douglass's followers abruptly seemed far less committed to stay and fight for their lives than he did. A journalist watched with astonishment as Douglass, fighting "like a trained pugilist," took on scores of white men. Casting men off him, Douglass "cleared through the crowd to the rostrum, which he clutched with an air that indicated his determination to hold to his place."

Police officers swarmed around him, taking hold of his body, one jerking Douglass by his hair. The officers were now emotionally with the crowd instead of protecting the speakers, and some angered officers took hold of Douglass and dragged him to the edge of the Tremont Temple stage. They then violently threw him down the stairs. Still conscious and fighting, Douglass rose to escape as his assailants pursued him until he was out of the hall.

With Douglass and his followers seemingly routed, the southern sympathizers now set to write new resolutions denouncing the incendiary abolitionist assembly which was now effectively in shambles. Still, it was not over. From the back of the auditorium, astonishingly, Douglass walked back in with clothes torn, hair disheveled, and eyes blazing with rage. To the shock of the crowd, he walked right down the aisle. No eyes left him and no hands touched him. Once he got on stage, he looked around for a few moments and then situated himself. Sitting in silent resolve, it was clear that Douglass would not be moved until he was ready to leave on his own accord. The police chief confirmed that, on orders of the mayor, this meeting was over.

The horde did not let up during the day, knocking down any black men they found, beating and trampling them, and smashing the windows of black households. One free man fought back by hacking at a white man's leg with a hatchet. Abolitionist orator Wendell Phillips and women he was walking with on the Common were stalked by men howling, "Stone him!" "Hit him with a brick!" "Hang him!"[24]

That night, abolitionists reconvened at the Joy Street Baptist Church, which for decades, in an alleyway on the backside of Beacon Hill, had been the heart of Boston's black community. Furious white men were outside the church, lobbing rocks at the windows. When it was Douglass's turn to speak, the lessons of that morning were clear. The topic of that meeting had been "How Can American Slavery Be Abolished?" The fury Douglass had seen in the New England whites left no doubt as to both the staggering nature of the challenge they all faced—and the unavoidable solution. Now he would spend his life "in advocating John Brown's way of accomplishing our object."[25]

In further reflecting on Lincoln's election, Douglass was staggered that the South would bother with the secession movement. In assessing the Republican stance, he could not figure what the southern firebrands had to gain—if they just took Lincoln's platform at face value, they could achieve all that they had ever wanted. In believing that the new president in his moderation was in fact abolitionism's "most powerful enemy," he thought the new administration could well be "the best protectors of slavery," and if this were so, the South had nothing to fear. "Slavery will be as safe, and safer, in the Union under such a president, than it can be under any President of a Southern Confederacy." Only if they seceded would Lincoln "would then be entirely absolved from his slave-hunting, slave-catching, and slave-killing pledges and the South would have to defend slavery with its own guns, and hunt her negroes with her own dogs."[26]

The unsettling events of December, however, culminated with stunning news flashing through the telegraph wires on December 20 that the Union now truly faced its greatest crisis in the seventy-two years since the ratification of the Constitution. By unanimous vote at the secession conference meeting in Charleston, South Carolina formally dissolved its ties with the United States. With that vote, the visage of war loomed nearer than ever. The epicenter of disunion, Charleston was important because it promised to be the flash point of war in a more immediate way: The day after Christmas, Kentuckian Major Robert Anderson transferred his federal troops from Fort Moultrie to the more easily defended Fort Sumter in the Charleston harbor. It was one of few remaining federal redoubts in northern control, and the secessionists were clear that it could not remain.

The president-elect in this crisis atmosphere wrote a reassuring letter to an old friend, Alexander H. Stephens, knowing the Georgia congressman was publicly advocating against the wisdom of secession. As he had maintained so many times, Lincoln stated that he would never interfere with slavery where it already existed: "The South would be in no more danger in this respect, than it was in the days of Washington." Then he added a just summary of what was still dividing them all, despite these repeated vows of nonintervention. "You think slavery is *right* and ought to be extended; while we think it is *wrong* and ought to be restricted. That I suppose is the rub."[27] This point was the rub indeed, and the resulting friction was set to explode.

The final conflict that Douglass had so long predicted was now drawing closer. As December 1860 ended, the imminent secession of six other Deep South states looked inevitable, and eight other states pondered their course. Once secession began, Douglass was determined to command a national stage from which he would allow no man to remove him.

1861

CHAPTER 5

Mighty Currents

The four long months leading to Lincoln's inauguration were filled with anxiety, as South Carolina's actions sank in and the telegraph wires burned with more secession news. On January 9, Mississippi withdrew from the Union; the next day Florida; the next after that Alabama; on January 19 Georgia passed its ordinance of secession and on January 26, Louisiana; Texas followed suit on the first day of February. As the cascade of secession continued, federal forts and garrisons also fell, quickly creating the potential flash point of Fort Sumter in Charleston harbor as a lonely holdout to federal authority. Like others, Frederick Douglass felt acutely nervous over the course of events but for a reason few shared. What he most feared were last-minute concessions to the South that would deal a weighty blow to abolitionist interests. Douglass thought the antiabolitionist mobs in Boston, Philadelphia, Rochester, and elsewhere were furthering the South's demands and aggressive stance. He pleaded with those who blamed abolitionists for the nation's dire prospects to recognize the true threat, and he asked, "Now what disturbs, divides and threatens to bring on civil war, and to break up and ruin this country, but slavery. Who but one morally blind can fail to see it; and who but a moral coward can hesitate to declare it."[1]

Though it seemed an impossible political goal, Douglass still asserted that immediate and full emancipation was actually the only means to any lasting peace. Such a drastic measure was now "a matter of life and death."[2] The South more than the North seemed to understand this, and that was why they were so ready to fight, although in some sense their political position had never seemed so promising. Though the new president was still silent on the matter of emancipation, his long train of statements on allowing slavery to be protected where it already existed held steady. Still, it was possible, from the southern perspective that the president-elect's refusal to offer any sort of "compromise" (which abolitionists considered simple capitulation) indicated that Lincoln was indeed an enemy to any future that they imagined.

Either way, Lincoln's firm history of refusing slavery's expansion into the emerging western states meant that sooner or later the slave states would be overwhelmed in Congress by the further admission of free-state politicians. The South saw that their previous hold on the levers of power was now irretrievably broken. Even if the Republican agenda held firm, without touching slavery where it existed, few southerners felt sanguine about seeing the presidency and both houses of Congress move inexorably into the control of those who believed slavery was a moral wrong. Those advocating secession were looking not simply at Lincoln's election, but at the meaning of his election for decades to come.

From the northern perspective, however, this view of things seemed strange and close to paranoid. The rise of the Republican party did not signal that abolitionism was anything more than a fringe movement, and there was little taste for anything abroad other than keeping the widely unpopular Fugitive Slave Law, a draconian measure that allowed slaveholders to take black people into the South with virtually no legal recourse. As Douglass had seen all too well, there was in fact a rising tide of hope in the North that an overarching compromise such as Henry Clay's 1850 effort could somehow yoke the clashing sections together one more time. Douglass spoke for many abolitionists when he implored the North not to give in again. He called the efforts of politicians for such compromise as "cowardly, guilty and fantastical."[3]

But compromise efforts did emerge, including one that proposed to write slavery into the Constitution. The Crittenden Compromise was introduced to Congress on December 18. Kentucky senator John Crittenden, a man whose admiration of Henry Clay was as great as Lincoln's, spoke on the floor of the Senate on January 9, 1861, in favor of the multifaceted plan, and though its prospects seemed dim, others were hoping the president-elect would eventually break his silence to support it. On the surface, its chief provision was to reimpose the old 1820 Missouri Compromise limits on slavery, only allowing slave states below the 36°30' latitude, but it also proposed a new constitutional amendment stating slavery in its current states would be free of federal intervention forever. Since Lincoln was clearly against expansion of slavery into the western territories and had based his whole reentry into politics on this sole idea, it was improbable he would endorse any new slave states, north or south of that famous line. But would he support the amendment that preserved slavery in perpetuity? There was no word from

Lincoln, and by January 16, it appeared dead in the Senate, but there was a long period still until the new president was inaugurated.

Douglass saw this as one of the most dangerous threats yet seen to possibly ending slavery in America. He was appalled that Republicans he had championed, such as William Seward, seemed increasingly comfortable with such ideas. Douglass warned his readers, "We are, therefore, now in danger of having an open palpable Covenant with Death, and Agreement with Hell." Though he did not believe the Constitution to be inherently proslavery, work in Congress was now moving forward to change that forever. This was, in the abolitionist's eyes, a moment of extreme peril. As frightened politicians thought to fix the Union, it seemed the rejoining "must be again cemented with the slave's blood." If the North relinquished what antislavery principles it had, "The plantation rule will thus extend itself over the North, and the Negro will be hated, persecuted and despised as never before." Further, Douglass feared for the safety of any abolitionist around the country.[4]

In a strange quirk of history, the presidents-elect of both the North and South left their homes on the same day, February 11, for their places of inauguration, Lincoln from Springfield and Jefferson Davis from his Mississippi farm. A week later in Montgomery, Alabama, Davis was sworn in as the first president of the Confederate States of America. Despite these events, Lincoln's twelve-day train procession to Washington was marked by a strange series of statements along the way. In Columbus, Ohio, he told the state legislature, "I have not maintained silence from any want of real anxiety. It is a good thing that there is no more than anxiety, for there is nothing going wrong. It is a consoling circumstance that when we look out there is nothing that really hurts anybody. We entertain different views upon political questions, but nobody is suffering anything."[5] In Cleveland, he added, "I think that there is no occasion for any excitement. The crisis, as it is called, is altogether an artificial crisis . . ."[6]

Artificial or not, it seemed real enough to detective Alan Pinkerton, who after death threats against the president-elect whisked him overnight into Washington and deposited him at Willard's Hotel at six A.M. The train tour was over, and Lincoln had nine days until Inaugural Day to pull together a speech, a cabinet, an administration, and a nation.

One of the few hints that Lincoln was apprehensive of what awaited him was when he had admitted earlier in New York, "It is true that while I hold myself without much mock modesty, the humblest of all individuals that have ever been elevated to the Presidency, I have a more difficult task to perform than any one of them."[7] The frightening results of the folly and indecision of the last administration much less the southern insurrection certainly made this statement hardly hyperbole. The new president would take office with the military in pitiable shape, most of the talented West Point graduates already in the process of joining the Confederate army, many of the Union's forts and ports wrenched from his control, a significant proportion of Congress absent or soon to be, the Treasury's coffers virtually empty, the chief justice his sworn enemy, and the nation shorn in two. George Washington had formed a government from nothing; Abraham Lincoln had to form a government from chaos.

A few days before the inauguration, Douglass was feeling hopeful about Lincoln's intentions, as the man had given no indication that he would in any way capitulate to the South's demands. The editor took this as a sign that Lincoln would not betray the ideals upon which voters elected him. If he was correct, he knew the South would never accept this president, that "the context must now be decided, and decided forever, which of the two, Freedom or Slavery, shall give law to this Republic. Let the conflict come."[8]

Abraham Lincoln was inaugurated the sixteenth president of the United States on the early morning of March 4, in a tense city where blue winter sunshine could not disguise its gloom. Troops lined the streets and snipers were arrayed atop federal buildings. As Lincoln rode from the White House to the Capitol, one spectator commented, "It seemed more like escorting a prisoner to his doom than a President to his inauguration."[9] Despite the ominous atmosphere, Lincoln in a dry and coolly reasonable address sought to appeal to his countrymen, principally to his southern listeners (if there were any at that point) to save the Union. He stoutly maintained that "the Union of these States is perpetual." Secession was, in this sense, an illusion that his government would never recognize as legitimate. As president, sworn to uphold the nation's laws, he would address the insurrection by fulfilling his oath. That need not mean war—"In *your* hands, my dissatisfied fellow countrymen, and not in mine, is the momentous issue of civil war. The government will not assail *you*."

Yet he was more than willing to meet his disaffected countrymen halfway. There would be no interference with slavery or any state's "domestic institutions." He would enforce the Fugitive Slave Law (as odious as he found it). He would even support the draconian Crittenden constitutional amendment permitting slavery (like the existence of the Union) in perpetuity. Lincoln essentially offered to make the entire basis of the Civil War a nonexistent factor.

In a shift of tone, he concluded with an evocative flourish: "The mystic chords of memory, stretching from every battle-field, and patriot grave, to every living heart and hearthstone, all over this broad land, will yet swell the chorus of the Union, when again touched, as surely they will be, by the better angels of our nature."[10]

As the day ended, Lincoln walked into his office for the very first time, and he was greeted with the news that Major Robert Anderson felt he did not have the supplies to hold out until the Union navy could resupply him. Fort Sumter was the first item on the desk, and there was no time left to compromise.

Douglass had had high hopes that the new president would step into the leadership void, but he was severely disappointed when he read Lincoln's inaugural address, both for the coldness it displayed toward the slaves and the conciliatory, even kind, attitude offered to the South. The words he seized upon were "I have no purpose, directly or indirectly, to interfere with the institution of slavery in the States where it exists. I believe I have no lawful right to do so, and I have no inclination to do so."[11] It seemed to him that the adding of the word "inclination" was superfluously callous, if not morally obtuse.

In his rage, Douglass declared that Lincoln had begun his presidency by "announcing his complete loyalty to slavery."[12] In regard to a constitutional amendment that would write slavery permanently into the nation's constitution, Lincoln said he favored such a step, saying "[H]olding such a provision to now be implied constitutional law, I have no objection to its being made express, and irrevocable."[13]

From Douglass's vantage point, what kind of antislavery president was this? Lincoln spent a considerable amount of his speech reassuring the South that he would indeed enforce the Fugitive Slave Law.

In this straightforward signal to the South that even slave laws would be faithfully served, Douglass declared in his April *Monthly*, "what an excellent slave hound he is . . ." Douglass saw what his radical allies had been saying all along in their opposition to the Republican candidate, and he furiously turned on Lincoln, condemning his "slave hunting, slave catching and slave killing pledges." Sickened, Douglass felt he had been betrayed. A livid Douglass wrote,

> Some thought we had in Mr. Lincoln the nerve and decision of an OLIVER CROMWELL; but the result shows that we merely have a continuation of the PIERCES and BUCHANANS, and that the Republican President bends the knee to slavery as readily as any of his infamous predecessors.

Douglass felt humiliated by Lincoln's weakness. This attitude of benevolence and conciliation would only embolden the southern traitors when Lincoln should "blast their high blown pride." Sadly, Douglass concluded, "Mr. Lincoln opens his address by announcing his complete loyalty to slavery in the slave states. He stands upon the same moral level, and is in no respect better than they."[14]

Yet somehow, these same slaveholders did not hear in this speech any such moral similarity. What they read in Lincoln's appeal was another antislavery screed, and so the nation moved headlong into a bloodbath.

Lincoln was acutely aware that the stakes of the war extended beyond the nation and its borders. The Confederacy's hope to expand and create an empire based on the model of southern slavery had been openly espoused, most notably by Alexander Stephens, his old friend who was now vice president under Jefferson Davis. Stephens proclaimed these states formed only "the nucleus of a growing power, which, if we are true to ourselves, our destiny, and high mission, will become the controlling power on this continent."[15] The annexation of Cuba often had been discussed before the war, and if the South were to win its liberation, that expansion effort would likely continue, with an eye to countries in Central America.

Prior to the war, Alexander Stephens had served with Lincoln in Congress, and they continued a correspondence up to the war and communicated about tentative peace offers during the war itself. In a March 1861 speech in Savannah, Stephens attempted to interpret why this great collision had come, admitting that slavery was, as Thomas Jefferson had predicted long ago, the "rock upon which the old Union is split." But he doubted that Jefferson had fully understood the true nature of slavery, falsely believing it to be an evil, a social institution that the nation would find a way to outgrow. This was "fundamentally wrong," Stephens proclaimed; Jefferson's error was believing in "the equality of the races": "Our new Government is founded upon exactly the opposite ideas; its foundations are laid, its cornerstone rests, upon the great truth that the negro is not equal to the white man, that the slavery, subordination to the superior race, is his natural and moral condition." Stephens added that his new government "is the first, in the history of the world, based on this great physical, philosophical, and moral truth . . ."[16]

Lincoln understood what powerful elements of the Confederate government coveted and why this demanded a war waged until such ambitions were checked. He made it clear, however, that if war came, it would not be from his hands. Yet, the unthinkable seemed more likely each day as state after state left the Union, and rushed steps toward establishing a new Confederate States of America proceeded, most notably with elected representatives and newly appointed president Jefferson Davis preparing an army for their "nation's" defense. The hastening dynamic of secession seemed inexorable.

William Lloyd Garrison and Wendell Phillips, leading radical abolitionists, had for more than a decade advocated disunion, ridding the northern states of the taint and corrupting influence of slavery. After espousing this course for so long, many abolitionists were shocked that what they had wished for was coming to fruition. With a clearer mind, Douglass viewed these events as nothing less than a calamity. He had always been more than a little dubious of his fellow abolitionists (particularly those who had never been personally exposed to slavery nor had been slaves); their proclamations had often smacked of moral posturing rather than a way of freeing slaves.

For the North to secede from the South would have been to abandon forever the slaves to their fate, leaving abolitionists basking in their moral purity. It reeked of recklessness, and now they were tasting their own disunionist remedy. Douglass asked a question that demanded a realistic answer: "Will the South become less intensely slave-holding, and the North more antislavery?" Douglass thought not. In these drastic times, Douglass wanted Lincoln to speak forcefully on how he would fight to hold on to all parts of the country. Not to do so would quickly create for northern abolitionists a powerless situation that his English abolitionist friends had long experienced as they looked on American slavery, as "a thing of foreign interest over which we have no power, and therefore, no responsibility." Successful southern secession would "end the thirty years moral warfare with the accursed slave system." As the nation dissolved, patriotic feelings stirred in him. In his writings he evoked "the mighty rivers and fertile fields that bind it together" and other patriotic images to help Americans understand that true separation was impossible.[17]

It was a strange time of political limbo as the southern states fell, one by one, like dominoes, into the seduction of separation. In this void, the president seemed a nonentity. Douglass was vexed by the president who seemed neither strong enough to preserve the Union, nor moral enough to champion emancipation.[18] In Rochester, New York, the *Democrat and Chronicle* reported, "On no occasion since the days of the Revolution have our citizens undergone the same degree of anxious exciting suspense that characterizes every hour of the day."[19]

In the middle of the night of April 12, 1861, firebrands in South Carolina let loose sustained artillery fire upon Fort Sumter, the spectacular cannonade lighting up the Charleston harbor. The suspense at last over, the war that so many had predicted, and so few envisioned in its future course of savagery, was upon them all. Douglass exclaimed, "Thank God!—the slaveholders themselves have saved our cause from ruin!"[20]

Confusion gripped cities and towns around the country. Six days after shots rang out at Fort Sumter, at a public meeting held in Rochester, thousands of citizens crowded the City Hall. Speaker after speaker called on free men to defend the Union, to enlist and respond to Lincoln's call for volunteers. Douglass described these days as "deep, intense, heartfelt, widespread and thrilling excitement."[21] He welcomed war because, as he told a friend in words similar to Lincoln's, "I have little hope of the freedom of the slave by peaceable means."[22] As he awoke in the morning and as he tried to fall asleep at night, his thoughts shifted from buoyant expectations of what this war could beget to despondency on whether the immense opportunity at hand would be lost in compromises by feeble leaders. He feared premature capitulation by the North, before the war could engulf slavery.

On the day the first local soldiers would depart Rochester, American flags hung from every building in town and patriotic designs flew from telegraph poles. The first eight companies from Rochester left on May 3 on trains bound for Elmira. Douglass was one of the twenty thousand who crowded State Street to watch the troops parade. His emotions swelled as he watched wives embracing departing husbands and heard the mournful cries of mothers who did not know if they would see their sons again. Though it was not a thought held by many in this throng, he held slavery responsible for every aching moments in these families' lives.[23]

But this was not his only emotion as the men marched to their destinies. The black man also watched these boldly outfitted men with envy, wondering when and if the country would afford the same opportunity to his people. Douglass wrote that he was ready to go and would have gladly marched in these ranks. Only days before, he had told residents to "let a few colored regiments go down South and assist in setting their brothers free, and they could and would do this work effectively for our government." Someone stopped Douglass in the street and asked what his people would do in this conflict. Douglass responded, "Would to God you would let us do something!"[24]

Intimately understanding how the social structures of the South worked, Douglass told audiences that it would quickly and efficiently put black men to work building fortifications and doing other hard labor to aid the war effort. Clearly, the Union was not taking equal advantage of the vast resources his people could offer. He detested the racism he saw in the North's refusal to employ black men, asking northerners why they thought that they were too aristocratic to march by the side of a black man.[25] He also predicted, "If this conflict shall expand to the grand dimensions which events seem to indicate, the iron arm of the black man may be called into service."[26]

His life mission of destroying slavery now had a means and purpose—to put free blacks into the battle. To do so, he encouraged blacks to organize themselves into martial societies and companies, to buy arms and learn to use them. Douglass declared, "Let's not only be ready on call, but be casting about for an opportunity to strike for the freedom of the slave, and for the rights of human nature." He began articulating these goals in monthly lectures on Sunday afternoons at the Spring Street A.M.E. Zion Church in Rochester. Every month the crowds grew, until church leaders realized they needed to find a larger space if they were going to continue sponsoring Douglass's addresses. Along with his monthly newspaper, these speeches gave him the opportunity to push for an abolition war.[27] He told an audience on April 28, ". . . the control of events has been taken out of our hands . . . we have fallen into the mighty current of eternal principles—invisible forces, which are shaping and fashioning events as they wish, using us only as instruments to work out their own results in our National destiny." The understanding of freedom and the war that Lincoln would come to would be strikingly similar. Douglass predicted in April, "But the time may yet come when the President shall proclaim liberty through all the land." This was a conflict that "will, and must, if continued, take on a broader margin. The law of its life is growth."[28]

Though the Lincoln administration would resist emancipation for a time, the war would change because the "'inexorable logic of events' will force it upon them in the end; that the war now being waged in this land is a war for and against slavery; and that it can never be effectively put down till one or the other of these vital forces is completely destroyed."[29]

For years, Douglass had dismissed colonization plans. He clung to his dreams of black people living free and equal in the United States, so whether white or black people advocated these schemes of a mass exodus, he did not accept them. However, in the months before war broke out, the prospects had been discouraging enough for him to begin entertaining notions of leaving America. When James Redpath, who had organized the Tremont Temple debacle, offered him a free trip on a steamer chartered by the Haitian Bureau to investigate whether his people's future might be more promising on this revolutionary island, Douglass justified the trip to his readers: "We propose to act in view of the settled fact that many of [the black population] are already resolved to look for homes beyond the boundaries of the United States."[30]

Douglass was unconvinced about emigration plans but was unabashedly elated to stand "upon the soil of San Domingo, the theater of many stirring events and heroic achievements, the work of a people, bone of our bone, and flesh of our flesh."[31] Over the years he had often spoken of the thirteen years of blood-soaked slave rebellion in Haiti that had ended in the creation of a free black republic. Behind the fearless leadership of men such as Toussaint L'Ouverture, the enslaved people battled their French oppressors from plantation to fiery plantation. By 1804, Haitians had won the right to rule their own country and determine their own destiny. The world had never before seen a slave uprising create a free nation. This uprising had long been an inspiration to Douglass's struggle in America, as it repudiated myths of black cowardice and ignorance. He wanted to experience a government administered by black people more than fifty years on from their revolution. If American blacks were to emigrate, at least Haiti's proximity to their native land would mean they remained "within hearing distance of the wails of our brothers and sisters in bonds."[32] Although emancipation had swept throughout Europe, slavery continued in the United States, Cuba, and Brazil. Haiti was the ultimate beacon of hopefulness.

Douglass had scheduled a six-to-eight-week trip for May with his daughter Rosetta and Ottilie Assing. The trio were to set sail to Port-au-Prince from New Haven, Connecticut, on April 25. But when war broke out at Fort Sumter on April 12, Douglass faced a monumental decision. With the war at hand, could he afford to lose writing and speaking time by being abroad? Could this conflict eventually create an everlasting home for his people in a form he could only dimly envision? What kind of message would it send if Douglass left America now, instead of springing into advocacy for an abolition war?

When readers opened their May edition of *Douglass Monthly*, it was bewildering. On its opening pages was a detailed review of Douglass's journey to Haiti, shocking enough since he had not previously mentioned the trip and had been such an avid colonization foe. Douglass topped his personal bombshell with the news of real bombshells falling upon Fort Sumter. And in the last paragraphs of the paper, in type set at the last moment, he announced the cancellation of his trip.

Douglass reported, "The last ten days have made a tremendous revolution in all things pertaining to the possible future of colored people in the United States." He vowed that he would "stay here and watch the current events and serve the cause of freedom and humanity in any way that shall be open to use during the struggle now going on between the slave power and government." He predicted that while northerners were confident of a quick and easy war, they would soon become better acquainted with the barbarity of slaveholders.

He predicted, "The revolution through which we are passing is an excellent instructor." Once that happened, "they may be willing to make war upon [slavery], and in that case we stand ready to lend a hand in any way we can be of service. At any rate, this is not time for us to leave the country."[33]

As tempting as the trip to free Haiti appeared, in the end it was impossible for him to tear himself away from a conflict that had the potential to make freedom real. Douglass would give America one more chance. Whether the nation would fulfill his long-deferred dreams or break his toughened heart was another question. At any rate, his decision was clear: He would hope again.

On the first day of May, Douglass wrote to a friend of his twenty-year activist career: "The clouds and darkness which surrounded its morning—and which have brooded over it most of the way—seem now disappearing in the opening prospects of my long enslaved people . . . We have drifted into the deep current of Eternal Laws—and must be carried where they lead."[34]

CHAPTER 6

Remorseless Struggle

Fighting had hardly begun when Douglass published heroic accounts of black soldiers in the American Revolution and the War of 1812 in the May 1861 issue of *Douglass' Monthly*. His message was unmistakable: LET THE SLAVES AND FREE COLORED PEOPLE BE CALLED INTO SERVICE AND FORMED INTO A LIBERATING ARMY.[1]

Realizing intense racism would make the prospect of free black men in blue a daunting sell, the editor began the long appeal to northern whites to think of their own welfare, to be practical about how to win this war they had stumbled into and must somehow finish. He did not share the widely held belief that the war would be quick, with a symbolic battle or two to teach the secessionists that they could achieve their goals politically. (Many Union politicians were anxious to pacify the new Confederacy once war had been tasted and found unpalatable.) Arming blacks in the South who were newly freed by Union soldiers would instantly rob the Confederacy of its chief labor source—each freed slave was one less worker for Jefferson Davis, and each gun in the hand of a black soldier further increased the Union odds. To resist this logic was senseless: "We are still hugging the delusion that we can crush out treason without hurting the traitors."[2]

Douglass wrote of Union generals who, in infuriating contrast to this logic, turned fugitive slaves away from their lines, thus depriving themselves of crucial intelligence sources. He predicted the physical result would be a land drenched in blood, as the enslaved would awake from a long stupor with prodigious force. The old vision of John Brown still tugged at Douglass, who was captivated by the enticing notion of free black regiments marching into the heart of the South with a stunning effect on its morale.

He was by no means the only black man wanting to fight in this war.

Black men met and passed resolutions offering to fight for their country in cities such as Boston, Providence, Cleveland, Detroit, Pittsburgh, New York, and Washington. In Philadelphia, men began drilling outside of their Masonic Hall.[3] Wherever the volunteer offers came from, the Lincoln administration was fierce and unrelenting in response: Their services were not needed or desired.

Meanwhile, the Confederacy was not so blind and took full advantage of their vast pool of enslaved labor, with every worker freeing up a white southern man to fight. The Memphis *Avalanche* reported, "Upwards of 1,000 negroes, armed with spades and pickaxes, have passed through the city within the past few days."[4] The rebels need not send them to battle, but the Confederacy was making use of their black population to do manual labor in a way that the North refused to do. Douglass knew this would be the case when he wrote in June, "The very stomach of this rebellion is the negro in the condition of a slave. The negro is the key of the situation—the pivot upon which the whole rebellion turns."[5]

The North was very far from understanding this pivot, but unfortunately it was not the only problem going unaddressed. Douglass used his unquestionable knowledge of the psychology of the enslaved (as well as those who had wrenched themselves free of it) to assert that if the North did not offer slaves their freedom, give them something to entice them, they would numbly continue to serve their masters and that government. In the first months of the war, he made a case that he would repeat to Secretary of War Edwin M. Stanton in two years: "Who can blame them? They are men, and like men governed by their interests . . . capable of love and hate. They can be friends, and they can be foes."[6] The current policy was making them foes, when they could be inestimably valuable friends.

Douglass believed that to alter this policy, the Lincoln administration needed to be swayed in any way possible. It required more antislavery meetings, abolition agents, editorials, and personal letters, and a mountain of labor for himself. Most of all, in this time before any battles had been fought, Douglass hoped that Lincoln would learn to assert himself and develop the kind of inflexible firmness associated with such presidents as Andrew Jackson.[7] Lincoln, wholly inexperienced in government organization, military knowledge, and diplomatic expertise, somehow had to exercise the authority to forcefully remind the South that he was still the lawfully elected president, that their claims of creating a new nation were false, and that the United States was in a state of fractious rebellion, not dissolution.

To that end, Lincoln was pushing General Irving McDowell and the unproven Union army to engage the equally unproven Confederate forces.

Everyone was anxious for action. As Douglass wrote at the beginning of July, "The war has made little progress, physical or moral."[8] At last, the Union army departed Washington on July 16, intent on engaging and quickly snuffing out the rebellion. Their path intersected with the Confederate army at Manassas Junction, next to Bull Run creek, twenty-five miles south of Washington, close enough so that politicians and other prominent Washingtonians traveled down and set up picnic parties for what they believed to be the first and last battle of this war. In the heat of July 21, the killing commenced.

Union forces were close to breaking through the Confederate flank on the lush green Henry House Hill, but an eccentric Virginia Military Academy professor named Thomas Jackson arrested their progress, earning the nickname "Stonewall" for his stand. J. E. B. Stuart, a dashing cavalry dragoon in a purple-plumed hat, and his men charged out of the woods at the perfect time, running into the jammed-in Union army and slicing their way through northern companies outfitted in their distinctive blue and white Zouave uniforms. The rout was on. The North's lack of military discipline was dangerously apparent as its ranks gave way to bloody chaos. The federal army did not formally regroup until back in the District of Columbia, with many men retreating at a run, never stopping until they saw the sight of the Capitol. The fantasy of an undemanding war was over. Douglass hoped that this shock of losing would not lure back "the dark shadow of compromise."[9]

In a panicked Washington overrun by shaken soldiers, the next day the House of Representatives passed a resolution stating that ending existing southern institutions was not the goal of this war. The conflict, they said, was only to preserve the Union and the Constitution. The Senate passed a parallel measure three days later. They were making it clear to both sides that the war was not over the eradication of slavery.

If the country could achieve peace, it would because they had "bound up the fate of the Republic and that of the slave in the same bundle, and the one and the other must survive or perish together," Douglass had written in May 1861. Slavery was a national affliction shackling both races: "The Republic has put one end of the chain upon the ankle of the bondman, and the other end about its own neck." In effect, both races needed emancipation to truly be free.[10]

Months later, with the war going badly, and with frustration growing in the North, Douglass would still claim, "No President, no Cabinet, no army can withstand the mighty current of events."[11] His message was consistent. Slavery caused this war, so it must end with the destruction of the cruel custom, otherwise the war would end in true defeat. There was no alternative, and it was fanciful to think otherwise.

Since Douglass's early assessments of how the war would play out proved so accurate, it is difficult today to understand how radical and unpopular these ideas were, though the incident at Tremont Temple indicates the reality Douglass faced. Prejudice toward blacks twisted views of the conflict in powerful ways. Astonishingly, the *New York Times* wrote that the war would be occurring even if there were not a slave in America because "The issue is between anarchy and order,—between Government and lawlessness,—between the authority of the Constitution and reckless will of those who seek its destruction." *National Intelligencer* echoed this sentiment with these stark words: "The existing war has no direct relation to slavery."[12]

In 1861, the notion of black men fighting in the war was laughable. The *New York Times* mockingly proposed "to Jeff. Davis that if he will rendezvous the whole of his black warriors somewhere on the coast of South Carolina, they will be delighted to meet them and him *there*, on any day he may name—he to general the black revolutionary cohorts, and Fred. Hannibal Douglass to lead the enemy." Such sallies would seem not just shortsighted in two years, but foolhardy from any sound strategic view. The North would find "black warriors" to be a necessity in victory, and Douglass would be a leader in recruiting them.[13]

Northerners were surprised and uneasy that European governments expressed little support for their cause, indicating the possibility of foreign recognition or even military support for the Confederacy. This would be a disaster for the Union. Douglass believed that the key to holding off foreign recognition of the Confederacy lay with the slavery issue. If the North could find the will to declare that they were fighting to expand freedom, other nations would then support them. As things stood, foreign governments saw the war as having no overarching moral dimension, as just the battling of states in conflict, a matter they cared little about (although the South did hold the trump card of King Cotton on their side). These nations needed some sort of well-defined differentiation of the North's goals from those of the slave-holding South.

Douglass, having been in Britain for five months in the previous year, knew that European countries were unclear as to what was driving the North in this war. He explained, "A lukewarm cause deserves only a lukewarm sympathy. When we deserve more, we shall receive more." Douglass believed a government indifferent to the malevolence of slavery would not attract allies, for "that attitude deprives us of the moral support of the world." His words were rather like Lincoln's from seven years earlier, speaking about slavery to a Peoria crowd, "I hate it because it deprives our republican example of its just influence in the world." The North was now blindly squandering its own "just influence" and paying the price.[14]

As a new president overwhelmed at the complexity of his task, Lincoln, of course, saw his way forward very differently. In his assessment, the possibility of foreign powers recognizing the Confederacy was a problem that could be dealt with as the war moved on, but there was one absolute pressing imperative that made Congress's recent vote on war goals compatible with his views. Every day, Lincoln was engaged with a delicate political balancing act to keep border states such as Kentucky, Tennessee, and most of all, Maryland in the Union. He felt the war was winnable (he hoped) with the states aligned as they were, but the loss of any of the border states tipped the equation and the war became an exercise in futility. Douglass never accepted this logic or this imperative, and he steadfastly advised, "Make this an abolition war, and you at once unite the world against the rebels."[15] Political leaders in Europe, who were inclined to favor the South since it served to weaken America in the play of world events, would have a difficult time justifying their opposition to that.

Lincoln, on the way to the White House, had declared at Independence Hall in Philadelphia that he "never had a feeling politically that did not spring from the sentiments embodied in the Declaration of Independence . . . It was that which gave promise that in due time the weights should be lifted from the shoulders of all men, and that *all* should have an equal chance."[16] Douglass too turned to the Declaration for inspiration. The guarantee to "life, liberty and pursuit of happiness" was something that he believed outweighed any legal backing America had subsequently bequeathed slavery. Douglass asked the government to "unsheathe the sword to make this truth the law of the land to all its inhabitants and it will then deserve, and will receive the cordial and earnest sympathy of the lovers of liberty throughout the world."[17]

On August 6, a law passed both houses of Congress calling for the confiscation of property used "in aid of the rebellion." This little remembered statute was important because it started the long train of steps to the adoption in 1865 of the Thirteenth Amendment to the Constitution freeing all slaves. Perhaps the reason it is so overlooked is that the so-called Confiscation Act concerned not property at all, but human beings. Even abolitionist-leaning members of Congress were hamstrung by fierce resistance to the conflict being tied in any way to slavery, so the law dealt with the increasing tide of blacks freeing themselves and fleeing into Union lines in terms that their former owners would have recognized—as property. Still, for radical senators and representatives, this was an important first step in coping with the hundreds (and as the war continued, thousands) of black people that the Confederacy was depending on to assist the rebellion. The Confiscation Act was enacted in a vacuum of leadership from the Lincoln administration, which was choosing to let individual Union generals on the ground deal with the problem as they wished. These same politicians would play an important role in goading Lincoln forward, as they possessed legislative powers that agitators such as Douglass did not.

The Radical Republicans (labeled Jacobins by Lincoln's secretary John Hay) were actually a fairly diverse group, many of whom came to their convictions not through devotion to abolitionism but to a free-soil ideology aimed at the economic advancement of white men. Thus, many of the radicals, though they pushed hard at Lincoln's perceived slowness, in fact did not share Douglass's views on black equality. One of slavery's strongest foes, Senator Benjamin F. Wade, a mercurial Ohioan whose temper made him always willing to duel for his honor, swore that if the war "continues thirty years and bankrupts the whole nation, I hope to God there will be no peace until we can say there is not a slave in this land." Yet, like President Lincoln, Wade was also a firm proponent of colonizing black Americans out of the country. Even as he worked for emancipation, he hoped "to hear no more about Negro equality or anything of that kind. Sir, we shall be as glad to rid ourselves of these people, if we can do it consistently with justice, as anybody else."[18]

On the other hand, there were dedicated men like Representative Thaddeus Stevens and Senator Charles Sumner, each of whom had long fought for racial equality. Sumner had grown up living among the free black community of Boston on the back slope of Beacon Hill, and had teamed with black attorney Robert Morris to argue the first school desegregation case, *Roberts v. the City of Boston*. A humorless dandy of cosmopolitan tastes and acute intellect, Sumner was relentless, fearless, and did not mind causing offense. He was sometimes called, in his reckless and determined abolitionism, the "John Brown of Congress." Of Sumner, Douglass said, "none has uttered the feelings of the black man so well; none have hurled at slavery such a succession of moral thunderbolts as he."[19] He hurled many such thunderbolts at Lincoln, serving as a conscience and a goad. After the disaster at Bull Run, Sumner spent until midnight at the White House trying to convince Lincoln that it was time for full emancipation, that he had been advised by John Quincy Adams that in these war circumstances, the power to do so was his. Lincoln did not agree, but Sumner would be back. While delivering a eulogy for Senator Edward Baker, a friend of Lincoln killed at the battle of Ball's Bluff, Sumner used the joint session of the Senate and House to assail slavery. He

Senator Charles Sumner

looked right at Lincoln when he named slavery as the murderer of Lincoln's late friend. Lincoln stared back stonily. Yet the two men, as different as they were, developed an odd sort of friendship and mutual respect.[20]

After the defeat at Bull Run, during the doldrums of the summer of 1861, it was difficult for abolitionists like Douglass and Sumner to see any prospects for improvement. Douglass did not know how to write about this event without giving comfort to the rebels, but it was impossible to deny things were not going well. He urged his readers to pressure the government "through the press, by petitions, by letters, by personal representations, and in every way, in a manner to convince it that the people of this great Republic are ready" for emancipation. Douglass demonstrated his grasp of presidential legal history, noting John Quincy Adams's theory that the government could abolish slavery as a war measure during a time of conflict. He believed this to be all the justification needed for Lincoln to take the great step. Indeed, it was this same point that Charles Sumner hammered away at with Lincoln, to no avail.[21]

At times Douglass felt beside himself, speaking to a nation in such painfully obvious denial. He kept hearing a national refrain that this was not a war about slavery; it was a "sectional war." What qualities about these two sections would produce war, Douglass wondered? Not the two languages, climate, or soils, "not a quarrel between cotton and corn—between live oak and live stock." In fact, "There is nothing existing between them to prevent national concord and enjoyment of the profoundest peace, but the existence of slavery." If they were going to wage war against the South, why not eliminate the only thing that truly divided them? So he pushed on to "make the Government and people an abolition Government and abolition people."[22]

Douglass poured his frustration into a letter to Rev. Samuel J. May. It was as though the government was convinced that "no good shall come to the Negro from this war." Why was a slaveholder bearing arms against the government treated better than a slave? Not closed to optimism, he still confessed "that it seems much like hoping against hope." He would keep waiting, but "Whenever the government is ready to make the war, a war for freedom and progress and will receive the service of black men on the same terms upon which it receives that of other men I pledge myself to do one man's work in supplying the Government."[23] This pledge would come to pass, though in ways he could not have imagined in the first months of war.

On the day Douglass wrote this letter, August 30, one general in the field was at last taking action to change the tone and tenor of the war. General John Frémont issued an order declaring martial law in Missouri, and then declaring slaves owned by disloyal citizens free. Frémont was a household name because his western odysseys before the Civil War had captivated America's imagination. Frémont had a gift for translating the unbounded, previously unexplored beauty of the West onto maps, and these heroic exploits catapulted a man whose surveying skills exceeded his political ones into the Republican nomination for president in 1856. Four years before Lincoln's election, the country had not been ready for a party hostile to slavery's extension to win the White House. Now Frémont the Pathfinder was leaping far ahead of Lincoln's policies by conferring freedom to slaves in a crucial border state, and the president was ashen when he heard the news. This radical move was the last thing his border state policy needed. However, in Rochester, Douglass shouted for joy when he read the proclamation. He elatedly believed that the Pathfinder had found a trail to victory in this war, striking right at the rebellion's heart.[24]

Lincoln responded quickly, telling Frémont that his actions "will alarm our Southern Union friends, and turn them against us—perhaps ruin our rather fair prospect for Kentucky." The vision of his birth state seceding and raising arms against the Union was of continual torment to Lincoln. Frémont responded that

Lincoln of course could overrule him, but he would not modify his order because "it would imply that I myself thought it wrong."[25]

Frémont's wife, Jessie, as bright as she was outspoken, met with Lincoln in a late night meeting to plead her husband's case. According to her, Lincoln coldly responded, "It was a war for a great national idea, the Union and . . . General Frémont should not have dragged the Negro into it." Lincoln felt he had no choice but to officially withdraw the order, not only because it so frightened the border states, but because he realized a new president must maintain control of his prerogatives and policies. He could not have his generals seizing the initiative.[26]

Douglass's resentment of Abraham Lincoln was growing. In disgust, Douglass described "the weakness, imbecility and absurdity of this policy . . ." Frémont's proclamation had been another test that Lincoln failed, as the lawyer inside him outweighed the warrior. When Douglass heard that Lincoln was considering relieving Frémont of duty, he thought the idea suicidal for the war effort, and that Lincoln only contemplated it because a much bolder man was threatening Lincoln's ambition. The Radical Republicans in Washington were irate; Douglass predicted, "In *three years more* the people will call for the man and his principles *to end this war!* and *then* they will sanction the death of slavery in the man of their choice." The comment would prove to be half-right.[27]

Regardless of what Lincoln did to Frémont, the issue of slavery was not going away. More than any politician, general, or activist, the slaves were themselves forcing the issue. Wherever the Union forces moved into southern territory, their advancing lines made closer and more attractive the prospect of freedom. It was almost as if the Promised Land was coming to them, the fabled North Star steering their way. Though such an exodus made perfect sense to the slaves, the North seemed unprepared for them to flood military lines. If Lincoln was determined to keep slavery out of this war, the message had not reached these travelers.

The fat, pugnacious General Benjamin Butler had dealt with this question of what to do with them by classifying them, innovatively, as war's "contraband." It was a racist, but clever, way to deal with a contentious issue, as those who opposed emancipation liked a term that continued to keep blacks labeled as property, even as those who favored freedom knew it was, in fact, a significant softening toward an emerging reality of emancipation. After all, who would not be in favor of taking away valuable property of an enemy? Moreover, the offensive phrase held practical value for abolitionists, helping to shift the prior policies of many Union generals who had cheerfully sent slaves by the hundreds back to their masters in the first months of the war.

With decidedly mixed feelings, Douglass parodied the ridiculousness of it all by telling the story of an escaped black man in Clarksville, Tennessee, whose owner found him within Union lines and accused him of stealing a horse to aid his getaway. A federal officer responded, "I don't see how that can be. One piece of property steal another?"[28]

As the fall began, Douglass imagined a scenario: "If persons so humble as we could be allowed to speak to the President of the United States, we should ask him if this dark and terrible hour of the nation's extremity is a time for consulting a mere vulgar and unnatural prejudice." The article shows no sign that Douglass actually believed a meeting like this could ever occur. In his fantasy, Douglass said he would tell Lincoln of black soldiers who fought alongside General Jackson at New Orleans and how Jackson, cruel as he could be, did not deny their bravery. He wanted to enlighten the president on the black man's service in the Revolutionary War, or of the bravery of men like Nat Turner who struck at slavery without regard for their own life. In unmistakable terms, he wanted to tell the president what Douglass was proclaiming in all his public addresses, that "this is no time to fight only with your white hand, and allow your black hand to remain tied." No one had greater motivation to fight slaveholders than those they enslaved. Douglass asked, "Is he not a man? Can he not wield a sword, bear a gun, march and countermarch, and obey orders like any other?"[29]

If Douglass needed a reminder about his status for some in America, he received it in Syracuse, New York. He was slated to give a lecture entitled "The Rebellion, its Cause and Remedy" at Wieting Hall on Thursday and Friday, November 14 and 15, 1861. During the week, residents saw a hand-bill posted around the town. The title was "Nigger Fred Coming." It warned citizens of the upcoming lecture and asked, "Shall his vile sentiments again be tolerated in this community by a constitutional-liberty loving people? or shall we give him a *warm* reception at this time, for his insolence, as he deserves?" The writer made clear what they wanted done to this "*coward* and *traitor,*" galvanizing antiabolitionists to "Rally, then, one and all, and *drive him from our city!*"[30]

The city was on edge in the hours leading up to Douglass's lecture. Violent mob action was on Syracuse's mind. Mayor Charles Andrews, a Republican, busied himself with preparations to see that a repeat of the Tremont Temple disaster would not happen in his city. He was serious enough to allocate $300 for the task. He organized the regular police and appointed a fifty-man special force for the occasion. The county sheriff and his resources joined in the efforts and those training troops at nearby Camp Munro assembled their men to take action sooner than the new soldiers would have thought. The owner of the hall refused to be frightened into canceling the lecture.[31]

When Douglass arrived at the hall to speak, he was stunned at the sight of a double guard of soldiers at each entrance. In fact, they had been there since late afternoon, standing with bayonets fixed. When it was time for Douglass to rise, Mayor Andrews locked arms with him and walked him to the podium, while soldiers presented themselves in the hall led by a particularly overweight major. The conservative *Syracuse Daily Courier and Union* railed against the Republican show of force that "*beggared* all description—all to protect a negro from 'mob-violence,' fill the house with people, Fred's pockets with *ten cent pieces*, (at the expense of the city Government!)." They added that every disloyal Douglass speech was worth a thousand men toward the Confederate cause.[32]

For Douglass, the lead-up to his speech felt all too reminiscent of the previous December's speech in Boston. Yet he walked away from this event heartened, because this time those around him defended his right to speak. The effort that this mayor had taken to shield him was a promising sign in troubling times.

Some still hated and feared Douglass, but others were increasingly offering support and protection. Douglass's schedule of lecturing picked up, and he pressed his message wherever he could. He battled through frequent colds as he continued to suffer from chronic bronchitis. As his British friend Rosine Draz reminded him, "Do take care of your health. Do not use your voice when your chest is weak." Draz, his most active English correspondent, knew Douglass pushed hard into his work reframing this war because he believed in the cause, but she also believed that if he paused, his grief from Annie's death would threaten to overwhelm him again.[33]

As much as possible, Douglass focused on his work. In the *Monthly*, he printed a letter supporting full and immediate emancipation that he implored supporters to sign and mail to Congress, and petitions that he directed abolitionists to take from house to house to accumulate signatures. He hoped these letters and petitions would arrive in congressional offices "in such numbers, and in such arguments, as to leave no room for the Government to escape from the great work of liberation."[34]

A year to the day, Douglass was back on the same Tremont Temple stage where he had last done battle with words and fists. It was bitter December in Boston. Making a speech on the anniversary of such an ignominious occasion was in itself a statement of defiance for Douglass. But surprisingly, the speech he prepared did not remotely resemble the themes he had spoken of last year. His lecture was on the emerging art form of photography.

The lecture series, known as the "Fraternity Course," had featured some of the greatest minds in America—Emerson, Beecher, Phillips, and Sumner. Douglass's insecurity speaking on such a topic was evident immediately, as he professed that this type of address was hardly his area of expertise. With uncertainty in his voice, he began tracing the history of the captured image, this new art and its innovators. It had been only twenty-five years ago that Daguerre had first manipulated light to record pictures, and now this advance was being practiced all over the globe. Douglass was having a hard time focusing the speech, drifting into philosophical ramblings on the femininity of photographical subjects to the medium's impact on politics, religion, and art. He theorized, "The whole soul of man is a sort of picture gallery." He wondered if photographs make their subject less or more glorious. Douglass seemed to lack a unifying theme for his thoughts.

Douglass had been speaking for the better part of an hour and was failing miserably. One correspondent in attendance thought that at this point the speech was "near being a total failure." Expounding on how a young Shakespearean character might look in a picture, he seemed to have a moment of realization about why he was really here. Then, his sense of mission took over.

With a sharp oratorical turn, he gave up photography and took the speech in an utterly different direction. For an overflowing crowd of such distinction and power, the images of Daguerre seemed trifling in comparison to the usual themes Douglass knew and cared about, victory and freedom. Douglass recovered the power and passion audiences knew him for, painting his own picture of a country where "every pillar in our great national temple is shaken . . . War and blood have burst forth with savage ferocity among brothers." He was setting up the message he infused into every issue of his paper. It was not sectionalism destroying the United States but something infinitely worse: "We have attempted to maintain a union in defiance of the moral chemistry of the universe."

His audience awakened, ready to engage the mercurial speaker. "We are striking with our white hand, while our black one is chained behind us." Proclaiming that the government must recruit black men to win this war, the country was now "catching slaves instead of arming them." With a growing rhetorical cadence, Douglass alleged, "We are endeavoring to heal over the rotten cancer, instead of cutting out its death dealing roots and fibers." He told the assembly he wanted to fight, now, but could only go to war as an officer's servant.

Then he recalled the events of the year before, the cries of hatred, the streets that were blocked, the doors shut to black men fleeing their assailants. Those firebrands had called for his blood, but he asked, where was that mob tonight? Bostonians and many across the North were starting to understand, "Nothing stands today where it stood yesterday. The choice which life presents, is ever more, between growth and decay, perfection and deterioration. There is no standing still, nor can be. Advance or recede, occupy or give place." The nation was heading toward final freedom for his people. He finished by linking this back to technological innovation. He endeavored to tie two virtually disparate speeches together, explaining that photography and ending slavery were both part of humanity's progress, their never-ending journey toward something better.

As Douglass stepped down from the dais, the crowd gave a powerful and enthusiastic ovation. For a second year, Douglass had saved himself in Tremont Temple.[35]

The year 1861 had been painful for Douglass. Three days before Christmas, he wrote to Gerrit Smith about "our rotten government." He found himself "bewildered by the spectacle of moral blindness infatuation and helpless imbecility which the Government of Lincoln presents. Is there no hope?"[36] The president's first Annual Message to the Congress (a tradition that later evolved into the State of the Union address) was another dagger to his hopes, as Lincoln wrote at length about sending blacks "at some place, or places, in a climate congenial to them."[37] Almost worse than realizing that this idea that echoed Henry Clay's old notion to colonize the black population was still alive in the war atmosphere was the new president's stated determination that, however he prosecuted this conflict, he was determined to keep it from degenerating "into a violent and remorseless revolutionary struggle."[38] Then what was this? If not a "revolutionary struggle," then was this a deadly crisis without a moral center? Douglass had not gone to Haiti because his belief that America could redeem itself was alive again. Now what?

The *New York Times* argued earlier in December that emancipation would be a public opinion disaster: "*The time for the safe and successful treatment of the Slavery question*, in its broadest aspects, *has not yet come*."[39]

1862

CHAPTER 7

Different American Destinies

A month after the New Year began, Douglass was in Boston again. He was the fourth speaker in a series of talks hosted by a new group, the Emancipation League. Abolitionists founded the association to promote emancipation as a moral and military necessity. The group's leadership was dominated by the allies of William Lloyd Garrison, so it was notable that Douglass was invited because he and his former mentor were still estranged. Garrison had never been one to tolerate dissent, yet now the nonviolent Garrisonians were all for winning the war and fighting against the division of the nation. Douglass could hardly hide his satisfaction, believing that these events proved him ten years ahead of them in his thinking.[1]

His February 1862 speech centered on the need for the nation to solve the issue of slavery, which, he said, involved "the whole question of life and death to the nation." Despite his brief flirtation with the idea of Haitian resettlement, Douglass was utterly committed to being an American. He clearly stated a message intended for Abraham Lincoln and every American who shared Lincoln's views: "In birth, in sentiment, in ideas, in hopes, in aspirations, and responsibilities, I am an American citizen."[2]

Douglass traveled from Philadelphia to Milford, Massachusetts, to Jersey City, to Naples and South Livonia, New York, telling white Americans, "We have sought to bind the chains of slavery on the limbs of the black man, without thinking that at last we should find the other end of that hateful chain about our own necks." He recounted the distinguished history of black troops in previous conflicts, comparing the Union's mediocre generals with national heroes who had been glad to have black soldiers under their command. He had traveled more than two thousand miles in January alone, battling throat problems and colds, no small matter for a man who often spoke for three hours a night.[3]

Rosetta Douglass

As he traveled, his family's letters trailed him. His eldest daughter, Rosetta, was twenty-two, and knew well the more vulnerable Douglass that her father kept hidden from the world. After the Civil War she would write, "You say you are a lonely man no one knows it better than myself and the causes." From an early age, she assumed a strong role in her father's life and corresponded with Douglass's female reformer friends. She also proved talented at the piano, mellifluous sounds the fiddle-playing Douglass loved to hear. He would respond by singing for her and neighborhood children on summer nights, often favoring "Nelly Was a Lady" and "My Old Kentucky Home."[4]

When she was a little girl, several weeks into her education at a school in Rochester, she described her day to her father, which included the faculty isolating her the whole time, allowing her inside the building only when the white girls went outside. Although no white parents had asked for the separation, the principal did this in deference to the racial feelings of local citizens. Douglass was livid that anyone would humiliate Rosetta, and he boycotted the schools by hiring private tutors for his children. Desegregating the city's schools became one of his long-term projects, and nine years later segregation ended in Rochester schools. By then, Rosetta had finished her education at the progressive Oberlin College preparatory school.[5]

After graduation, Rosetta went to the Philadelphia area to teach. She found teaching to be difficult, and the shadow that her famous father cast made the prospects of failure more depressing. Her wish to please her father made her struggles teaching and her dislike of the family she was staying with even harder. She wrote, "I did not know I could be so unhappy . . . I would like to come home but—feel ashamed because I did so very much wish to get—school and pay my board and I then could feel independent."[6]

Her father also was unhappy. Douglass lamented what the renewal of the stalled war might bring. "It is enough to exhaust the patience of Job, to read every morning that 'all is quiet on the Potomac.' "[7] After the disaster of Bull Run, Lincoln had appointed young General George McClellan to mold an army that would be prepared the next time they went into conflict. McClellan was adept at drilling and sluggish in moving his men toward battle, much to Lincoln's frustration. Lincoln and his newly appointed secretary of war, Edwin M. Stanton, struggled to make the conservative general engage the enemy. Lincoln wanted to win; McClellan was content to force a draw, one that would make the South able to rejoin the Union with slavery intact, its social institutions untouched.

The general's contentment to let slavery go unharmed made him anathema to abolitionists like Douglass. Yet, the longer Lincoln retained McClellan as his general, the more Douglass took Lincoln to be a confused man. At New York City's Cooper Union Institute in February, a crowd of more than two thousand heard Douglass speak. He was convinced that people he encountered over the previous months were changing their views, seeing emancipation in a new light. But would Lincoln?[8]

There were strains in Lincoln's life that had nothing to do with the war. On February 20, his beloved son Willie died of a fever. A gifted, bright, and sweet child, said to be the most like his father of the four sons, this was a heavy blow, particularly to his wife, whose grief would border on madness for many months. Both Douglass and Lincoln went through the very personal devastation of losing children who were close in age. But the swift and pressing current of national affairs propelled Lincoln's life onward, despite grief.

Those in favor of emancipation were still trying to get a good read on Lincoln. On January 20, Lincoln met with two such men, Moncure Daniel Conway, Unitarian minister and outspoken abolitionist, and William Henry Channing, nephew of the illustrious minister. After their meeting with

Lincoln, Conway reported that Lincoln told them that it was their responsibility, not his, to move public sentiment in support of the action they desired. In order to raise this enthusiasm for freeing the blacks, Lincoln told them they could "say anything you like about me, if that will help. Don't spare me!" After he finished laughing, he more seriously told them that action on this account was possible in the future.[9]

Meanwhile, Lincoln was not totally idle, quietly following his long-held belief that a cautious, long-term solution to the conundrum of slavery was the way forward. He was working on gradual, compensated emancipation plans. He wanted to pay slave owners fairly for their loss of "property," and in demonstrating his math for a senator, he wrote: "Less than one half-day's cost of this war would pay for all the slaves in Delaware at four hundred dollars per head." Further, "less than eighty-seven days' cost of this war would, at the same price, pay for all in Delaware, Maryland, District of Columbia, Kentucky and Missouri." He suggested a date in 1882 by when slavery would be over in these states. Lincoln felt it was better to spend this money on freeing people as opposed to killing them. To his bitter disappointment, however, his arranged meetings to press these ideas with border state representatives went nowhere. He would need another approach.[10]

Word of these efforts finally reached Douglass, and he took them as grounds to cautiously believe in Lincoln's sincere, though flawed, efforts again. As infuriatingly moderate and hesitant as these plans were, they were the first time in his life that he had seen a sitting American president advocate any form of freedom for his people.[11] Writing in an English newspaper, Douglass revealed that during February he had thought Lincoln a man intent on "repressing all anti-slavery sentiment at the North, and so to manage the war as that slavery should receive no detriment." He wanted the English to know, as they evaluated helping the Confederacy, that this news changed the equation. Douglass did not champion dealing with slavery in mild terms, as Lincoln's plans on gradual emancipation did, but the fact that the president was taking positive steps, however subtle, made Douglass consider the notion that "we have fairly reached the turning point of the moral struggle involved in this terrible war."[12]

Lincoln would need more pressure. Yet, Douglass optimistically told a Rochester audience in late March, "A blind man can see where the President's heart is . . . He is tall and strong but he is not done growing, he grows as the nation grows."[13]

This movement on gradual emancipation wasn't the only encouraging news for Douglass. Lincoln steadfastly upheld the execution of Nathaniel P. Gordon, a sea captain caught with 893 black people on a ship bound for the

United States from Africa. Though domestic American bondage remained intact, international human trafficking was piracy; however, up to now no president had enforced the ultimate penalty for those involved in its perpetuation. Many thought Lincoln overzealous for demanding the life of this Maine man with a young wife and child, but as sympathetic a man as Lincoln was, he thought stealing souls from their native land for slavery's dark purposes was not forgivable in this world. The execution penalty stuck.[14]

For abolitionists, this was a matter beyond one man's life—it reflected, instead, a position on whether people could continue fueling slavery with new blood and not fear the consequences. After Gordon's execution, Ottilie Assing contentedly wrote, ". . . the captain's execution is therefore the first blow directly aimed at the trade itself in this country."[15]

Meanwhile, the Lincoln administration had also signed off on a measure backed by Charles Sumner, chairman of the Senate Foreign Relations Committee, to bestow full diplomatic recognition to two black republics, Liberia and Haiti. There were critics of this action, but Lincoln was again showing a reformer spirit. James Redpath relayed the message to Haiti's president that the United States would not object to a black ambassador being sent. Lincoln's wording to Redpath still reflected his Illinois roots, quipping, "You can tell the President of Haiti that I shan't tear my shirt if he does send a nigger here!"[16]

Words like these made Douglass cringe, but he was more interested in action, especially when he heard Congress was considering a bill to abolish slavery in Washington, D.C. Douglass explained the symbolic importance of slavery's preservation in Washington in the March *Monthly*, stating ironically that it "must be kept alive as a token to all the world that America, after, as before the rebellion, is under the dominion of the slave power." The result was a "damning inconsistency of a free country with a slave capital."[17] Many white Washingtonians, with their southern sensibilities, dreaded the measure, believing it would bring an influx of shiftless free black people into their city. Lincoln had encouraged Sumner to push such legislation, which the House and Senate shortly after passed. However, even if he was ready for the underlying reality of the measure, Lincoln may have had concerns about the mechanics of this emancipation.[18]

In the days between the measure's congressional approval and the president's signature, Bishop Daniel A. Payne of the African Methodist Episcopal Church, physically slight but spiritually powerful, visited Lincoln and expressed his wish that Lincoln's pen would meet this paper.[19] The bill was passed on Friday night, April 11. On the following Monday, Payne met with Lincoln in the company of Representatives Elihu Washburn and Carl Schurz.

The four sat by a fire and Payne asked, "I am here to learn whether or not you intend to sign the bill of emancipation?" He continued, "Mr. President, you will remember that on the eve of your departure from Springfield, Illinois, you begged the citizens of the republic to pray for you." They had done so and had also prayed they would be delivered from this wicked institution, he said. Lincoln, whom Payne found warm but not fluent in his conversation, responded, "Well, I must believe that God has led me thus far, for I am conscious that I never would have accomplished what has been done if he had not been with me to counsel and to shield." Yet he would not say whether or not he would sign the bill. After twenty minutes, Payne left for Lincoln pamphlets on what the A.M.E. Church was doing to improve the lives of black people, then departed.[20]

On April 16, as McClellan was just beginning his achingly slow advance on Richmond and the nation was still absorbing the vast number of deaths suffered in the near-loss of the battle of Shiloh in the west the week before, Lincoln signed the act abolishing slavery in the capital. It was something he had expressed support for since he was a congressman more than fifteen years ago. In a message to Congress, Lincoln wrote, "I have never doubted the constitutional authority of Congress to abolish slavery in this District; and I have ever desired to see the national capital freed from the institution in some satisfactory way."

He signed the act, but more troubling words followed. Lincoln was gratified that "the two principles of compensation, and colonization, are both recognized, and practically applied in the Act."[21] Part of the act's language concerned funds for black people to emigrate elsewhere. Douglass would soon learn more about Lincoln's affinity for programs that took black people out of the country. For now, however, he focused on the positive, as did the seventeen black churches all over Washington, whose worship services on Sunday thundered with rapturous praise as never before. Celebrations like this happened in free black communities all over the country, so long starved for news this splendid. In a letter of gratitude to Senator Sumner, Douglass revealed, "I trust I am not dreaming but the events taking place seem like a dream."[22]

Douglass had no doubt that this was the most significant result of the war thus far. Douglass sought to capitalize on the momentum. In an article titled, "Shall We Look Back?" he reminded readers that when something is set in motion, it tends to keep rolling—but its corollary was equally true, if that motion ceases, it is all the more difficult to get the object moving again. He pointed to this time of extraordinary opportunity that abolitionists could not let pass without pushing on. Emancipation in one city was a great boon, but the District of Columbia was small in comparison to a vast land where every sunrise brought more agonizing toil.[23]

The constant goal that Douglass pressed for was the still somewhat incredible notion that black men could fight for their own freedom in this conflict. It was no secret that encampments of black people who had taken flight from slavery were swelling by the thousands, and Douglass recommended that the government start furnishing "ARMS, NOT ALMS FOR THE CONTRABANDS."[24] He was encouraged by the actions of General David Hunter, whose respect for authority was at best questionable. Working in Union-occupied parts of the South Carolina sea islands where white owners had abandoned their plantations, Hunter took charge of organizing the black men left behind. Instead of farming crops, he decided they would be more useful preparing to fight. On May 9, he issued a general order that freed those enslaved in Georgia, Florida, and South Carolina. Because Hunter believed military necessity forced martial law, which he declared to be incompatible with slavery, he thought he could accomplish what John Frémont had failed to do.

When news of Hunter's ambitious experiment reached the North, Douglass was elated and reprinted Hunter's letter to Secretary of War Edwin Stanton in his paper. Hunter maintained that black men would make fine soldiers: "The experiment of arming the Blacks, so far as I have made it, has been a complete and even marvelous success." Describing these men as eager to fight and attentive to military discipline, Hunter was seeking to challenge the deeply held racist belief that these men would be too dense and cowardly for the training of a soldier. Though these disorganized regiments would never take the field, the ramifications of the order were immediate and long term.[25]

Much of the nation felt very differently than the determined General Hunter. The *New York Times* wrote that arming black men was "laden with possible dangers to humanity." Peter Sturtevant told Lincoln from New York, "This act has done us more harm than a loss of two battles and has made Kentucky & Maryland almost against us if not wholly."[26]

On the other hand, German-American Republican Carl Schurz wrote to Lincoln that while the president could well feel it was necessary to annul this declaration, it was an issue that was not going away: "As our armies proceed farther South the force of circumstances will drive us into measures which were not in the original programme, but which necessity will oblige you to adopt." He hinted that freeing and arming black men might have to be part of a new program.[27]

Though he was well aware of this dynamic, Lincoln publicly distanced himself from the situation as thoroughly as he could, quickly issuing a proclamation stating that he "had no knowledge, information, or belief, of an intention on the part of General Hunter to issue such a proclamation." He made it clear that this action was void.

Yet Lincoln's document did not have the terse, cross quality he had addressed to Frémont after his declaration of freedom in the area he commanded. The ensuing months had seen an evolution of Lincoln's thinking on the matter, a change clearly indicated in the second paragraph of his nullification.

> I further make known that whether it be competent for me, as Commander-in-Chief of the Army and Navy, to declare the Slaves of any state or states, free, and whether at any time, in any case, it shall have become a necessity indispensable to the maintenance of the government, to exercise such supposed power, are questions which, under my responsibility, I reserve to myself, and which I can not feel in leaving to the decision of commanders in the field.[28]

It was as much an assertion of the president's powers to emancipate people, a contentious issue, as it was a rebuke of Hunter. Was Lincoln opening the door to something?

As the spring of 1862 wore on, the president a told a group of clergymen inquiring about emancipation, "I can assure you that the subject is on my mind, by day and night, more than any other." Sumner was keeping it that way. At every opportunity Sumner, often with Thaddeus Stevens and fellow Massachusetts senator Henry Wilson, kept pressing the reluctant president. However, Lincoln said in April, "Well, Mr. Sumner, the only difference between you and me on this subject is a difference of a month or six weeks in time." At the end of May, Lincoln predicted that an emancipation measure might come within two months. Lincoln still felt the essential risk of action in the face of a nation that he sincerely believed was not ready to support emancipation. If several of the border states responded to emancipation by joining the Confederacy, if the morale of Union soldiers plummeted, the Union might be lost forever.[29]

Lincoln prided himself on his finely calibrated sense of where the public was, and he was seldom wrong once the war commenced. Midterm elections were in a few months, and Lincoln's reelection was only two years away. What would emancipation do to the rise of the first party to oppose slavery's extension? Moving ahead of public opinion could mean a very deep cut in their turnout, spelling disaster when coupled with his administration's ongoing military defeats. Lincoln told Sumner during this summer that a freedom de-cree would mean "half the officers would fling down their arms and three more States would rise." As he told a delegation from Congress when they pressed him, "This thunderbolt will keep."[30]

Many factors affected Lincoln's consideration of emancipation. His le-gal justification would have to be military necessity. Another concern was the nagging question of diplomatic necessity. After suffering defeat after defeat, he realized something had to change, that the path to victory he had sworn to follow was failing—and that failure would allow Britain and France to at last weigh in on the side of the South. He would later tell the painter Francis Carpenter, "Things had gone on from bad to worse, until I felt that we had reached the end of our rope on the plan of operations we had been pursuing; that we had about played our last card, and must change our tactics, or lose the game. I now determined upon the adoption of the emancipation policy . . ."[31] But Lincoln did not want to play his hand just yet.

Clearly, something powerful was stirring in the frustrated president. On June 19, Lincoln happily signed a measure ending forever slavery in all west-ern territories, thus bringing to an effective close his long-ago debate with Stephen Douglas. A week later, with the Seven Days' battles beginning, a delegation of progressive friends visited with a request that slavery be ended. He answered, very uncharacteristically, that sometimes he thought that he "might be an instrument in God's hands of accomplishing a great work."[32]

As June progressed, Lincoln was handling two sensitive issues that tended to reinforce one another. Behind the scenes, even as he was pro-gressing with an early draft of the proposed Emancipation Proclamation, he had to deal with the failure of General McClellan's much vaunted and painfully slow Peninsula advance on Richmond. In the seven pitched battles within sight of the church steeples of the rebel capital, the newly appointed Confederate general Robert E. Lee had confused and then thoroughly de-moralized McClellan's much larger army. Despite coming so close to an overwhelming victory, McClellan felt forced to withdraw his army from the Peninsula campaign, and the efforts of the previous six months came to nothing.

Douglass was to give an oration on the Fourth of July in Himrods, New York. Upon arriving particularly early that morning, he could hardly believe he was in the right place. After stepping off the train, he surveyed his surroundings and took in about six cottages on a hillside, all painted white and about equal distance apart. In addition to the railroad station, there was a church and a grocery, and the economy of this backwoods village could evidently support two taverns. If this was not inauspicious enough, Douglass quickly realized that there was no one here to greet him and provide assurance that he had not gotten off at the wrong train stop.

Considering his limited options, he started off toward the small cluster of buildings. It did not take long for a resident to hail Douglass down and to apologize that in the town's haste to prepare for the celebration, they had forgotten the task of meeting their speaker. The friendly Himrods native took Douglass to the residence of his hosts, the Ayers family, where he could prepare for his address. As the morning went on, Douglass started to see the sleepy place come to life. American flags were unfurled everywhere, old men in military uniforms started drilling, pretty women in pink dresses looked on, and a band whose enthusiasm exceeded their talent struggled with some patriotic ditties. Now, every train that came into the station conveyed huge crowds of people, as did wagons from all directions. In a matter of hours, this hillside had gone from being empty to having two thousand people waiting for him to speak.[33]

Surrounded by pine trees and under a spotless blue sky, Douglass began his talk. Ten years before, he had given his famous Fourth of July speech in American history in Corinthian Hall in Rochester. On a day when Americans celebrate the liberty that unites them, Douglass had then used the occasion as a poignant protest for what separated his people from that vision:

> What, to the American slave, is your 4th of July? I answer; a day that reveals to him, more than all other days in the year, the gross injustice and cruelty to which he is the constant victim. To him, your celebration is a sham; your boasted liberty, an unholy license; your national greatness, swelling vanity; your sounds of rejoicing are empty and heartless . . . [34]

Ten years later, much had changed. Now he declared, "We are torn and rent asunder, we are desolated by large and powerful armies of our own kith and kin." Race was almost beside the point, as he deemed southerners his wayward American kin. He called the American Revolution a struggle "which your fathers, and my fathers began eighty-six years ago."

After recounting the growing role of slavery's power in the nation's history, Douglass moved on to the present. His evaluation of this administration was a taunt: "An Administration without a policy, is confessedly an administration without brains." Tellingly, Douglass listed Lincoln's rejection of the black man as a soldier in this war as his most salient mistake, and his second mistake was not issuing some kind of proclamation rendering all slaves free. In fact, it seemed Lincoln's abiding goal was to reconstruct the Union "on the old and corrupting basis of compromise." If Lincoln continued to pursue only one goal on a national basis, this Fourth of July would very soon be "a day of mourning instead of a day of transcendent joy and gladness."[35]

Despite the trio of positive signs from the spring, Lincoln still had not redefined the war's purpose. Furthermore, General McClellan's grand plans to capture Richmond had ended in seven days of battle marked by indecision on his part and the bold assertion of the Confederacy's new military leader, Robert E. Lee. As the discouraged federal army headed back to Washington, changes were in store for the beleaguered administration, some evident, like the demotion of McClellan, and some hidden. After the subsequent defeat of General John Pope in the second battle at Manassas, Lincoln made a hesitant, and surprising, move. On a carriage ride to a funeral, Lincoln had startled Secretary of State William Seward and Navy Secretary Gideon Welles by sharing his rumination that he was seriously considering sending a warning to the Confederacy—a presidential proclamation declaring their slaves free.

On July 22, he shocked the full cabinet by stating his intention and then proceeded to read a preliminary version of the decree. None of his cabinet members responded with enthusiasm, even the abolitionist and treasury secretary Salmon P. Chase was lukewarm. Seward, in his languid way, offered the shrewd observation that the president should only issue such an emancipation order upon some future Union victory, otherwise the world would look upon the proclamation "as the last *shriek* on the retreat."[36] The president agreed, putting the revolutionary measure in his desk, awaiting events.

August 14, 1862, was the first time a delegation of black men met with the president of the United States. Lincoln knew it was an important meeting and invited a reporter from the *New York Tribune* to make a full transcription. Reverend James Mitchell, an Indiana activist for colonization for fifteen years whom Lincoln had appointed commissioner of emigration within the Interior Department, was responsible for selecting these five black visitors—none were well-known black abolitionists. Mitchell had recently authored a pamphlet entitled *Letter on the Relation of the White and African Races in the United States, Showing the Necessity of the Colonization of the Latter* that described present troubles and future calamities if the two races were to share the same land. The document reflected the author's near-obsession with sex and racial purity, as Mitchell deplored "this repulsive admixture of blood" and "possible admixture of inferior blood."[37]

The "Deputation of Negroes," headed by District of Columbia's black leader Edward M. Thomas, was there more as a backdrop for Lincoln's remarks than for a conversation. Lincoln was not interested in their ideas or an exchange of dialogue. He was advancing an idea to their brethren around the country and meanwhile reassuring white people of his sincerity on colonization. It was the chief executive's chance to lay out a case to African-Americans for their voluntary exodus of the country. Lincoln did not mince words. He moved hastily through pleasantries as they sat down and stated that Congress had appropriated a large sum for their resettlement and that he favored this idea. Why should they leave this country? In answering this first question, Lincoln stated, "You and we are different races. We have between us a broader difference than exists between almost any other two races." This fact was "a great disadvantage to us both." Kindly, Lincoln admitted that blacks had had to "suffer very greatly." And whites, how had they suffered? The answer was simple, ". . . ours suffer from your presence." If this was conceded, "it affords a reason at least why we should be separated. You here are freemen I suppose."

One of them replied, "Yes sir."

The president added that their people were suffering "in my judgment, the greatest wrong inflicted on any people." He accurately described the daunting prospects they all faced. Go where they will in the United States and "the ban is still upon you." Lincoln then described the evil effects of slavery, not upon blacks but upon the white race. The most pressing was the war itself, "our white men cutting one another's throats, none knowing how far it will extend . . ." The five men listened as Lincoln added, "But for your race among us there could not be war, although many men engaged on either side do not care for you one way or the other . . . It is better for us both, therefore, to be separated."

The problem of colonization, as he saw it, was that free blacks, such as the men before him, were too comfortable to contemplate leaving for a foreign land. They might believe that upon winning freedom, social and financial advancement in this country was possible, but Lincoln emphatically said that was not the case. Lincoln reasoned that only the sacrifice of "intelligent colored men, such as are before me," by packing up and leaving, could convince whites to allow full emancipation to move forward. By staying, free blacks were in effect holding their enslaved brethren hostage. If they would free themselves of their attachment to America, they could go to Liberia, for example. Then he offered a home a little closer than Africa. What about Central America? It was hot enough, "thus being suited to your physical condition."

Thinking he had made a fair offer, Lincoln wanted to know how many people around the country they thought would be interested in making this readjustment. Could the president count on "a hundred tolerably intelligent men, with their wives and children, to 'cut their own fodder,'" and if not, then perhaps fifty? Even twenty-five men would "make a successful commencement."

Thomas told the president that the group "would hold a consultation and in a short time give an answer."

Lincoln responded, "Take your full time—no hurry at all."[38]

Douglass was furious when he read the transcript. At his most generous, he called Lincoln "silly and ridiculous." But the depths of Douglass's hurt and acrimony were better captured when he wrote that Lincoln acted as an "itinerant Colonization lecturer, showing all his inconsistencies, his pride of race and blood, his contempt for negroes and his caning hypocrisy."

Lincoln was using his bully pulpit to advance arguments that Douglass had been fighting hard against for two decades. Douglass thought the message to his people boiled down to, "I don't like you, you must clear out of the country." Douglass reiterated that the cause of this increasingly horrific war was not black people but the institution of subjugation that was trapping them. Douglass reviled ideas that he should abandon dreams of peace and opportunity for his family in America.[39]

Yet Douglass's writing in the *Monthly* after Lincoln's crude effort to highlight colonization was frankly more about his overall disillusionment with this president than about countering these specific arguments. After all, these colonization hopes of Lincoln were common, even among vehement abolitionists. To be antislavery was not always to be abolitionist, and to be an abolitionist did not always mean that, having freed black people, one wanted them staying around. Twelve years before, Salmon Chase, an early supporter of emancipation, wrote to Douglass that he had "always looked forward to the separation of the races," suggesting South America as a promising destination for them. Like so many of slavery's detractors, Chase simply did not think anything should have brought these two races together. This was one of Lincoln's essential points, and he was using this theme of colonization as a means to justify the release of his proclamation.[40]

In October, Douglass engaged in a public exchange of letters with Lincoln's postmaster general, Montgomery Blair, who, like his chief, felt the war should somehow move along the separation of the races. He tried to explain that American culture, with all of its flaws, was still the place, with its familiar customs, that felt like home. With pain apparent, Douglass pleaded, "But why, oh why! may not men of different races inhabit in peace and happiness this vast and wealthy country?"[41] He thought no idea hurt his people more than the one making "Africa, not America, their home. It is that wolfish idea that elbows us off the sidewalk, and denies us the rights of citizenship." Douglass battled this resettlement idea during the Civil War— even supposed allies had to be made to understand what connected black and white and bonded them together in this country was more than just slavery. Douglass tried to make them see that the bond was freedom and equality.[42]

The racism inherent in the Lincoln administration's colonization reasoning was consistent with the racism of the president's hesitant actions over the past year and a half. The *Tribune* report of this meeting left no doubt in Douglass that Lincoln was "quite a genuine representative of American prejudice and negro hatred and far more concerned for the preservation of slavery, and the favor of the Border Slave States, than for any sentiment of magnanimity or principle of justice and humanity." Most damning was how this caused Douglass to appraise Lincoln as a man. Reading the president's words, Douglass felt, "The genuine spark of humanity is missing in it, no sincere wish to improve the condition of the oppressed has dictated it."[43] To Douglass, Lincoln did not seem to be a public figure he would ever be able to trust or think of as an ally. Just ten days before his meeting with the black men, Lincoln said no to another delegation of "western gentlemen" who offered to raise two regiments of black soldiers to represent Indiana, adding that the Union could still use the men as common laborers. On the twenty-fifth, Secretary of War Stanton somewhat mitigated that refusal, authorizing the acceptance into service of some five thousand black soldiers in the Deep South to act as guards.

On August 25th, the hugely popular *New York Tribune* published a letter from the president. Lincoln was hastily responding to editor Horace Greeley's recent article "The Prayer of Twenty Millions," in which he had called for emancipation and chastised Lincoln for not enforcing the Confiscation Act with more vigor. Lincoln wrote,

> My paramount object in this struggle *is* to save the Union, and is *not* either to save or to destroy slavery. If I could save the Union without freeing *any* slave I would do it, and if I could save it by freeing *all* the slaves I would do it; and if I could save it by freeing some and leaving others alone I would also do that. What I do about slavery, and the colored race, I do because I believe it helps

to save the Union; and what I forbear, I forbear because I do *not* believe it would help to save the Union. I shall do *less* whenever I shall believe what I am doing hurts the cause, and I shall do *more* whenever . . .[44]

His formulation of what he could and would do is classic Lincoln rhetoric, appearing straightforward, clear. But it was highly discouraging to those waiting for a document to free the slaves, those unaware that the Emancipation Proclamation was waiting in his desk, written and already discussed in cabinet session. The real truth behind the letter *is* there, almost in a code not easily broken, hidden in a logically ordered yet tangled thicket of words that serve ably the goal of misdirection. Nothing as written is strictly untrue, but anyone taking it at face value would have been totally misled as to what the future held for emancipation. The key words were ". . . and I shall do *more* whenever . . ." That "whenever" was fast approaching, but Lincoln felt no need to say so.

For Douglass, reading these words in the *Tribune*, seemingly relegating the moral issue to whatever course was most expedient for the Union, was dispiriting. Yet, he found something very promising in the last two lines of Lincoln's letter to Greeley and, by extension, to the public: "I shall adopt new views as fast as they shall appear to be true views. I have here stated my purpose according to my view of official duty; and I intend no modification of my oft-expressed personal wish that all men every where could be free."[45] Lincoln drew a distinction between his understanding of the constitutional powers of a president and the ideals he held. By Lincoln's explicit affirmation, an openness to new views meant for Douglass that there was still hope that they could somehow move Lincoln.

Or that they already had.

Rosetta's time teaching was not getting any better and she told her father, "I hate this school. I am thinking of leaving." Douglass often sent her money, never inquiring to how she spent it but hoping her spirits might improve. Rosetta took comfort in thinking of Rochester, her parents and brothers, and knowing Douglass would welcome her home if that were her decision. She was struggling with long teaching hours, a mile and a half walk to and from the school, the unruly nature of her students, missing meals and sometimes feeling on the verge of fainting in front of her charges.[46]

Rosetta came as close as anyone to understanding her father's guarded nature. "I often think of your loneliness," she wrote, empathizing with his lack of close friends. Knowing that while he was a famous man with thousands of acquaintances all over the world, he was emotionally connected to few. She could sense his depression in the letters he sent her; as she told him, "Please don't grow despondent and write soon." She also possessed unusual sensitivity. It is common to find in her letters friendly words such as, "My love to Ms. Assing." Douglass worried that she was too careless in speaking of certain family business, but she reassured him, "father you are mistaken in supposing that I spread family differences." In the end, nothing could change her having "too great a family pride, pride for yourself to say anything to make people acquainted with such things with which they have no business."[47]

Douglass's old ties still held strong, particularly those to his British supporter Julia Griffiths Crofts. Douglass wrote her about the challenges of the war and even domestic issues, such as his worries about Rosetta's teaching problems. Griffiths Crofts also understood the severe stress Douglass felt over whether this war could bring about his ultimate goals. By virtue of the unpredictable nature of recent events, she described him as being in a "constant state of excitement." One possibility she dreaded was that Douglass might enlist if indeed his long-held dream of black soldiers became a reality. She warned, "Do not I *beseech* of you, be hurried *away* into taking up arms . . . your work is with your *pen not* with a sword or guns!"[48]

Unaware that their enigmatic president was sitting on a measure that would dramatically recast the war, the Radical Republicans in Congress continued to press the administration to confront slavery. The passage of the Second Confiscation Act was a considerable blow aimed at the heart of the Confederacy. This act was based on the practicalities that General William Sherman, utterly unsympathetic to abolitionists, articulated to an old Confederate friend: "Even without the Confiscation Act, by the simple laws of War we ought to take your effective slaves. I don't say to free them, but to use their labor & deprive you of it."[49] The act decreed that the enslaved of those found guilty of treason toward the United States were free, and that those engaged in rebellion could be imprisoned and executed. The duty of the president was to seize rebels' property, which now meant their slaves. Congress instructed the Union army to stop returning those escaping from their chains back to their masters—unless their owner was loyal to the United States.

Toward the end of the Second Confiscation Act, Congress authorized Lincoln to "employ as many persons of African descent as he may deem necessary and proper for the suppression of this rebellion." This could mean merely manual labor—the common interpretation—yet the tantalizing allusion to organizing black troops was unmistakable. On the other hand, the act also permitted and allocated money for the president's desire to encourage black colonization.

In the second year of the war, with the Union armies thwarted on the field except for some signal victories along the Mississippi River, from New Orleans to Fort Donelson, it seemed that every positive step forward was accompanied with the poison pill of colonization, even the prospect of arming freed black people. In the same vein, Sumner presented Lincoln with a copy of George Livermore's *An Historical Research: Opinions of the Founders of the Republic on Negroes as Slaves, as Citizens, and as Soldiers.* As casualties mounted in the war, Lincoln also heard support for black troops from those who were hardly champions of racial justice. Governor Samuel J. Kirkwood of Iowa told Lincoln's chief general, Henry Halleck, that he would have no regrets if part of the Union dead would be black "and that all are not white men."[50]

Sumner believed that in their moments together, he glimpsed the careful and deliberate thought that Lincoln was bringing to an emancipation decision. To those who harped on criticisms of Lincoln, as Douglass did, Sumner wrote, "I am confident that if you knew him as I do, you would not make it."[51]

The future of the nation resided on his long sloping shoulders. As a student of history, Lincoln fully understood the importance of making the right decision on emancipation. For better or worse, what he decided would determine the fate of this democratic experiment, and the decision would send reverberations through the world for hundreds of years to come. As he said in his second annual message, the outcome of the war was "for a vast future also."[52] If the wrong move caused any border states to shift to the Confederacy, he would be responsible for the loss of his country. He had only the slimmest margin for political miscalculation in the months that led up to the Emancipation Proclamation. At the commencement of a cabinet meeting on September 2, Lincoln expressed half-jokingly that he was almost ready to hang himself.[53]

CHAPTER 8

On the Wire

September 17, 1862, was the bloodiest day in American history. The instinct of Robert E. Lee was to be always on the offensive, and he had invaded the North for the first time in the war. Around the peaceful fields of Sharpsburg, Maryland, where the Antietam Creek ran, Lee encountered George McClellan's significantly larger Army of the Potomac. After the remarkable good fortune of finding Lee's battle plan wrapped in discarded cigar papers, McClellan should have had a decided advantage. Yet, fearing that the Confederate invaders possessed overwhelming numbers, McClellan hesitated for crucial hours. When battle did begin on the morning of September 17, a lack of Union coordination created almost three separate battles, a godsend to Lee, who was able to shift and adjust in response.

At five thirty A.M., the fighting started with Union forces advancing toward a modest, white German-American Baptist church. Vicious fighting filled the cornfields, with the advantage changing hands repeatedly. Storms of lead ripped apart crops and soldiers. Then the battle shifted to the center of the Confederate's entrenched position in front of a sunken piece of ground, worn down from years of wagon traffic. In a few short hours, more than five thousand casualties lay in a long trench that had become a conduit of blood. As in the fighting at the cornfields and church, there was no firm advantage either way. In midafternoon, the third phase of the battle centered on the incompetent Union general Ambrose Burnside attacking the southern end of the Confederate line, by attempting to cross the creek over a narrow stone bridge. Had he done it hours earlier, it could have won the day decisively, but one delay after another gave Lee precious time. The bridge itself became a deadly holdup for thousands of federal soldiers crossing it. General A. P. Hill's men had been on a wearing seventeen-mile trek from Harpers Ferry and

Lincoln meeting with McClellan at Antietam, Maryland,
October 3, 1862. Photograph by Alexander Gardner.

arrived at just the right moment. At four thirty, they threw themselves into
the progressing Union army and pushed Burnside's men back to the bridge
across which they had just fought their way.

Over twenty-two thousand Americans were casualties on the day. Had
McClellan attacked the next day, he might have been able to inflict fatal
damage on the outnumbered and ailing Confederate forces, but he was too

cautious and troubled by the ghastly nature of the day before. General Lee's loyal and damaged army turned back for Virginia. Though a military stalemate, the fact that it ended Lee's northern invasion rendered the battle a success for the Union. By virtue of not being an utter defeat, it seemed the closest thing yet to victory for the North in this theater of the war.

And it was all Lincoln needed. Five days after the armies clashed, Lincoln issued a document proclaiming his intention to fully emancipate all enslaved people held in rebel territory within three months. The text pronounced that as of January 1, 1863, all those held in slavery within any state rebelling against the government would be "forever free." Because the legal basis of the order was weak to the extreme, the whole act rested upon the doctrine of military necessity; thus, the border states were exempted from this emancipation since they were not at war with the federal government. In fact, several Union states, notably Maryland, preserved slavery within their borders until late in the war. In another oddity borne of its war footing, any southern state that reentered the Union would also be exempt from the act, thus "saving" slavery in the state.

The Emancipation Proclamation was always conceived as a ramshackle, temporary measure that, at best, moved the country along until a constitutional amendment could firmly and finally eradicate slavery. If the war ended quickly, even with a Union victory, the actual legal status of slavery was not clear—and with the United States Supreme Court still in the hands of Chief Justice Roger Taney, a case could be made that the war would have been fought to no abolitionist purpose whatsoever.

Lincoln's proclamation also declared that "such persons [former slaves] of suitable condition, will be received into the armed service of the United States to garrison forts, positions, stations, and other places, and to man vessels of all sorts in said service."[1] Lincoln did not state that black men would be fighting, but accepting them into the armed forces for these tasks was a monumental step.

Provisional or not, cautious and full of half-measures or not, the announcement was a bombshell for North and South. It certainly took Douglass by total surprise. Only days before, he had written to Gerrit Smith, "Your gloomiest predictions have been even now more than realized—and I shudder at what the future may still have in store for us." He felt that Lincoln was beholden to conservative army figures such as McClellan, who had no interest in emancipation. His letter continued, "I think the nation was never more completely in the hands of the slave power," and Lincoln was "doing his utmost to destroy the country."[2]

As the summer of 1862 ended, however, things looked infinitely more promising, and Douglass understood the Emancipation Proclamation's true revolutionary nature in a way that Lincoln's detractors ignore. Well understanding its limitations, Douglass cried, "We shout for joy that we live to record this righteous decree." To all those who had labored for freedom throughout the South, Douglass told them to "lift up now your voices with joy and thanksgiving." Not all was forgiven for this president, as "Abraham Lincoln may be slow, Abraham Lincoln may desire peace even at the price of leaving our terrible national sore untouched, to fester on for generations." Yet here was a sizable step forward.[3]

The idea of a proclamation that freed people in places Lincoln had no power over while it left black people in bondage in places that Lincoln could touch disturbed Douglass, but he "saw in its spirit a life and power far beyond its letter." Though the dry legal language belied it, Douglass sensed an expansive moral power being unleashed, a power that neither Lincoln nor anyone else could really control.[4]

Reactions of soldiers throughout the country were diverse. Consider the contrasting statements of two New York soldiers—one noted that the Proclamation had some soldiers "threatening to abandon the service, declaring that they came to fight for the Union and to maintain the Constitution," and another wrote, "Thank God . . . the contest is now between Slavery & freedom, & every honest man knows what he is fighting for." Others respected the practicality of the act. A Pennsylvania soldier made it clear, "I am no Nigger worshiper," yet slavery gave the South strength through labor so "nothing will end this war sooner" than emancipation.[5]

Douglass deemed that it would change how Europe viewed the war, putting the North finally on the right side of justice and civilization. From his own knowledge of Britain and his contacts there, he did not think these governments could now aid the Confederacy. An overlooked quality of Douglass's Civil War years was his influence on British public opinion, which was vital because their recognition of the Confederate States of America would have been disastrous. The elite of Britain had political and economic reasons to encourage the Confederacy. Britain was a world leader in antislavery advocacy, however, and the North could have lessened this lingering English sympathy for the Confederacy had they made emancipation an original war aim. No small debt is owed to abolitionists such as Douglass for the fact that the Confederacy never received the aid and recognition it desired from Britain during these first two years of war.[6]

Oddly, the initial reaction to the proclamation was not positive in England, where many viewed it as cold political maneuvering. The *London Spectator* observed, "The principle is not that a human being cannot justly own another, but that he cannot own him unless he is loyal to the United States." Some felt that out of desperate political opportunism Lincoln was inviting a gruesome racial war, something they should prevent out of an obligation to humanity. The *London Times* wrote, "the reign of the last PRESIDENT [was] to go out amid horrible massacres of white women and children, to be followed by the extermination of the black race in the South? Is LINCOLN yet a name not known to us as it will be known to posterity, and is it ultimately to be classed among that catalogue of monsters, the whole sale assassins and butchers of their kind." An English subscriber to the *Douglass Monthly* wrote a letter to Douglass in November on emancipation, asserting that "we see clearly this is not the object of the war."[7]

Ottilie Assing sent this perspective home to Germany: "As important and fateful as this proclamation will prove to be, one has to recognize that it again reveals itself as one of those halfway measures so characteristic of this president and his advisors." Douglass's friend Mary Carpenter, a distinguished reformer in her own right, wrote him, "I don't see that it can do very much as the slaves in the South will be *free* because Mr. Lincoln or all the people of the North declare them to be so." Douglass knew that, strictly speaking, she was correct.[8]

Douglass, in a long address to British readers in his October *Monthly*, explained what the Emancipation Proclamation meant in a larger sense. He thanked them for their moral support and the money they sent him for his antislavery efforts, and informed them that "Our arguments, appeals and entreaties combining with events, have at last moved the Government to this high duty, and opened up to the downtrodden millions the hope of speedy deliverance from a bondage whose horrors and crimes no pen can describe." The proclamation did not free anyone, but it showed that the American government, after sixty years, no longer placed itself on the side of slavery. Now they had turned the page to "the first chapter of a new history."[9]

Douglass had his British friend Henry Richardson send his writings on the proclamation to editors at the *London Daily News*, *Daily Chronicle*, *Newcastle Guardian*, *Leeds Mercury*, and other publications around the island. People all over England read Douglass's impassioned plea, full of vivid metaphorical imagery, that those in bondage would soon be free as long as the British did not extend their "potent and honored hand to the blood-stained fingers of the impious slaveholding Confederate States of America." It would take a few months for people to understand that the nature of the war had genuinely changed, and then British opinion shifted lastingly against intervention. Richardson told him, "I quite think there is a turn of tide observable, and that the Northern States are beginning to be looked upon with some favor. Your appeal has doubtless helped in this change."[10]

Still, there was danger lurking for the Union. William Gladstone, chancellor of the exchequer and a figure who was thought to be sympathetic to abolition, gave a surprising speech on October 7 proclaiming that the southern leaders "have made a nation." Winning the battle of Antietam had staved off disaster, but the Lincoln administration was not out of the woods. Any turn of events or another audacious victory by Robert E. Lee could send Britain to the side of cheap cotton and a divided America.

Lincoln knew that proclaiming the slaves free did not make them so; pushing the reach of their military and winning the war would. Finally despairing of McClellan's inaction and timidity, Lincoln and Stanton fired him, realizing that the Democrat might well oppose them in the upcoming presidential contest. Republicans had decided that the general was fighting to preserve the old nation on old terms, instead of smashing the Confederacy. Though Lincoln had held out longer than many of his advisors thought reasonable, Wendell Phillips said of McClellan that he might not have been a traitor, "but I say this, that if he had been a traitor from the crown of his head to the sole of his foot, he could not have served the South better than he has done as Commander-in-Chief."[11]

In mid-December, the armies in the eastern theater faced each other across the Rappahannock River. Fredericksburg, a picturesque Virginia town before war found it, was the scene of a grisly battle on December 13. In bitter cold, General Ambrose Burnside sent his soldiers across the river, through the town, and up the slopes toward Marye's Heights. Brigade after brigade bravely charged, but not a man reached a Confederate line entrenched behind a firmly built stone wall. From a position of cover, the rebel army unleashed blazing, merciless firepower. The Union suffered thirteen thousand casualties, far more than double the number of Confederate casualties. It was a massacre, and worse, an unnecessary and brutally incompetent one.

Lincoln grieved after the battle, "If there is a worse place than hell I am in it." Witnesses said when he heard the news of a disaster, he looked pale and in terrible pain. The governor of Pennsylvania remembered that he "groaned, . . . and showed great agony of spirit. He walked the floor, wringing his hands and uttering exclamations of grief . . ."[12]

In the wake of yet another military debacle, Douglass wanted badly to believe, as he had written earlier, that "Abraham Lincoln is not the man to reconsider, retract and contradict words."[13] Yet there was nothing firm yet about the issuing of the real proclamation at New Year's, and Lincoln was still signaling to many border state politicians that the offer of graduated, long-term emancipation was still on the table. For that matter, the act had been deliberately delayed for months so that even the South could reconsider the war itself (though not even Lincoln with his habitual good will believed they would).

The pressure had to be kept up, and Douglass showed his doubts when telling his readers, "Now for the work." Between late fall and the January date that the proclamation would go into effect, he asked every one of them to write, speak, and donate money to the cause of emancipation. The aim was to "make the North a unit in favor of the President's policy." They could leave "nothing to contingency, but work steadily to keep the public mind and heart up to the one grand object." If they did not do this, Douglass feared that Lincoln would not go through with his stated purpose. Many in the North did not share Douglass's joy at the action. The *New York World* believed Lincoln had betrayed the moderation of his inaugural address and was "fully adrift on the current of radical fanaticism." A wealthy Bostonian was appalled at the idea black people "should be made free by killing or poisoning their masters and mistresses."[14]

Uncomfortable with a proclamation that did not immediately take effect, Douglass in his articles urged Lincoln to put it into effect instantly, claiming that delay only aided the enemy by giving them time to move black people out of the reach of Union armies as well as to generate northern opposition. Beyond these valid concerns, what scared Douglass more was the idea of Lincoln backing out of this pledge. He wondered in a letter, "Are we not in danger of a compromise?" The thought that the North could give up was never far from his mind. His anxiety about whether this proclamation would become a reality was almost unbearable. John Jones, a friend from Chicago, wrote to Douglass, "we are held in suspense on the first of the month until we receive it." Douglass explained to another associate, "Oh! If one could strike December from the calendar."[15]

Few passages of Lincoln's have been as often quoted as his stirring ending to his second annual message to Congress. The political document for a moment reached out to express so much to all future Americans: "Fellow Citizens, *we* cannot escape history . . . The fiery trial through which we pass, will light us down, in honor or dishonor, to the latest generation." He said the ways to save the Union were known, and that the nation must "hold the power, and bear the responsibility." Then he expressed this salvation for the country: "In *giving* freedom to the *slave*, we *assure* freedom to the *free*— honorable alike in what we give, and what we preserve. We shall nobly save, or meanly lose, the last best, hope of earth."

Few words have been so inspirational, yet many ignore the direct context of the means to be employed to "nobly save." Preceding long passages provide a detailed outline of the gradual, compensation border state plan that Lincoln had been trying to sell, without success, for nearly a year. This plan, which offered to buy a way out of the violence of war, was closely allied to the colonization plan, which offered a means of "augmented, and considerable migration to both these countries (Liberia and Haiti), from the United States." He outlined, in passages seldom read by anyone other than professional historians, what each slave owner would get in return for the freedom of each slave in his possession, and added, "Congress may appropriate money and otherwise provide for colonizing free colored persons, with their own consent, at any place or places without the United States." He then estimated the length of this prolonged emancipation process: thirty-seven years. In other words, slave states (South and North) could participate in this compensation at any time until 1900. Lincoln noted that this plan would not please all equally but would, in his opinion, not only save the Union and stop the killing, but also save "both races from the evils of sudden derangement."[16]

What Lincoln wrote on December 1 brought Douglass only more anxiety. In his annual message, Lincoln affirmed, "I cannot make it better known than it already is, that I strongly favor colonization." Many radicals noted that Lincoln's annual message barely mentioned the possibility of a final Emancipation Proclamation, and instead discussed at length colonization and gradual, compensated emancipation. The annual message made Douglass question Lincoln's commitment to the proclamation, even if it was still part of his thinking.

Despite what Lincoln said in the message, abolitionists also noted the absence of any word on colonization in the preliminary Emancipation Proclamation offered in September, which they hoped was significant. For Lincoln's legacy and the memory of this order as a document of freedom, it was a fortunate omission. However, the omission was plainly not because Lincoln had abandoned these ideas. A far less remembered document that Lincoln signed the day before he placed his pen on the final Emancipation Proclamation is a contract applying federal funds to move five thousand black Americans to an island near Haiti.[17]

Compensated emancipation and colonization were concepts in firm partnership for Lincoln, mutually reinforcing one another. It was no coincidence that these acts were presented on consecutive days. Lincoln wanted to show white voters that emancipation would not necessarily mean free black people would be inundating their communities (an idea he also firmly rejects in his annual message). Indiana representative George W. Julian, writing of the proclamation, indicated that Lincoln "wished it distinctly understood that the deportation of the slaves was, in his mind, inseparably connected with the policy." In fact, Lincoln had told his cabinet as much the day after he released the Emancipation Proclamation, vowing, "the effort to colonize persons of African descent, with their consent, upon this continent, or else where, with the previously obtained consent of the Governments existing there, will be continued."[18]

Rosetta worried for her father, writing, "Are you entirely well or are you forcing yourself about." As she readied for a Christmas break from her school, she missed him and hoped he would find a way to visit soon. When she had a free moment, she loved to go into downtown Philadelphia to find a newspaper documenting her father's latest speech. More than anything, she longed to be in Boston on New Year's Day to see her father experience a crucial moment in all of their lives.[19]

Three days before the final proclamation was to be signed and sent out to the nation, Douglass spoke in his hometown. For December in upstate New York, it was uncharacteristically warm, and Douglass saw symbolism in this glorious weather. He told the crowd that it should not be a day for his words, but rather "a day for poetry and song, a new song."

Since he was a child he had been asking, "How long! How long oh! Eternal Power of the Universe, how long shall these things be?" He felt that God would reveal that answer in three days. He framed the Emancipation Proclamation as a definitive statement to and for a nation heading toward freedom, and Douglass wanted his audience to believe with him the abolition war he had relentlessly worked for had now arrived.

He also confessed, "The suspense is painful, but will soon be over." The range of opinions were so broad and passionate, Douglass saw that the "national head swings, pendulum like, now to the one side and now to the other. Alas, no man can tell which will prevail—and we are compelled to wait, hope, labor and pray." He believed that Lincoln, as inept as he had been, was not a liar. He estimated that Lincoln's word, "though clumsily uttered," was honest.[20]

Then again, just getting Lincoln to this point forced Douglass to compare the president to an ox that emancipation advocates were forced to drag along. The lack of enthusiasm in the preliminary proclamation's words still bothered Douglass; there was nothing resembling an "expression of sound moral feeling against Slavery." There was not a word of shame and regret for slavery's existence nor an extension of mercy. In the end, he suspected there was no motivation in this act that was moral as opposed to military necessity. And if this was indeed the case, Lincoln just might have few reservations about annulling the order.

The irony was that such a stated moral basis might have seemed far more shaky to Lincoln, whose principal governing instinct was to always first make an appeal to logic and reason; it was precisely the secure basis of military necessity that was keeping Lincoln so firmly on line, unbeknownst to Douglass. Somehow, Lincoln had to win this war, and he was convinced, though many in his administration were not, that the proclamation would help in the long run. It was a great gamble, but then again, with so many of his efforts coming up short, perhaps the time had come.

On January 1, Douglass was again at the Tremont Temple. Here he would learn whether Lincoln would force this turning point in the war. A staggering three thousand people crammed into the hall around ten A.M., brimming with enthusiasm. Looking back, he would write, "Our ship was on the open sea, tossed by a terrible storm; wave after wave was passing over us, and every hour was fraught with increasing peril." The Emancipation Proclamation was the lifeline he needed. Alone, it would not ultimately save them, with its questionable legal standing and inability to touch the border slave states, but it would keep them afloat for a while longer, and lead to a horizon no one could yet spy.[21]

One leader after another spoke from the stage, but most eyes kept checking the door for the telegraph messenger to come in with news of the proclamation. It was decided that they would break and reconvene at two P.M. At this time, Douglass spoke on the meaning of this day. He ruminated on the dark period they had passed through, characterized by the attack he had suffered in this very building before the outset of war. This proclamation was a ray of possibility that abolitionists must capitalize on. He reminded the audience that black men were keenly waiting for their chance to fight in this war.[22]

At seven thirty that night people gathered once again and the hours again passed by without information. Eight became nine and nine turned to ten. By eleven P.M., Douglass had been waiting for more than twelve hours, but he vowed he would not go home until morning. Douglass was growing frightened at this point. The crowd's optimism had given way to a pensive, apprehensive mood. Douglass wondered if Mrs. Lincoln's coming from a slaveholding family would cause Lincoln to relent. Perhaps Lincoln's tender nature was actually a weakness that some last-minute plea had swayed. How could he have overlooked the fact that Lincoln did not seem to be "a man of heroic measures"? For Douglass, "suspense became agony," as, "Every moment of waiting chilled our hopes, and strengthened our fears."[23]

The abolitionists had organized a line of messengers that extended to a telegraph machine in a local newspaper office. Finally, Judge Thomas Russell of Plymouth, Massachusetts, sprinted through the crowd, yelling, "It is coming! It is on the wires!!" The effect of his words was "startling beyond description." Old friends and strangers clutched each other, people prayed, sang, and cried to God all at the same time. In a moment, Russell had the proclamation in his hands. Lincoln had kept his word. As soon as black people could reach Union lines or Union lines could reach them, they were free. Douglass remembered, "I never saw enthusiasm before. I never saw joy before." People of all races, ages, and genders embraced. Hats and bonnets flew into the air. The noise was deafening. They shouted three cheers for Abraham Lincoln, while others thanked God with tears streaming down their face.[24]

Charles Slack stepped onto the stage with the proclamation in his hand and then read Lincoln's words above the joyous sounds. It was midnight and their lease on Tremont Temple was over. Someone suggested moving to Rev. Leonard Grimes's Twelfth Baptist Church, an appropriate place because aiding fugitives from slavery had been a cornerstone of this congregation from its inception. Grimes led a crowd almost delirious with excitement down the brick sidewalks of Beacon Hill, where the glow of streetlamps revealed his church on Phillips Street.

Douglass was in the heart of the celebration that packed every pew. They sung "Glory, Hallelujah," "Old John Brown," and "Blow Ye, the Trumpet Blow." One old black man stood up to say, "I was born in North Carolina, where my brother Douglass was born, thank God!" Douglass, laughing, did not have the heart to interrupt him with the information that he was from Maryland. The old man told the crowd that they had both escaped from the slavery and he had managed to take his wife with him. She was with him tonight to rejoice for this blow to the institution that threatened to tear them apart.[25] The party kept going until three in the morning and Douglass spoke for the third time during this emotional whirlwind of a day, but his mind was already moving on to other matters.

He was thinking about black troops. The black men he informally surveyed during the night said they were ready to fight. Was Lincoln ready to accept them?[26]

1863

CHAPTER 9

"Give Them a Chance"

If Frederick Douglass had learned one thing from his years as a slave, it was this: "Power concedes nothing without a demand. It never did and never will. Find out just what any people will quietly submit to and you have found out the exact measure of injustice and wrong which will be imposed on them, and these will continue till they are resisted with either words or blows, or both."[1] If black Americans were to become full citizens of the United States, Douglass was utterly convinced it would happen only after they had personally fought for it. The Emancipation Proclamation was just a step toward a freedom that they would likely have to earn through violence.

Douglass desperately wanted to be a part of this experience of liberation, no matter what it might entail. He told friends that his speaking around the country was to somehow shift the North to support, grudgingly or not, both emancipation and black troops. This effort might not be in vain, and he wondered if it was beginning to dawn on the president that "The slaves' liberation is the country's salvation." Less than a month after his exuberant night of celebration in Boston, Douglass captured how his life had not changed all that much in a letter to newspaper editor Theodore Tilton, "For nearly twenty five years I have been at work—toiling over the country from town to town—speaking to tens where I could find tens—and hundreds—when favored with such numbers. I shall as usual be in the lecturing field this winter." He headed as far west as Chicago, then back east for speeches throughout Connecticut. Before leaving he wrote to Samuel J. May, "the people hear me gladly."[2]

The Emancipation Proclamation would be meaningless if the Union did not win this war. Despite his sense that the proclamation represented a vital turning point, even if the Union's military fortunes radically improved soon and the war ended in victory, Douglass knew the act was still just a presidential order in military guise, not a constitutional amendment. True liberation would only come after black men fought. It was clear to him (and was beginning to occur to those in the War Department) that without black soldiers, the North could not close this contest.

Radical abolitionists saw another dangerous element to the proclamation. Upon closer examination, it clearly was far less radical than the Second Confiscation Act already passed by Congress. As positive a step as it was, it appeared to be a shrewd maneuver by Lincoln to outflank both the radicals in Congress who were pressing him hard on slavery and the conservative Democrats who wanted nothing done on slavery at all. It was Lincoln's way of taming two sets of critics with one act, and the president stoically took whatever criticism came his way, knowing that if he antagonized both sides equally, he was probably as safe as he was going to get.

Douglass's post-Emancipation Proclamation speaking series climaxed in front of a large audience featuring the nation's reformer luminaries at Cooper Union in New York City. He hoped Greeley's *Tribune*, read throughout the country, would publish his entire address. This was his greatest opportunity yet to shape the nation's understanding of the Emancipation Proclamation and of what must happen next in the war.

First, Douglass wanted all Americans to see the good of being emancipated from a curse upon their nation. He proclaimed, "We are all liberated by this proclamation. Everybody is liberated." Lincoln would have agreed with this appraisal of slavery's socially and morally corrosive effect. Thus, in Douglass's estimation, Lincoln had not created a new truth but offered "in this dark hour of national peril, to apply an old truth, long ago acknowledged in theory by the nation"—the radical concept that all are born equal. For this reason, Douglass considered the Emancipation Proclamation to be among the great acts not just of United States history, but in the story of all humanity.

By acknowledging this ideal, Lincoln's emancipation act could also free the Union army from the racial prejudice hindering its progress. He asked his audience if they would rather drown than let the black man save them. As glorious as his view of this presidential action was, if it was not accompanied by enlisting black men, Douglass said it would be "worthless—a miserable mockery." To conquer the rebels and win this epic conflict, the North would have to conquer their own prejudices first.[3]

As the Emancipation Proclamation approached, he had written to Julia Griffiths Crofts of his desire to finally give up the onerous burden of his paper and join the war effort in some regard. It is clear that he was envisioning a more direct involvement. In her response, she says she cannot stop thinking about his letter, and ends up pleading with him, *"you must not give up your paper."* Her exasperation is such that she wished to "fly over the water" and convince Douglass to stay out of any military involvement. Griffiths Crofts was one of Douglass's closest friends, and her opinion carried great weight. But in this case, she did not fully understand Douglass.[4]

In contrast to Griffiths Crofts, H. Ford Douglas, a black male abolitionist, well understood Douglass's inclinations. He agreed with Douglass that black soldiers—not the Emancipation Proclamation—would be the only thing that could put an end to Lincoln's colonization impulses. Ford Douglas knew that white America doubted black men would fight. He told his friend that he was in the most prominent position to prove this assertion wrong. As the most famous black American, there was real pressure on Douglass to wear the uniform.[5]

Many white people found the idea of black men fighting both offensive and unrealistic. The *National Intelligencer* argued that black people were too clumsy to handle guns. If there were to be black soldiers, they recommended arming them with pikes. The widely read *Harper's Weekly* thought the idea unworthy of a civilized or Christian nation. The *Dubuque Times* thought it to be an insane and cowardly concession of the North's weakness. Border state politicians predicted that it would lead to the rape and killing of hundreds of white women throughout the country. Even in Douglass's hometown, the opposition was vocal. The *Union and Advertiser* told citizens to disregard "whatever Fred. Douglass may say about this matter." They thought it impossible for black men to win in a fight with white southerners and, in any case, doubted that Douglass could possibly raise such a regiment.[6]

Abraham Lincoln had been one of the severest critics of using blacks as soldiers just six months ago. In August he had told a delegation that "if we were to arm [the Negros], I fear that in a few weeks the arms would be in the hands of the rebels." Now some profound change was happening. Lincoln's pragmatism began to outweigh his previous sentiments, as he found applying this previously unused element toward victory indispensable. In March 1863, he wrote Tennessee governor Andrew Johnson, "The bare sight of fifty thousand armed and drilled black soldiers upon the banks of the Mississippi, would end the rebellion at once."[7] Regardless of policy changes, Lincoln's earlier dismissive words would have stung Douglass, and probably led Douglass to plead at Cooper Union in New York City on February 6, "Give them a chance! Give them a chance. I don't say they are great fighters. I don't say they will fight better than other men. All I say is, give them a chance."[8]

Douglass's radical abolitionist allies had also been pushing for black troops on the ground, and none more so than Massachusetts senator Charles Sumner, who, like Douglass, had cried out in 1861 that the Union must "carry Africa into the war." Though he had unusual sway with Lincoln, and indeed had developed a real, though push-pull friendship with the president, nothing had happened—yet. But the mounting death toll of Union soldiers and the stunning succession of losses on the battlefield were beginning to create an internal logic to opening up black recruitment. The old refusals were starting to waver, especially with the Emancipation Proclamation as a new factor. On January 25, a group of longtime Boston abolitionists and supporters of John Brown arranged a meeting with Lincoln and his secretary of war, Edwin Stanton. Wendell Phillips, Moncure Conway, and other members of the Emancipation League trooped into the president's office and went through much of the same dance that abolitionists had gone through with the administration many times before. The Boston group entered exasperated and persistent, with the president polite, cautious, and nonforthcoming. When pressed to give their hero Frémont a greater role, Lincoln replied, "Suppose I should put in the South these antislavery generals and governors, what would they do with the slaves that would come to them?" Then an odd-looking, wealthy businessman, George Luther Stearns, whose flowing patriarchal beard made him look as if he had stepped in from the streets of Jerusalem instead of the meadows of Medford, Massachusetts, spoke up. "We would make Union soldiers of all who were capable of bearing arms." Not ready for that, Lincoln simply replied that his Emancipation Proclamation "knocked the bottom out of slavery." The impetuous young Conway said that without some military success, the bottom could be put back in.[9]

The discouraged group quickly learned upon their return to Boston that their state was in fact going to achieve their desired goal. During that same period, Massachusetts governor John Andrew (yet another thorn in Lincoln's side) had finally convinced Stanton to formally agree to a War Department–approved regiment of "volunteers of African descent."[10] The Massachusetts governor hurriedly headed home, hardly believing in the great shift in policy, and immediately hit a wall. His state had fewer than two thousand free black men. How were they to recruit such a historic regiment quickly, before the administration changed its mind?

Andrew wasted no time going back to George Stearns, aware that his deep pockets and fame as financial supporter of John Brown would make him a perfect leader in this effort (for the rich merchant's lead pipe business was doing better than ever in the war, though the radical admitted, "Emancipation has been very hard on my purse.").[11] Stearns quickly responded by forming the Black Committee to move beyond Massachusetts to the whole free North and even into Canada, and his energy and skill promptly confirmed Andrew's faith in him. The shy, slightly stuttering man came to life, believing that he at last was fulfilling the dream of John Brown that he had risked so much for years ago. Stearns wrote to Gerrit Smith that his work now was "to make this a true John Brown Corps."[12] At first, the announcement of the formation of the "Colored Regiment" produced only a tiny number of recruits, and Andrew despaired. Stearns said he would leave for the west the next day. He knew just where to go.

The chief reason that Stearns was the right man for the job was his faith in and long friendship with Frederick Douglass. Stearns boarded a train on February 23 to Rochester, intent on recruiting the orator as his chief spokesman. He simultaneously signed up many other black leaders to become recruiters, but only Douglass had the instant credibility and voice to spread the word. It seems incredible but true that it took only weeks to assemble such a vast national network of agents to sign up black recruits, with Stearns basing himself in Buffalo to direct his men like "pieces on a chessboard."[13]

The King he quickly employed was Douglass. Remarkably, Douglass's great recruiting speech, "Men of Color, to Arms!" appeared in print only three days after Stearns's visit. This suggests a rush of inspiration Douglass experienced after Stearns's call, although he may have already written notes toward such a declaration, whether or not the government asked for his people's help. In any case, Douglass's excitement was palpable. He was soon telling friends that filling up the ranks of the Fifty-fourth Regiment of the Massachusetts volunteer Infantry was the best possible service he could perform for the country's welfare.[14]

The recruiting speech was an impassioned call to his people that in retrospect reads as an addendum to the Emancipation Proclamation itself, with all the power and moral grandeur that Lincoln's document lacked. Douglass saw the opportunity to promote the abolition war he wanted. For months, he had been traveling virtually without pause, usually riding all night after an address to the next night's site. During the month, he covered over two thousand miles, speaking from Boston to Chicago. Every speech or conversation he had during the time revolved around one conviction: "the ABOLITION OF SLAVERY IN EVERY PART OF OUR COUNTRY IS THE BEST AND ONLY WAY TO RESTORE OUR DISTRACTED AND WAR-SMITTEN NATION TO PERMANENT PEACE."[15]

Douglass began his recruiting at home. The first two men enlisted for the Massachusetts Fifty-fourth were his sons Lewis and Charles. Douglass told a friend that his boys would "go to peril all for Liberty and country."[16] Douglass at the outset knew the risks of sending black troops to fight in the South. Armed black men, free or slave, violated the fundamental custom of

American society, and their danger was magnified in the South. A white abolitionist friend of Douglass's, Martha Greene, sent a son to war, but did so with the government's protection of him in the event of capture. Southern policy was already clear—blacks were not soldiers, merely insurgent slaves, and death would be their lot. She told Douglass that Charles and Lewis would have "halters about their necks," even more so in the event that rebels discovered exactly who their father was. She was amazed and almost dismayed over "the depth of earnestness it must require in you to send yours."[17] There was no hesitation now, however. His recruiting would be that much more effective with his beloved sons as leading examples.

Lewis was twenty-two and Charles eighteen when they signed up to begin recruitment for the Massachusetts Fifty-fourth. Douglass's middle son, Frederick Jr., was twenty at the time, and later in the year he signed on to assist in black recruitment in the Mississippi Valley. His father thought him the most practical of the brood, but this came from a cautious, hesitant nature. The fact that he chose not to fight fits with a pragmatism mixed with trepidation. Lewis and Charles were both slightly shorter than their father, with a darker skin tone and features that more resembled Anna's. Charles had a slender face, with innocent chestnut eyes like Rosetta's. Lewis had a more mature countenance, bearded and worn.[18]

Educated in Rochester public schools, the boys relished helping their father prepare his newspaper, as well as delivering it locally. Yet Douglass was often traveling during their childhood, and he wondered about the effect his being gone so much might have on them. He feared, and others noted, that they seemed to take after Anna more than him. Knowing the boys would likely struggle in his considerable shadow, he tried to offer his protection and care. Each had grown up reading the story of their father fighting back against the slave breaker Covey—perhaps all three sons saw the Civil War as the opportunity for their similar awakening to full manhood.

Lewis was the most confident and capable of them. Yet career prospects for a young black man continually discouraged him. Only a few months before the possibility of black enlistment, he was making plans to participate in a group emigrating to a Central American colony. The prospect of being in the vanguard of the black military represented a fresh start at proving himself on American soil, as his father had always hoped would be the case.[19] Though he was professionally stifled, he was finding himself increasingly successful in his courtship of the beautiful Amelia Loguen, daughter of one of the highest-ranking men in the African Methodist Episcopal Zion Church. Compared to her, he thought himself the "vilest wretch on earth," though an "undefinable force attracts me to you, and I have no means of resisting it and would not if I had." Amelia now found herself among the thousands of young women praying no harm would befall their beloved.[20]

Once March came, Douglass recruited all over New York state. He visited Auburn, Ithaca, Buffalo, Geneva, Oswego, Utica, Little Falls, Canajoharie, Glens Falls, Syracuse, Troy, Albany, and more. He did not have to strain hard to convey the fierce happiness he felt in this long-dreamed-of opportunity: "The iron gate of our prison stands half open. One gallant rush from the North will fling it wide open, while four millions of our brothers and sisters shall march out into liberty."

The government had long held back their "powerful black hand." Now the chance was here and it warranted their action. He explained that circumstances for enlistment were hardly ideal, but there was no time to delay. If white men won this war without their help, blacks would never truly gain their liberty. Worse, infinitely worse, if this war was lost, the opportunity to finally destroy slavery might never come again. Douglass cried, "Who would be free themselves must strike the blow."[21]

Regretting that it was not the state of New York calling them, Douglass told his black audiences to take up arms for Massachusetts. Sadly, at this point in his recruitment tour he transmitted erroneous information received from Stearns, who got it from Governor Andrew, who thought he had it from the War Department: Douglass assured them that they would have the same wages, rations, equipment, bounty of one hundred dollars, and the same government protection as white soldiers. Some were skeptical, but Douglass told them that his twenty years as an abolitionist should make him worthy of trust: "I have assured myself on these points, and can speak with authority."

Most of all, Douglass conveyed that regardless of race, they were men. Every man should see his duty in a contest where right and wrong were so clear. If black men did not enlist, it would only justify racist ideas that they were cowards. He told them to enlist for their own self-respect. Men who became soldiers would be able to defend themselves long after the war. Douglass wanted these young black men armed for an uncertain future. If they did not serve, Douglass foresaw a national retreat into compromise, complete with a revocation of the Emancipation Proclamation. He enticed them with the simple notion that the American government was at last giving them the chance to kill white slaveholders. These men could carry a bloody abolition dream to the heart of the South.[22]

Douglass concluded by raising the names of great men martyred for freedom: Denmark Vesey, Nat Turner, John Brown. Black men had the golden opportunity to ease away animosity against their people and to win the gratitude of the country. Douglass offered to pay their way to the camp at

Readville, outside of Boston. Some nights, when his words sent the crowd around him into a whirlwind of joy and jubilee, Douglass concluded by singing "John Brown's Body."[23]

In Syracuse, Douglass spoke at Zion's Church two weeks in a row, burning with energy. At the first meeting, twelve men came forward to serve. During the next week, word of Douglass's message spread throughout the community and seven more men signed up. When Douglass returned for his second speech, six more men volunteered, bringing Douglass's Syracuse total to twenty-five. They were poor men; one observer guessed that they arrived with about five dollars collectively among them. Yet they were attentive, smart individuals with strong, battle-ready bodies.

Ambrose Cook was only seventeen, green and impatient for a fight with a slaveholder. On the other hand, Thomas Leonard, with a grizzled white beard, was almost sixty. What he lacked in youthful spirit, he made up for with perspective on how valuable the chance to fight was. Leonard was disappointed when he found out from Douglass that there were not black officers. Douglass also felt this was a cowardly injustice on the part of the government, though not one outweighing the progress of being able to serve. Douglass compared that to a man refusing to touch water until he was a great swimmer. Leonard also thought better of it and remarked that they would fight so heroically that the government would be forced to change its mind about the officer question.[24]

Douglass paid a doctor fifteen cents per man to examine them a few days later. Once he approved them, Douglass sent his son Charles to put Leonard and the twenty-four other men on the train for Boston. Stearns had worked a deal with a railroad company by which the men rode in first class without disturbances at a reduced rate. Douglass gave them plenty of ham and bread for the journey. Charles spent a few weeks making these trips back and forth from New York state to Boston until it was time for him to stay in camp.[25]

Syracuse was a successful trip, but in smaller towns, Douglass would labor for only a few individuals. His trip to Little Falls produced four soldiers and Canajoharie provided two. Douglass sometimes felt frustrated by having to make these humble appeals for often small results. Nevertheless, he pressed on, knowing the larger matters at stake. In Geneva, seventeen men were ready to enlist after hearing the confident power of Douglass's oration. Yet in the hours that followed, more than half of the volunteers changed their minds, two at the last second before their train started. It took determined work to fill a regiment.[26]

Using a donation from Douglass's radical philanthropist friend Gerrit Smith, Stearns took care of Douglass's expenses plus ten dollars a week. Douglass privately felt it was not enough considering the demand of the work, but was too invested in the mission to grumble. Douglass wrote to Smith in the spring of 1863 that he saw "no hope for the American slave outside the salvation of the country." In the March issue of his *Monthly*, he wrote about the cruel possibility that Lincoln might rescind the Emancipation Proclamation for a compromise. He saw every recruit as being an argument against the possibility of returning black men to chains. By mid-April, he had sent more than one hundred men to the Fifty-fourth.[27]

Rosine Draz warned him that he was pushing himself too hard. She reminded him to pace himself because his people would need his strength for many years to come. She lamented that it was rare these days that he had time to return her letters, but did not want to jeopardize any minute he could spend on his quest. It was enough for her to pray for Douglass. Many of the prayers had to do with Douglass's letters about his going to war. She found the thought almost too horrible to contemplate, but assured him that she would do anything she could for his children if he did not survive the war. Her opinion was that his life was too precious for his people's welfare for him to sacrifice it. Julia Griffiths Crofts expressed these feelings more bluntly. Douglass sent her another letter declaring that if the New York legislature would sanction a regiment, he was ready to serve. She implored him not to accept any commission offered to him. Pleading for him to refrain, she continued, "*never go south*—or killed you *most assuredly* will be—you are, in many respects, a *marked man*."[28]

Douglass may have been tempted to serve because of letters from old friends who were in the service. George Evans, a white abolitionist who was able to fight from the beginning of the war, said that he saw the war transforming into an abolition war because of the determination of "the immense multitude of the flying fugitives" all over the Virginia countryside.[29]

As Douglass traveled to Boston to see his sons and the historic Fifty-fourth off to battle at the close of May, the North needed to find hope in something. As the other Army of the Potomac leaders had before him, Massachusetts's own "Fighting" Joe Hooker had missed his great chance. Against all classical military advice, the aggressive Robert E. Lee had brilliantly split his army in the Virginia wilderness and had sent Stonewall Jackson to surprise resting Union regiments. With federals running as if a force from hell had descended upon them, the Battle of Chancellorsville in early May had been a rout, another Union disaster. The only consolation, and it would prove to be a huge one, was that Jackson had been accidentally killed by his own men. Yet, this did not change the fact that the battle crushed confidence at home again. How is it possible to win a war when your army is thoroughly beaten over and over? How many more defeats like this could the North endure?

People around Boston desperately needed something to signal things were changing, that there was hope for their cause. The debut of the Massachusetts Fifty-fourth, the unveiling of the free black man as soldier, certainly signified something new. For Douglass, this was deliverance.

The Boston and Providence railroad ran a train along the great plain of Camp Meigs in Readville, where Massachusetts men trained to become part of the Union army. In the windy and muddy month of March 1863, white officers waited for the trains. At last the results of Stearns's agents produced a flood of recruits, who were promptly outfitted with their wool blue uniforms with the brass buttons that read U.S. and billeted in vast drafty and chilly wooden barracks. By March 25, four hundred men were in camp, and in eight weeks, the regiment reached full numbers at a thousand.

Stearns, in his offices in Buffalo, notified Governor Andrew that they were two hundred men above the limit. Could they go beyond Stanton's orders and create another regiment? Andrew dared and said yes, and the Fifty-fifth was born.

By mid-May, all had been trained to march and turn, wheel and salute. Moreover, they all now held Enfield rifles. The nature of the Civil War was about to change irrevocably. All they needed now were the regimental colors, and on May 18, Frederick Douglass joined a flood of dignitaries to watch as four Massachusetts flags were presented to Col. Robert Gould Shaw, a young man from a proud abolitionist family. Shaw, a white Beacon Hill Brahmin only twenty-five-years old, initially thought himself unworthy to lead such a significant regiment. He also feared the loneliness and social stigma that would come from leading black troops. Eventually his ideals outweighed these considerations, and he commanded with a maturity far beyond his years. At the presentation of the colors, Shaw said, "May we have an opportunity to show that you have not made a mistake in intrusting the honor of the State to a colored regiment—the first State that has ever sent one to the war."[30]

Andrew then handed him his orders from Stanton. They were pulling out immediately, to report to General David Hunter's Hilton Head headquarters on the Sea Islands off South Carolina. The army was stationing them south of Charleston, near Fort Sumter where the war had begun. No one on that proud day could envision what one month would do to the ranks of the men before them. It is not recorded if Douglass spoke that day. He would also be there when, ten days later, the Fifty-fourth marched through Boston to the waterfront to sail to their fate.

Lewis was a sergeant major, a noncommissioned officer. Charles was an orderly, but stayed behind ill at Readville. The regiment formed their line at six thirty A.M. and boarded a train at Readville bound for Boston. No previous regiment had elicited such awed reaction. Beacon Street was jammed with excited onlookers, one newspaper putting the number at twenty thousand. The regiment neatly marched along the Boston Common while women waved handkerchiefs from the windows of the fine red-brick mansions, with flags and shouts of encouragement filling the air. As they paused in front of the State House, Governor Andrew proudly sent up a hurrah. They entered the Boston Common by way of the Charles Street gate and drilled for the cheering crowd. Around noon, the regiment marched toward State Street in the direction of the wharves, while throngs sang "John Brown's Body." They passed over the exact spot where Crispus Attucks fell in the Boston Massacre. At the last moment reality intruded on this remarkable day, when ruffians at the tail end of the parade finally disrupted an otherwise ideal march. Lewis was among those who were spit at and beaten. Some white men tried to grab their weapons, but these guns were now firmly in black hands.[31]

Police held back well-wishers and family as the men boarded the steamer *De Molay*, headed for Port Royal, South Carolina. By four o'clock, the sun started to set over the Boston Harbor on a clear, cool spring day and the steamer left its dock. As it sailed away from the great crowd at the wharves, one family member was not ready to say goodbye. Douglass was allowed to board the ship. Besides his eldest son, the regiment also contained over a hundred young men who had put their trust in him. He did not know all of them well but knew some of their stories and the small towns they had left behind for this mission. He went throughout the boat, bidding farewell to these young men he felt connected to, offering words of encouragement and strength.[32]

In a larger sense, the whole regiment was the product of Douglass's dreams, and they were his children. He had cried out for black troops from the outset of war. The faces of this sharply outfitted and well-drilled fighting force embodied Douglass's vision. Throughout the day, Douglass could hardly believe how grand they looked. It was understandable that he wanted a more intimate goodbye. The sight of land was fading when it was finally time for Douglass to board a tugboat and head slowly back to shore.[33]

Lewis Douglass stared at the long treacherous stretch of South Carolina beach. A fresh breeze blew through the ranks of six hundred men of the Fifty-fourth

The evening battle of the 54th Massachusetts regiment,
depicted in *Storming Fort Wagner* by Kurz & Allison, 1890

crouched down in the wet sand. Fog gathered over the sea as the sun set.
Thunder mixed with the sound of the preceding artillery barrage. Having
marched almost continuously for two days and having gone without food since
morning, the men wished the wait over, the orders to charge now.

At the end of the narrow sea path facing them was the confederate
stronghold of Fort Wagner. Made of quartz sand and palmetto logs and
stretching for the width of the island at that point, it was generously equipped
with cannon and bristled with determined defenders. Ingeniously designed,
Fort Wagner was a death trap, as Shaw and his men well knew, but the way to
Charleston was through it—there was no way around. The dashing young
man's face looked pale as he called out, "Now I want you to prove yourselves.
The eyes of thousands will look on what you do tonight."

As they rose to start their long advance, the fort seemed to explode with
fire. Lewis kept pace with those around him. Every few seconds he saw a shell
clear a deadly space of about twenty feet in the ranks. He did his best to close
the gaps around him. Trying to ignore the screams of downed comrades, at
times he pressed through waist-deep water. After running the equivalent of
ten football fields among flying lead, they reached the base of Fort Wagner
and knelt in a long ditch. The time had come for Colonel Shaw to offer what
officers must. His men followed as he ran on a pathway leading to the fort,

Lewis Douglass

yelling "Forward, Fifty-fourth!"[34] He scrambled up the bloodied sloping sand wall to the parapet, and then, his shadow set off by blazing gunfire, he rose up with his sword out. His regiment followed behind him with bayonets ready, but his bullet-ridden body fell.[35]

With grape, canister, shell, and mines exploding around him, Lewis pushed forward toward the fiery rampart. Men fell all about him, with the returning fire savagely effective. A bullet grazed his leg, completely obliterating his sword sheath. The regiment gained the crest of the fortress through their hand-to-hand combat. However, they were outnumbered and trapped. Confederates were pushing back their progress. Lewis felt the battle was in the balance. He desperately looked behind him for reinforcements that he did not see. The fort's occupiers deliberately moved forward until Lewis had no choice but to join the retreat. He dodged shells and other missiles on the agonizingly long run back to safety. Badly wounded men who did not make it all the way back would drown during the night, as the tide continued to rise. It dawned on Douglass's son that he had no idea how he could have survived what had just happened.[36]

Lewis quickly understood the larger importance of what they had achieved. The Fifty-fourth may have failed to take Fort Wagner, but they validated the courage of black soldiers for all who saw the attack. Two days after the battle he wrote to Amelia, telling her that not a man flinched and their reputation would be of a fighting regiment. He also bid her farewell in the event of his death. He thought it highly unlikely that he could survive another such slaughter. He told her that "if I die I die in a good cause. I wish we had a hundred thousand colored troops we would put an end to this war."[37]

His parents were on his mind. Describing the regiment that his father helped to create as "cut to pieces," Lewis estimated that they had suffered three hundred casualties, including all but eight of the officers. He wrote to his parents, "If I die tonight I will not die a coward."[38] Douglass would later celebrate the importance of Fort Wagner, saying, "In that terrible battle, under the wing of night, more cavils in respect of the quality of negro manhood were set at rest than could have been during a century of ordinary life . . ."[39] This was undoubtedly true, and vitally important to his people and the eventual course of the war, but he kept his raw and immediate emotions under his usual steely control. Nothing survives that indicates how he actually received the news of the effective destruction of the regiment only a month into service, or of his son's almost miraculous survival. We do know how Stearns learned of his men's fate, however, and his reaction reveals the strain close to terror that these men were under as they worked twelve-hour days to send boys into the maw of battle.

Stearns was in Washington on July 19 arguing (with "great disgust") against Secretary Stanton about equal pay for the black regiments and the need for black officers. A friend asked Stearns as he entered the Willard Hotel if he had heard the news—the death of Shaw and half the officers, the shredding of the regiment. Hearing the words that they had been "cut to pieces," the businessman collapsed into a chair in anguished silence, clasping the newspaper report. His son Frank remembered never seeing his father so upset. Stearns immediately wrote Andrew, "My heart bleeds for our gallant officers and soldiers of the 54th. All did their duty nobly."[40]

The recruiting moved forward as the War Department closely watched the battles of Milliken's Bend, Mississippi, and Fort Wagner in which black troops fought. There was no willingness to pay the men equally or to commission black officers, but a basic policy was about to change, and so Stearns was sent for. To his amazement, Stanton was pleased at his and Andrew's audacious recruiting and wished to make official the work of the Black Commission by making Stearns an assistant adjutant-general with the effective rank of major. Accepting, he resolved to move his headquarters from Buffalo to Philadelphia.

The strain on Stearns's most effective agent was evident, however, especially to his old English friends. Rosine Draz saw the emotional strain this was taking on Douglass. After she sent Douglass money that she had raised for his causes, he tersely replied that she could have raised more, and that he ought to send the whole sum back until she could do better. She was shaken by his response and wrote back reminding him how much work had gone into these efforts and the joy she had felt sending the sum to him. To receive scorn instead of praise grieved her terribly. Douglass's uncharacteristically cross response reflected not only the anxiety he was experiencing for Lewis's trials but simple exhaustion. Mary Carpenter complimented his courage "not to shrink from any sacrifice that you may be called on to make or to hold back anything." She reminded him that his friends empathized and wanted to support him during the "trial of letting your sons join the army."[41]

How could Douglass stop when black troops were proving what he had long predicted? Nothing could help shift attitudes on slavery's ability to survive the war than what was being sacrificed on the field. The Massachusetts Fifty-fourth had unprecedented visibility as the first northern black regiment, but they were only one part of a larger movement of black soldiers proving their merit as spring became summer in 1863. Regiments largely composed of Louisiana natives fought fiercely at Milliken's Bend above Vicksburg and at Port Hudson on the Mississippi. At the latter, Captain Andre Cailloux, a wealthy, Paris-educated, free black man, shouted his orders in French, English, and Creole. With an arm almost totally shot off, he pressed on for up to six separate charges. Eventually it became clear that these charges were suicidal, but not before rebel guns had fatally struck Cailloux. Black soldiers found themselves holding the Union line under rebel assaults at Milliken's Bend. They protected it as the battle descended into vicious hand-to-hand matches. Both of these contests earned increasing praise from the generals sending reports back to Washington. However, nothing captured the country's attention like the Fifty-fourth's assault on Fort Wagner.[42]

Yet, Douglass was increasingly troubled. Slavery and equality were different matters, and what was disturbing Douglass was the continuing and obstinate discrimination against black troops. When Stearns asked him to come to Philadelphia to speak at the National Hall on July 6 to address the increasing resistance of black men to this evident discrimination, Douglass went.

Douglass had no trouble attracting a crowd—around five thousand black and white people packed the space to hear him. Greeted by thunderous applause, Douglass was more solemn than usual. On the question of whether black men should enlist despite this inequality, Douglass contended that fighting bravely would be the best way to gain equality. The speech came in a week that was probably the most crucial in the entire history of the war, as news filtered in about the defeat of Lee's invasion at Gettysburg, the capture of Vicksburg by Grant that put the Mississippi River under total Union control, and the outbreak of riots in New York City in resistance to the army draft.[43]

For three days and nights, dangerous mobs controlled the city and took out their anger on the black population. In one of the most impassioned passages from Douglass's *Life and Times*, he wrote:

> It spared neither age nor sex; it hanged negroes simply because they were negroes; it murdered women in their homes, and burnt their homes over their heads; it dashed out the brains of young children against the lamp-posts; it burned the colored orphan asylum . . . and forced colored men, women and children to seek concealment in cellars or garrets or wheresoever else it could be found, until this high carnival of crime and reign of terror should pass away."[44]

In a career of close calls, this was one of Douglass's narrowest, as he was passing through New York when the riots broke out and, as he noted, his fame as the Union's most prominent recruiter would have made him a double target of rage.

In his Philadelphia talk, even as these momentous events were swirling around them, Douglass once again tried to motivate the potential black recruits in the face of blatant inequality. As they faced death, why could they not receive equal pay? "I shall not oppose this view. There is something deep down in the soul of every man present which assents to the justice of the claim thus made, and honors the manhood and self-respect which insists on it . . . I am content with nothing for the black man short of equal and exact justice." But there was one thing that needed to be considered—the ghastly existence of slavery itself. If the South won, or stalemated, or exhausted the North, it lived on, and nothing excused that. "Do not flatter yourselves, my friends, that you are more important to the government than the government is to you. You stand but as the plank to the ship. The rebellion can be put down without your help. Slavery can be abolished by white men, but liberty so won for the black man, while it may leave him an object of pity, can never make him an object of respect."[45]

All this, before the July 18 assault on Fort Wagner.

As the recruiting continued, the ranks of the Union army swelled with the infusion of thousands of blacks. Many white soldiers at first, and not surprisingly, resented fighting alongside black men. A dispute broke out in a New Jersey regiment stationed in the Sea Islands of South Carolina over going into battle with black men. When a captain contended that they were an inferior race, a comrade countered, "What do you say of Frederick Douglass, who has raised himself from slavery to a high position?" The captain had no response to that, but was still not convinced.[46]

Charles Douglass had learned that wearing the uniform only increased racism toward him when, as he was boarding a train to leave a Fourth of July celebration in Boston to return to camp with the Massachusetts Fifty-fifth, a group of Irishmen overheard him making disparaging comments about former Union commander George McClellan. One stepped in front of him with his fists up and swore, "McClellan's a good General, you black nigger. I don't care if you have a uniform on." With his father's audacity, Charles ran right at the considerably larger man and fought him until a police officer pulled them apart. Charles was livid, believing he could have whipped a dozen more men. With a loaded pistol on him, Charles wrote his father that he would use it the next time a white man laid a hand on him.[47]

This racism would have saddened Douglass, not surprised him. Before he had started recruiting, he had written words that presaged those of W. E. B. Du Bois before World War I: "We shall be fighting a double battle, against slavery at the South and against prejudice and proscription at the North . . ."[48] Although he believed that no one who saw fifty thousand well-drilled soldiers could possibly retain their old notions of black inferiority, with so much blood already spilled, what increasingly made him share the anger of those young men he was lecturing was the formal and calculating way that the government was discriminating against black troops. This inequality took different forms.

The administration paid black men the wages of laborers instead of soldiers. White men received thirteen dollars per month and black men received ten dollars, minus a three-dollar clothing allowance. The administration claimed to be obeying the laws as they were then written, though many thought this was passively done out of deference to those still against black troops. It seemed that every letter a member of the Fifty-fourth received contained accounts of how their families were suffering. One soldier pleaded, "My wife and three little children at home are, in a manner, freezing and starving to death . . . How can men do their duty, with such agony in their minds?" Another soldier wrote to Lincoln, telling him of the battles they had fought on the South Carolina coast. He continued, "Now the main questions is. Are We *Soldiers*, or are we LABOURERS."[49]

Sergeant William Walker of the South Carolina Third Infantry (Colored) learned the tragic answer. He, like around 80 percent of the black men who fought, had escaped slavery.[50] For these men in particular, the three dollars were critical for financially fraught families. He led a group to the tent of their commander where they stacked their weapons in protest and peacefully returned to their tents without their weapons. For this act, officers charged Walker with inciting a mutiny. A few weeks later, his life ended in front of a firing squad. Governor Andrew lamented, "The Government which found no law to pay him except as a nondescript and a contraband, nevertheless found law enough to shoot him as a soldier." Scholars often herald Lincoln's softhearted tendency to commute execution sentences. One then wonders why Walker was not worthy of such mercy?[51]

Private Wallace Baker of Charles's Massachusetts Fifty-fifth met a similar fate when his anger over the issue boiled over and he struck an officer. A witness remarked, "No man ever met his death with less trepidation than Wallace Baker." One inequality led to another, with black men making up 8 percent of the Union fighting force but more than 20 percent of the executions. As well, there were still no commissioned black officers, and this inequality was now the cause of almost as much unrest. The Lincoln administration believed this prohibition was a way to soften the shock of employing blacks as soldiers at all. One soldier wrote, "We want men we can understand and who can understand us . . . we want simple justice."[52]

Finally, and most deadly, soldiers did not feel protected by the government in the event of their capture. In December of 1862, Confederate president Jefferson Davis ordered southern armies to turn over captured black men to state governments which would deal with the prisoners according to state law. These laws punished black insurrections with death. However, the reality was that wounded or surrendered soldiers would not even make it that far. Members of Lewis's regiment were found bound and executed near the sites of their South Carolina battles. One black soldier captured in Virginia escaped to recount that he watched as defenseless friends were led away to the woods and hung, executed on the banks of a river, and had their skulls crushed by the butt ends of muskets.[53]

Confederates themselves left the most chilling accounts of what happened to black soldiers after battles. G. W. Grayson, serving in Florida, compared the aftermath of a battle to quail hunting. Rebels combed through fields first and, ignoring cries for mercy, executed whom they found. They then proceeded to a nearby creek where black men hid with only their noses above water. Grayson thought his comrades seemed like wild beasts as they dragged the black men out of the water and murdered them.[54]

Hannah Johnson was the mother of a Massachusetts Fifty-fourth private whom she had brought out of slavery in Louisiana to raise in upstate New York. After her enormous efforts to ensure a better future for him, she was reluctant to let him fight. Eventually she did because she believed "Mr. Lincoln will never let them sell out colored soldier for slaves . . . he will rettallyate and stop it." In a letter to Lincoln, she told him that her son had proved himself as a man at Fort Wagner and deserved his protection. Although it seemed cruel, she implored him to react in kind or the Confederates would not end their brutality. She also asked him about rumors that he would rescind the Emancipation Proclamation. Begging him to never do such a thing, she added, "When you are dead and in Heaven, in a thousand years that action of yours will make the Angels sing your praises I know it."[55]

The discrimination pained Douglass on a number of levels. It jeopardized not only the lives of his sons, but also the lives of young men whom he had publicly and prominently promised would have equal treatment. This is what Stearns had understood to be the arrangement, but that did not change how those who believed his assurances would view him. As reports of these discriminations reached the North, recruiting became more difficult.

At a New York City recruiting meeting at Shiloh Church, Douglass finished his recruitment oration and, like a preacher saving those who would come forward, Douglass asked who would join the army. Only one man stood up. Douglass was appalled and called the audience cowards. A man named Robert Johnson stood up and told Douglass that it was not weakness that kept them from enlisting but respect for their manhood, that Johnson would not subject himself to such unfairness. This argument left Douglass in a quandary: No one more than Douglass had asked black men to assert and protect themselves.[56]

Such addresses were masterful and compelling, but Douglass could not keep making them. The sickening realization of betrayal crept over him. On August 1, he wrote a letter explaining why Stearns would not see him at an upcoming recruiting event in Pittsburgh. Douglass's dream had confronted a painful reality. He so badly wanted to keep recruiting black men to fight, but until circumstances changed, he could no longer be the one to tell them to ignore discriminations that could well cost them their lives. Thinking of all the abuses these young men already suffered, Douglass felt he owed them that much. His recruiting was supposed to come from his heart and without qualification. He had let his own sons prepare to sacrifice their lives for a callous government unwilling to protect them. Perhaps he had been naïve, too eager to think clearly, or had just overestimated the humanity of the commander in chief. Douglass's letter had nothing but love for Stearns. He was very clear as to who was solely responsible for his disillusionment: Abraham Lincoln.

In the first months of his recruiting, he had thought Lincoln's silence on inequality and Confederate ruthlessness belied strong action to come. After all, issuing the Emancipation Proclamation had sent Douglass's hopes soaring. That faith was nearly gone. There were so many moments when Lincoln could have asserted himself against such obvious wrongs. Douglass asked, "How many 54ths must be cut to pieces, its mutilated prisoners killed and its living sold into Slavery, to be tortured to death by inches before Mr. Lincoln shall say 'Hold, enough!' " Deafening silence was the response. He believed that Lincoln felt nothing at the thought of black men massacred. Until the North executed southerners for every black life taken, Douglass held Lincoln as responsible as Jefferson Davis. Douglass's guilt mixed with sadness and anger, for he had been complicit in allowing young men to be "betrayed into bloody hands by the very Government in whose defense they were heroically fighting."[57]

Stearns knew Douglass was right about the administration needing to take a firmer stand. He also knew how devastating Douglass's denunciations could be for the war effort. Fortunately, Stearns was a very clever man. He wrote back that if Douglass's issues were with Lincoln, then he should address them to Lincoln. Face to face.

Douglass had written that abolitionists should "speak out trumpet-tongued in the ears of Mr. Lincoln and his Government." Stearns took this literally and thought Douglass should lead the way.[58]

Douglass liked the idea.

CHAPTER 10

First Meeting

August of 1863 was oppressively hot, with temperatures climbing to 104 degrees, streets steaming. There was no refuge from mosquitoes that found the filthy, odorous waterways to be an ideal home in Washington. The miasmic smell of sewage and garbage was thick in the air. The sewage draining into drinking water made many sick, including Willie Lincoln, who possibly died from typhoid fever. Along Pennsylvania Avenue, there were cheap saloons, slaughterhouses, and markets. Fish and oyster peddlers stood on the corners, geese and hogs roamed through the streets. Through the city wafted the stench of dead horses, cows, cats, and other animals decomposing in and around the canals that ran close alongside the city's blocks and within easy sight of the White House.

The wounded and dying soldiers in the makeshift hospitals all over the city reinforced the overpowering stench of death, making it impossible to forget that the nation was at war.[1] Wounded men lay in unsanitary quarters in what had been mansions, schools, federal buildings, churches, and hotels from Judiciary Square to Washington Circle. Crippled men hobbled on their new crutches, adjusting to a life without limbs. They were the lucky ones. For many of their companions, these sweltering, putrid spaces would be their last images of life. The profession of undertaker burgeoned everywhere; Dr. Hutton & Co. on E Street between Eleventh and Twelfth bragged, "Bodies Embalmed by us NEVER TURN BLACK!"[2]

Journalist Noah Brooks estimated that Washington was the dirtiest city in America. He thought the moral sleaze rivaled the physical filth. Drunks and scoundrels of every kind overran what was virtually an urban military encampment. In the month before Douglass arrived, there were seven murders in one week. Going out at night in Washington, which had a feeble police force, was not recommended. The most frequented whorehouses were close to the White House, in mansions around Lafayette Square and the south side of Pennsylvania Avenue. A city official estimated that there were 450 brothels and five thousand prostitutes.[3]

Charles Dickens, visiting twenty years earlier, mockingly wrote that Washington had "spacious avenues that begin in nothing, and lead nowhere; streets, mile-long, that only want houses, roads, and inhabitants; public buildings that need but a public to be complete." Washington was then the fourteenth largest American city, with just over sixty thousand residents. Before the war, congressmen had felt they were living in a village with half-built markers of a great city. One could find a good baseball game near the Potomac River, but not the sophisticated entertainments of New York, though perhaps John Ford's new theater would bring some cultural development.[4]

Slavery had ended in the city only a year ago. Under the "black code," if white authorities caught a free black person without a residence permit, they could sell them into slavery. Offenses as trivial as bathing in the canals or flying a kite in the wrong place could be met with lashes. For black soldiers who passed through, rocks and the fists of civilians were hard realities. Many still called the local jail the "Washington Slave Pen" because of the manner in which Lincoln's friend and appointee Ward H. Lamon kept escaped blacks. Emancipation was a great boon, but Washington was still a repressive city.[5]

On this Monday morning, August 10, the *Daily National Republican* reported that Navy Yard engineer James Robinson had dragged a black man named James Wedge from his house and beaten him so severely that Wedge was left crippled. For this assault, Robinson was fined $5.94. If Douglass had wanted to reach the White House by the rickety, horse-drawn streetcars, he would have had to find one that had a sign, COLORED PERSONS MAY RIDE IN THIS CAR.[6]

Early this morning, Frederick Douglass arrived in the office of Kansas senator Samuel Pomeroy. Douglass carried with him a note from George Stearns charging Douglass with representing him for business related to recruiting for the government. Pomeroy was a man whose courage was not in doubt. Washington was so racist that Douglass believed it would be a daring act for Pomeroy to walk down the street with him. Though Pomeroy was a Massachusetts man and had served as a state representative on Beacon Hill in the early 1850s, he had moved to the Kansas territory as it erupted in violence over whether it would enter the Union as a free or slave state. When the town of Lawrence was under attack from slavery supporters, residents chose Pomeroy as chair of a committee of public safety. He did all he could to stem the powerful attacks of "border ruffians," but despite his efforts, the town was eventually pillaged and burned.[7]

Douglass considered the abolitionist Pomeroy a friend but did not endorse his work on voluntary black emigration plans. When his son Lewis wanted to go with a group Pomeroy was organizing to Central America, Douglass wrote with sadness to Pomeroy, "To see my children usefully and happily settled in this, the land of their birth and ancestors, has been the hope and ambition of my manhood." Douglass could see neither justice nor wisdom in the colonization project. As Lincoln pushed the idea to colonize Chiriqui (in Panama) in 1862, he turned to Pomeroy for help. The project was on hold by October 1863, but this was more because of the resistance of Central American governments and the corruption of some of the proprietors. Still, it was not at all clear at this time that either Lincoln or Pomeroy had terminated the initiative.[8]

Douglass and Pomeroy headed over to the War Department. Douglass's first meeting of the day would be with Secretary of War Edwin Stanton.[9] Despite his far-flung travels, Douglass had not been in Washington before, and he was thrilled to look up for the first time at the Freedom statue that adorned the Capitol dome, recently set in place. The great dome had been half-finished at the beginning of the war, and despite the tightness of the federal budget, Lincoln decided that work should go on—that its completion would be a morale boost to the country in the midst of war.[10]

Assistant Secretary Charles Dana greeted Douglass and Pomeroy. Douglass had known Dana since the idealistic Harvard graduate had lived on the Brook Farm in Massachusetts, a utopian experiment steeped in socialism. They had continued their friendship during Dana's fifteen years at the *New York Tribune*. Dana now served as Stanton's watchdog on Ulysses S. Grant, the controversial new luminary of the Union army who had won Union control of the Mississippi River after the recent victory in the long siege at Vicksburg. Rumors of Grant's fondness for drink dogged Grant, but since he seemed to be the only Union general who won victories, Lincoln was inclined to leave him alone on this subject (and even talked of sending a case of whatever it was Grant drank to his other generals). Taking time away from these and other matters, Dana walked Douglass into the office of his incisively sharp and usually irritable superior, located on the second floor and behind a constantly crowded reception room.[11]

Edwin Masters Stanton was the sort of man who always seemed to have had a poor night of sleep. The short, thick, impressively gray bearded and usually sweaty Quaker glanced at Douglass through his round wire-rimmed glasses with little interest. It took Douglass only seconds to realize he was

Secretary of War Edwin Stanton

dealing with a man with little concern for niceties. Lincoln's secretary John Hay said that he would rather suffer pox in a hospital than ask Stanton for a favor. His flat eyes conveyed time was of the essence, and Douglass imagined him thinking, "Well, what do you want? I have no time to waste upon you or anybody else, and I shall waste none. Speak quick, or I shall leave you." It did not increase Douglass's ease that Stanton was standing at his tall desk during the entire meeting, as he did with all visitors. The impatient but brilliant secretary of war found it was a none-too-subtle way of shifting power to his side of the room.[12]

Stanton's stern abruptness served to shield Lincoln from things and people he preferred not to confront, and the president himself said, "I want to oblige everybody when I can; and Stanton and I have an understanding that if I send an order to him which cannot be granted, he is to refuse it. This he sometimes does."[13] (This system would perhaps be exercised toward Douglass himself in the next month.) Stanton was close and intensely loyal to his chief, although before the war Stanton, a Democrat, had ruthlessly mocked him. Few people liked the secretary of war, but Lincoln liked his utter focus on winning the war, and so they spent countless hours together in the War Department and the Telegraph Office, waiting for word from distant battlefields.

Douglass quickly contemplated how he could keep this meeting as brief and clear as possible. He laid out the matters he was intending to bring to the president's attention: unequal pay, no black officers, and the frightening lack of protection for black soldiers. The status of this last issue had, however, changed substantially in the last eleven days. In Douglass's resignation letter to Stearns, the main issue he had bemoaned was lack of protection for black troops. Douglass's patience had run out at just the moment Lincoln finally took action. On the last day of July, the administration published an order from the president that, regardless of class, color or condition, the government would try to protect soldiers of color. To put a black soldier back into slavery (particularly if that man had been free in the North) was "barbarism, and a crime against the civilization of the age." For each Union soldier executed, they would deal with a Confederate in kind. Further, the administration would respond to any Union soldier sold into slavery by placing an enemy soldier in hard labor.[14] Douglass had long pleaded for the administration to do something—and Lincoln had done it. Yet because so many hopeful acts, such as Congress's Second Confiscation Act, had previously floundered in execution, Douglass still planned to press Stanton and Lincoln on this visit to ensure that they would put the brutal order into action.

Douglass then chose to elaborate on a larger point. He told the Secretary of War that there were two extreme opinions hurting his people. While some painted them as demons, others saw them as angels. Some people's expectations were crushingly low, others naïvely high.

Stanton did not follow where he was going with this. In what respect did Douglass mean?

Douglass went on to explain the reason he was saying this to the man ultimately responsible for all black soldiers was because there would be ambitious, brave soldiers, but there would also be base, cowardly fellows. Douglass implored the secretary to treat them all simply as men, and as normal men who reacted and responded to the same things that affected white soldiers. Why would they enlist if the government would not pay them fairly? Why would they perform well if there was no chance of their advancement in the ranks? In this, they were no different than others.[15]

Stanton's manner changed as he seemed to understand the kind of man he was dealing with. Comprehending Douglass's intelligence, his formerly skeptical and curt manner seemed to melt a bit. Stanton sincerely explained how difficult a position the administration was in when it came to supporting the simple idea—and then reality—of black soldiers. No one had to explain to Douglass the extent and depth of the prejudice that his young men faced. In addition, Stanton offered, the administration was dealing with the laws as Congress had passed them. He felt Congress had yet to codify that black men were no longer entitled simply to the benefits of a laborer. His personal wish was that black troops could soon obtain equal treatment.[16]

Then Stanton stated a startling proposition. Would Douglass go south as an assistant adjutant to Adjutant General Lorenzo Thomas to recruit and organize black troops in the Mississippi valley?[17]

Douglass was taken aback. He explained that he was already working for Stearns's recruiting in the North (not mentioning the fact that he had actually resigned a week and a half ago). That led Stanton to Douglass's second surprise. Stanton said he and Stearns had already discussed the idea, and that Stearns was behind it. Douglass reported to Stearns a few days later that Stanton was "imperative in his manner," telling Douglass that he would send him the commission and travel instructions immediately. Stanton asked how long Douglass needed to get ready. Douglass estimated that he needed two weeks to prepare. That was fine with Stanton, who agreed to send the papers to Rochester. Their meeting had lasted thirty minutes. Stanton concluded without the pleasantries he so detested.[18]

Douglass readily understood the importance of what was being asked of him, and the sacrifice he would need to make to go South. There was a clear limit to the number of potential free black soldiers, but the vast Mississippi delta could become the Union army's mother lode, providing a torrent of men freed from slavery who sought military service as a way into freedom. Lorenzo Thomas and Douglass came from vastly different backgrounds. Although Thomas had spent the last forty years, his entire adult life, in the military, he had not spent them in the field but in War Department offices, meticulously managing regulations and rules.

Stanton found General Thomas useless, suspecting the bottle had helped him through all these years of pedantry. He had been looking for a way to get rid of Thomas, so when a project far away from Washington that needed superior organizational skills arose, he knew just the man for the job. Stanton gave Thomas twenty-four hours to pack up and head west. Yet Thomas took on the project with more passion than anyone ever dreamed the elderly paper-pusher possessed. He spoke with sincere passion to prejudiced white officers whom he wanted to lead the freedmen, as well as to the "contrabands" flooding into Union lines. Many thousands were now living in makeshift camps where the conditions were appalling. Without proper food, clothes, or shelter, with vermin eating away at their bodies, the dead were piled into carts for mass burial. Thomas quickly visited these hellish places, appalled and ready to change these people's dire prospects. He was no Douglass, but his efforts were relentless and soon began yielding great gains in enlistment. Lincoln commented that Thomas seemed to be the perfect instrument for a task he wanted done vigorously. Thomas pressed himself so hard that sickness and exhaustion nearly killed him in the searing Mississippi sun.[19]

Frederick Douglass

The job Douglass accepted would be a dangerous one. Lieutenant Eben White was engaged in a similar endeavor while strolling around a Maryland plantation. When the farm's patriarch and his son discovered what White was doing there, they ran into their field with a shotgun and blasted the Union officer in the chest. Standing above his dead body, they shot him twice more and bashed in his head with the butt of their gun. Equally horrifying was the fate of Lieutenant Oscar Orillion, who was leading twenty black soldiers on a recruiting mission in Louisiana. The unit was captured by a Confederate cavalry force, and they were later found hung, their bodies cut to pieces. These killings sent a clear message about how the Confederacy felt about recruiting their slaves to carry a gun.[20]

The areas that Stanton intended Douglass to recruit in were along the Mississippi River, where entire social structures were being turned on their head and the Civil War was rapidly revolutionizing American life. The people who fled slavery to find Union lines—their sacrifices and risks—remain a largely untold story, yet was as vital to the course of the war as any battle. Archy Caughn was one of these men who ran toward federal troops in Tennessee. A furious owner named Bartlet Ciles recovered the captured and petrified Caughn. Ciles tied Caughn's hands, took him to nearby woods, removed his left ear with a sharp knife, and then castrated him. Sometimes even reaching a northern force did not mean safety. A Union officer named Thomas Ewing Jr. remembered a group of three black men, a woman, and a young girl, and boy who had escaped slavery. They followed behind the regiment that was sheltering them, but fell too far back during one particularly arduous march. When someone rode back to check on them, he found only lifeless bodies murdered by rebel guerrillas.[21]

It was not just those who trekked to the perilous lines around the Union army that suffered, but also those they left behind. Patsey Leach was a slave in Scott County, Kentucky, when her husband Julius ran away to join the passing Union army. For Julius's decision, their owner Warren Wiley whipped her continuously and mercilessly. While she bore his punishment, her husband was outfitted in the Union blue and placed in a regiment. Julius's unit passed the Wiley estate three weeks later. Three weeks was all it took in this new world for a master to see his slave empowered as a soldier. Wiley watched Patsey as she proudly saw her husband march by. Only a week later, Julius was killed in battle. When Wiley heard of his former slave's fate, he took Julius's inconsolable widow into their kitchen and tied her hands. He ripped off all of Patsey's clothes and bent her naked body over so he could whip her to within an inch of life. Wiley told her this was what she deserved for letting her husband kill white people.[22]

This was an abolition war, and it was being fought in ways that West Point generals could have hardly dreamed of.

Anyone could stroll across the White House lawn and pass through the imposing columns of the vast portico where people of all classes lingered. The front foyer fed into a long, beautifully carpeted hallway where a bronze screen separated the public White House from the family sphere. Upon his arrival, Douglass waited like all other supplicants for the president's time in a reception room painted elegantly in dark blues, decorated with blue furniture laced with silver satin, broadly framed mirrors, a fireplace festooned in marble, and a velvety blue carpet. The room was crowded, which was not unusual. It was often filled with everyone from senators seeking counsel to scalawags looking for jobs.[23]

The president rose hours before facing the onslaught of people—guests, diplomats, office seekers, generals, and common soldiers. His staff thought him mad for exposing himself to so many people on a daily basis, but Lincoln insisted. He called the exercise "taking a public opinion bath." Lincoln usually wrote for two hours before a moderate breakfast of an egg and coffee at nine. In this peace before the storm, he could answer letters and muse on subjects that confounded him. Then it was time to open himself to the multitudes. The visitors sent business cards in to him and a servant would return to the reception room and read out the name of the party Lincoln would see.[24]

Douglass pressed his way through the crowd and handed his card to one of Lincoln's attendants. He looked about him at a room of only white faces staring at him with puzzlement. Douglass tried to ignore their gazes and retreated into his thoughts at how he might be received. He expected to wait for most of the rest of the day, though he had heard of people waiting here every day for a week. Douglass also pondered the possibility that Lincoln would not invite him in at all. He remembered bitterly how the delegation of black men who had visited Lincoln in 1862 received only callous comments and then embarrassment, as Lincoln blamed them for the war. Douglass wondered whether Lincoln would turn him away, tell him to leave these questions to others. He thought about how, under the *Dred Scott* decision, the Supreme Court still did not consider him to be a citizen of this country, yet here he stood. It could have been a glorious feeling but was not. It felt like a terrible responsibility to bear, and he wished he could leave and have someone else take his position along with this duty.[25]

"Mr. Douglass!"

The voice of Lincoln's messenger cut through the room. Douglass was being invited in. He could hardly believe it. It was only about two minutes ago that he had handed over his card. Now he pushed the self-doubt to the back of his mind and elbowed his way forward. Someone mocked, "Yes damn it, I knew they would let the nigger through." The jealous crowd laughed around him. Douglass would joke that his heckler was probably a Peace Democrat.[26]

Douglass caught Lincoln at a time when he should have been feeling somewhat relieved about the war. The previous month should have been the best of the war, with Grant ending the siege of Vicksburg and the Army of the Potomac defeating General Lee during three furious days in the quiet Pennsylvania town of Gettysburg. But Lincoln was far from cheerful, because there was another way to view the events of July. General George Meade had fought a victorious defensive battle at Gettysburg, then let the defeated army limp back across the Potomac. When Lincoln discovered that an opportunity to finally destroy Lee's maimed army had slipped away, he sadly resolved that the war would go on. The draft riots in New York reflected surging popular sentiment that a compromise should end this war. The Confederacy could certainly bide its time for thirteen months until an election would end his presidency and the war effort. With General Lee's men now recovering in Virginia, had the best and last chance to win the war just slipped away?

Having to work through an August like this did not help his mood. It would have been far more pleasant to be with Mary and his sons Robert and Tad, who were staying in the White Mountains of New Hampshire. Lincoln kept them updated on what they were missing in Washington. Two days before Douglass visited Lincoln, the president complained about the stifling heat and described his distress over Tad's favorite goat being missing. Lincoln played detective in recounting that the "Nanny Goat" was last seen chewing on his young son's bed. The gardener had also complained of the animal's effect on the White House lawn. The affectionate goat's whereabouts were unknown.[27]

The president's office was adjacent to the reception room. It was a small and simple square-shaped office. Surprisingly few secretaries were there to assist the president, as they scurried around their leader. One of the two doorways led to the office of John Nicolay, one of these secretaries, while the other opened into the hallway where the servant holding the business cards sat. The only decorations were documents and military maps strewn extensively around him, his toil. They were in such disarray that Douglass thought perhaps Lincoln was in the midst of some kind of reorganization project. A muddle of papers obscured an oak table's cloth covering. Against the south wall, a desk with pigeonholes for papers stood. There were two unadorned sofas and an assortment of chairs scattered throughout the room. A poor, discolored picture of Andrew Jackson—no friend to Douglass's people—hung above a fireplace. Nothing in here denoted ceremonial regality. Two windows allowed Lincoln and his visitor to look out at the Potomac with the mansions of Arlington, Virginia, beyond. In peaceful days, Robert E. Lee had lived just beyond that river.[28]

His name was announced to Lincoln as he walked through the door. The president's face brightened when he heard the name. He was sitting rather informally in a low armchair between the two windows with his expansive legs seeming to reach into different parts of the room. Douglass hesitated until Lincoln's eyes lifted from the paper he was examining. As Lincoln stood up, it seemed to Douglass like a rather extensive process, as the man's long, lean frame kept rising and rising until finally Douglass was looking up at the president. There was never any spring in Lincoln's step, never landing or departing on his heels, but keeping them parallel to the ground. A body that looked like it needed oiling just went up and down again. Lincoln's chest was too narrow for the long, bony arms that hung down. While Douglass's build was mighty, Lincoln's thinness seemed out of proportion. Lincoln was eight years older and aging faster than Douglass, his health reflecting the anxieties that plagued his mind. He was down to 180 pounds, which, at six foot four inches, meant "the great emancipator" looked nearly emaciated.[29]

The president looked overworked and tired. Quickly examining the long lines of care sketched deeply in Lincoln's features, Douglass saw a patient man whose suffering was thinly veiled. A joke Lincoln identified with concerned two hunters meeting and one telling the other that he had vowed to shoot any man he ever met uglier than him. The other hunter scanned him and exclaimed, "If I am any worse looking than you are, for *God's sake shoot me* and git me out of the way!" And when political rivals had called Lincoln two-faced, he wryly asked why he would have chosen to wear the face he did. Yes, Douglass thought, Lincoln was homely, but in a very human sense. These eyes, he reflected, evoked the tenderness of a mother, while his pronounced nose, cheekbones and ears suggested the fortitude of a frontier father.[30]

Douglass was tense at first, but Lincoln's warm smile and the open extension of his great hand put Douglass at ease. Douglass started to tell the president who he was, but Lincoln blandly interjected, "Mr. Douglass, you need not tell me who you are. I know who you are. Mr. Seward has told me all about you." Secretary of State William Seward had first subscribed to Douglass's paper more than a decade ago. They had corresponded during the years that Douglass had published in the then-senator's state.[31]

Lincoln offered Douglass a place beside him. As Douglass sat down, the waves of misgiving he had felt minutes before disappeared. He wrote later of an immediate sense that he was in the presence of an honest man doing his best to save a nation. Douglass wanted to keep his opening words short and began by telling Lincoln how recruiting black men for service had started fruitfully. Now it was becoming unachievable because black men did not trust Douglass's words on the government's treatment of them. Douglass would cleverly frame the discrimination issues as harming Lincoln's interests in attracting soldiers. He stated, "Mr. President, I have been recruiting colored troops, and if you want me to succeed I must be able to assure them . . ." Lincoln asked Douglass to be more specific.[32]

Douglass began feeling freer to reveal his opinions, seeing that Lincoln was ready to listen. He stated the three issues he hoped to bring to Lincoln's attention. In Douglass's opinion, black men "while in the service shall have pay equal to that of white soldiers." Douglass almost expected Lincoln to interrupt, but Lincoln did not. He continued, "secondly, that when they shall perform acts of bravery in battle, which would secure promotion to white soldiers, the like promotion shall be accorded colored soldiers." Douglass thanked Lincoln for his recent order to protect the troops. Yet it was not enough just to issue this warning. Douglass was asking for something more, sternly uttering, "If the threat of Jefferson Davis is carried out, you, President Lincoln, will retaliate in kind."[33]

Douglass finished laying out his protests and Lincoln contemplated them before speaking. Lincoln, still silent, looked troubled. He was a careful thinker who preferred to consider a point in his own mind before he articulated it. Douglass was surprised by the way the president didn't hide that his own mind was working its way through these vexing issues. Douglass equated this with openness to new ideas.[34]

Lincoln finally replied, "Mr. Douglass, you know that it was with great difficulty that I could get the colored soldiers, or get colored men, into the army at all. You know the prejudices existing against them; you know the doubt that was felt in regard to their ability as soldiers, and it was necessary at the first that we should make some discrimination against them; they were on trial."

It was not an ideal answer, but Douglass knew it was a candid one. Lincoln reminded Douglass of the larger picture. Black men being able to fight in the war was a great gain for the entire race. It was against serious risks of popular opinion that Lincoln had allowed this to go ahead. Some were angered that black men had equal uniforms and others bemoaned that blacks no longer just held pickaxes and shovels. Lincoln honestly felt that men should be enlisting under any conditions considering the exceptional nature of this opportunity. He still viewed it as an experiment that could succeed or fail. Be that as it may, the pay discrepancy was a concession to those that opposed their presence in the military. Lincoln impressed Douglass with how candidly he was speaking. The president felt that they would end up with equal pay before the end of the war. He finished, "Nevertheless, though we cannot offer them at present the same pay as we pay the white soldiers, that will be done, Mr. Douglass, and you may say to your people that they will eventually be paid . . . dollar for dollar, equal with other soldiers."

Going on, Lincoln related that he found the protection issue to be thornier. Douglass glimpsed how hard it was for a tender man to preside over a bloodbath, as he saw pain in Lincoln's eyes and voice. Lincoln simply asked, "Where will it stop?" Lincoln had issued the order but trembled at the thought of a cycle of endless retribution killings between the two governments. He confessed, "If I could get hold of the men that murdered your troops, murdered our prisoners of war, I would execute them, but I cannot take men that may not have had anything to do with this murdering of our soldiers and execute them."

The thought of killing one man for the crime of another was sickening to Lincoln. It was his reluctant conclusion, "No, Mr. Douglass, I don't see where it would stop; beside, I understand they are beginning to treat our colored soldiers as prisoners of war."[35]

Lincoln wanted to believe in the "better angels" of the Confederate's nature. Unfortunately, neither man had yet seen the worst barbaric behavior that the war would bring. Douglass was in a hard position because he found himself moved by the spirit of mercy Lincoln was expressing. He did not think the president's logic was right, but knew that Lincoln himself was right. Lincoln was essentially telling him that he did not intend to follow through on the document Douglass had so long wanted him to issue. He argued back that Lincoln would ultimately be saving more lives if he could bear to go through with some executions. Why issue it at all if he did not have the grit to enforce it?[36]

As to the officer question, Lincoln simply said that he would sign any commissions that Stanton sent him, regardless of the soldier's color. It was a slightly evasive answer, deferring action on the issue. On the other hand, Douglass understood this to mean he would sign off on the commission Stanton had only hours before said he would issue to him. Once Lincoln confirmed Douglass's new position, this would in effect make public the president's new support of black officers.

Then Lincoln revealed he knew more about Douglass than he had initially let on. Douglass was taken aback when Lincoln mentioned a speech he had read of Douglass's given somewhere in New York; Lincoln had stumbled across it in a newspaper he was perusing. Douglass had declared in the speech that it was not the military and political disasters that disheartened him the most. It was, Lincoln quoted Douglass, the "tardy, hesitating and vacillating policy of the President of the United States." This was from Douglass's Cooper Union speech, which had run in the *New York Tribune* on February 13, 1862. Lincoln did not bring up this critical speech with any hint of acrimony in his voice. His next statement stuck with Douglass more than anything else said that afternoon. Lincoln knew people called him tardy and hesitating concerning these matters, but he wanted Douglass to remember, "No man can say that having once taken the position I have contradicted it or retreated from it."[37]

This launched them into a discussion on his retaliatory proclamation. Although Douglass may have felt it was late, Lincoln asserted that had he issued it earlier, critics would decry executing white men for the good of black men. He needed the bravery and success of black soldiers to prime public opinion for government action. Lincoln called this the "preparatory work" for the order. If the order came too early, the result would have been more hatred poured upon Douglass's people. It was a difficult answer for Douglass to accept, but he could not deny that it affirmed a point he had pressed for months: Courageous conduct by black soldiers would transform America.[38]

It had been a stimulating exchange for both of them. Douglass told Lincoln of the commission Stanton had just offered and said he would accept it. Douglass was full of newfound faith in the kindness of the nation's leader, and Lincoln revealed how much he valued Douglass's thoughts. Lincoln then wrote for Douglass a pass that identified Douglass to be a "loyal, free, man, and is, hence, entitled to travel, unmolested,—We trust he will be recognized everywhere, as a free man, and a gentleman." This pass would have protected Douglass in his journey to recruit in the Mississippi Valley.

As Douglass rose to leave, Lincoln remarked in his affable manner, "Douglass, never come to Washington without calling upon me."[39]

CHAPTER II

"Clenched Teeth and Steady Eye"

Lincoln's assurance that he did not retreat from his actions was a sincere commitment, but the president, in private reflection, realized that harsh circumstances surrounding him meant he might not be able to fulfill his promises. Others knew that too; three days before Douglass came to Washington, Charles Sumner sent Lincoln a letter expressing his own fears that the Emancipation Proclamation would be abandoned. The stubborn senator told Lincoln that when justice was done for the black man, the country might then deserve success in the war effort.[1]

A reflection Lincoln wrote to himself in August considered what he would do if the Confederacy made an offer to return to the Union under the condition that slavery could remain as it had been before the Civil War. Dreading a new lease on life for slavery, he knew it would be a nightmarish political dilemma. How could he justify the continuation of killing for a cause many of his fellow citizens did not support? Support for the war, as it currently existed, was wearing thin despite the July victories. He finally resolved to himself that his government would never return a free person to bondage. Even so, he could imagine the Supreme Court, still under recalcitrant Roger Taney, forcing him to do so.[2]

Then too, the election was a year away.

Even if the future was in doubt, Douglass felt his meeting with the president had been gratifying. Being a guarded judge of character, especially when it came to white men, Douglass was impressed by Lincoln's sincerity. Douglass predicted that Lincoln would go down in history not as great, wise, or eloquent, but certainly as an honest man. During the visit, he had been received as a gentleman. Never did Douglass feel reminded of their difference in color by either compliment or condescension. He did not take this fact lightly, being unable to remember a similar occurrence during his dealings with powerful men over the past twenty years. During a speech in Philadelphia, he summed up his feelings on the meeting: "I tell you I felt big in there."[3]

Lincoln had been giving much thought to black soldiers during the week they met. The day before Douglass visited, Lincoln composed a letter to General Ulysses Grant on the importance of recruiting black soldiers in the West. He found it to be "a resource which if vigorously applied now, will soon close the contest . . . It works doubly, weakening the enemy & strengthening us." Lincoln felt that with the Mississippi valley and delta in their control, the region along the mighty river was ripe for recruiting. One hundred thousand black troops would provide great relief to the white men who were already fighting.[4]

Grant replied to Lincoln on August 23, concurring with Lincoln's assessments and declaring that, from what he had seen in the field, emancipation was "the heaviest blow yet given the Confederacy." He viewed the black man as a powerful ally and was pleased with what he was seeing in terms of their fighting abilities. The Confederates would do all they could to prevent black men from joining the army, but Grant would send recruiting officers wherever the army extended.[5]

Lincoln told visitors to the White House on August 19 that black men were now so vital to the effort that the war would be lost in three weeks if they abandoned this new drive. Emancipation had given him two hundred thousand men who could be soldiers, and it would provide more. Senator Zachariah Chandler wrote to a fellow senator, "Every Negro regiment of a thousand men presents just one thousand unanswerable arguments against the revocation of the President's proclamation."[6]

On September 3, Springfield, Illinois, hosted a rally to show support for the war that their native son was struggling to sustain. Three months earlier, Lincoln's hometown, situated in a county that leaned Democratic, witnessed one of the largest midwestern peace meetings. James Conkling asked Lincoln to come home and stand with those who still believed the war was worth fighting. Returning to the warmth of Springfield to articulate a validation of the war was tempting. Lincoln's secretaries observed how eagerly he cherished the hope of speaking to adoring crowds as he had done so many times before. After two weeks of deliberation, Lincoln forlornly concluded his responsibilities in Washington were too pressing to go. Instead, he sent a carefully crafted letter that he wanted his old friend to read on his behalf. Throughout his presidency, Lincoln spoke very rarely in public and came to rely on written messages, sometimes in letters to political allies, sometimes to newspapers, and in this case, in a speech to be read by someone else.[7]

After a night to think it over, he sent a second draft and gave Conkling some speaking advice: "Read it very slowly." Three days later, he sent a third draft that included a reference to Grant, a man who had never supported abolitionist causes but was now a successful and rising general and believed that emancipation was strengthening the Union cause.

In the speech, Lincoln uncharacteristically went right to the jugular of his opponents. He asked his critics to choose between peace and union. Compromise was not possible, and if they thought he should let the Confederacy go, then they ought to come out and say it. Springfield was packed with somewhere between forty and seventy thousand people from all over the state, many having slept the night in their wagons. They thronged to hear Conkling read Lincoln's blunt truth as he had come to see it: ". . . to be plain, you are dissatisfied with me about the negro."[8]

Lincoln conceded that there were different opinions on the issue. He wished all could be free; others felt differently. Some thought the Emancipation Proclamation was unconstitutional; Lincoln considered it otherwise. He continued in a devastating deadpan note, "You say you will not fight to free negros. Some of them seem willing to fight for you; but, no matter."

Keep fighting to save the Union, Lincoln implored, as he had issued the Emancipation Proclamation to aid in just that goal. But they needed to keep in mind one central fact of human nature, that black men were serving under a promise they would be made free, for "Negros, like other people, act upon Motives." If they were risking their lives based on this pledge, how could the nation retreat from it?

When the day of freedom arrives, "there will be some black men who can remember that, with silent tongue, and clenched teeth, and steady eye, and well-poised bayonet, they have helped mankind on to this great consummation." On the other hand, there would be white men who would not forget that "with malignant hearts, and deceitful speech, they have strove to hinder it." Lincoln had never before spoken so powerfully about black soldiers. The contrast of white men who would so cowardly compromise and black men in the field so nobly sacrificing makes this speech a true line of demarcation in Lincoln's public conviction that he could never allow slavery to continue after all that these black men had dared. These words were widely republished in every northern newspaper. His assistant William O. Stoddard remembered Lincoln reading a version of the letter before he let it be mailed, with Lincoln putting particular emphasis on the line about the gallantry of black soldiers.

The administration's offer of a commission to Douglass to recruit in the Mississippi Valley was of great comfort to him. The pay issue was not resolved, but his meeting with Lincoln had led him to have faith in the "educating tendency of the conflict." He was convinced that Lincoln was honest, and that allowed him to go back to his recruiting efforts. One of Douglass's other major objections had been that by resisting black officers, the administration was not open to opportunities for these men. Yet by offering Douglass this position, the administration had done exactly what Douglass had advocated. His earlier resignation letter had made very clear that Douglass wanted to continue this work but could not until certain circumstances changed. Stanton may have caught Douglass off guard, but he was offering Douglass something that he had long coveted.

After his monumental days in Washington, Douglass returned to Rochester to tie up personal and professional matters. Stanton had said it would not take long for the commission to arrive. Douglass now faced a weighty decision: What to do with his monthly paper? Through sixteen long years, harsh financial times, and days when he was exhausted from the speech the night before, through all this he had kept the paper going. No matter how far his public engagements had taken him, he always made it back home to keep publishing. This valuable monthly transatlantic platform was at stake. The fact that he was giving up his paper conveyed how much the commission meant to him.

As he composed a farewell letter to his readers, "emotions are excited for which I shall not attempt to find words to give suitable expression." He felt like a huge chapter of his life was closing, one that had brought him tremendous joy. Moreover, for many of his closest friends who lived an ocean away, the paper was what had kept them connected. In its pages, they could keep track of their friend's activities from month to month.

He wrote that this felt like a painful parting. Part of him must have been relieved not to have the stress of the paper's financial precariousness, but it was gratifying to make clear that money trouble had not ended the paper, as this might reflect on the future viability of black-owned newspapers. Nor was there any intention on his part to stop writing on issues related to an evil that was not yet defeated.

The reason he was writing this farewell letter was simple: "I can better serve my poor bleeding country-men whose great opportunity has now come, by going south and summoning them to assert their just liberty, than I can do by staying here." He proudly reported his placement with General Lorenzo Thomas. Slavery had taken up the sword, so he predicted by the sword it would die.

Despite all the advice he had received from others that he should not join the war, he wrote that it was natural for him to play a part in the physical struggle to end slavery. Conceding that some would disagree with his decision, he could not hide his desire to be closer to where the blood of slaveholders would be shed. With a full heart, he brought a sixteen-year relationship with his readers to a close.[9]

With that emotional piece of business taken care of, Douglass waited for the commission that would take him south. After Edwin Stanton met with Douglass on August 10, the secretary of war had C. W. Foster of the Adjutant General's Office in the War Department write to a depot quartermaster to arrange public payment for Douglass's journey from Rochester to Vicksburg, Mississippi. Three days later Foster wrote to Douglass in Rochester, relating that Stanton now wanted Douglass to proceed to Vicksburg, Mississippi, where he would report in person to Brigadier General Lorenzo Thomas. Douglass found a copy of the order for his transportation at government expense, but something was missing in the envelope.[10]

There was no commission.

Waiting a few more days and receiving nothing, Douglass sent an anxious letter to Stanton, saying he was ready to meet Thomas in Vicksburg now that he had obtained the receipt of his transportation. However, before he left home, he wanted to know under what conditions he was entering the service. Straining to be polite, Douglass asked why there was no commission in the package. Stanton had clearly said he would be an officer under General Thomas. Had their agreement changed?[11]

In the days that followed, Douglass's confusion only increased. He had given up so much for this commission. On August 18, Douglass wrote his friend Thomas Webster, who was coordinating the recruitment of black soldiers in Pennsylvania, hoping to see him before he left for Mississippi. Still assuming the undertaking was happening, Douglass was uneasy. He wrote his friend that he was unsure about the conditions of his service, as well as the rank, pay, and duty. The agitated Douglass wondered if Stanton found it amusing to keep him in the dark about these critical matters. Did the administration think they were a monarchy, where they could command a man without regard to his life? The last thing Douglass needed was more worry, as he acknowledged that he lived in a state of constant fear for the safety of his sons. Perhaps realizing he was already divulging more sentiment than was typical for him, he reassured his friend that he would obey whatever Stanton decided.[12]

Stanton did not answer Douglass's letter; Foster did so but evasively. As if Douglass had written about money, which he had not, Foster responded that it would still be Stearns compensating him for his service. Douglass was utterly mystified. Who was paying his salary was not at all germane to the inquiry he had made. He simply wanted to know whether he was an officer of the United States military or not. They had stymied his query again. Yet Foster had implicitly answered the question. If Douglass were to be an officer, why would George Stearns be paying him, instead of the United States government?

Foster's letter concluded sharply, dismissing Douglass's questions and telling him "It is of course expected that you go." The War Department was not interested in a long discussion with a black man concerning rank. Foster restated the assignment—to aid General Thomas in recruiting black men—and expected him to get to it.[13]

It was not just the missing commission, but what Douglass perceived as a dismissive disingenuousness that angered him. He was offended by Stanton's refusal to level with him. He curtly wrote to the secretary of war that if he would only talk about who was paying him, that he might as well be conversing with that man on the status of his duty. He clothed the sentiment in courteous language, but the message was now coming clear. Stanton did not want to tell Douglass he was backing out of the understanding they had, so Douglass, in his sense of preserving his self-respect, had no desire to speak further with him.[14]

Ottilie Assing could not understand why Stanton did not have the courage to act on, or even address, what seemed to be originally his idea. What she saw happening was Stanton employing "petty excuses and intentional misunderstandings, so that Douglass, fully aware of the game that was being played, broke off the discussions completely disgusted and dismayed."[15]

Between Stanton's unwillingness to address whether or not Douglass would receive a commission and the time that lapsed as August became September, it became clear to Douglass that he would not have an opportunity that had come to mean much to him. Without answers, the theory he settled on was that the government was not ready to bestow any honors on a black man, and certainly not official military rank. Douglass said he did not doubt Stanton's sincerity in the moment of their meeting. He thought that after further reflection Stanton had decided it was too soon for such an action. It was not a personal rejection, but a rebuff to the black man's ability to be anything more than a private in the army, a grievance that after all had been so crucial to his Washington lobbying.[16]

On a personal level, he considered it a broken promise. It was his fond hope to go south to work, but he would not do it under these circumstances for a number of reasons. He felt the vulnerability of going into such dangerous territory without any rank to protect him. Douglass was still a marked man in much of America. More than that, seeing himself as a distinguished man in his mid-forties, serving without an officer's rank did not fit the part. It was an insult not just to himself but to the dignity of the people he longed to represent. In any case, his worth to his people as an advocate whose words were nationally received was more valuable than his laboring anonymously in the service. Furthermore, with two sons serving in the military and Frederick Jr. now helping recruit where his father would have gone, he felt that they embodied the sacrifice he was already making.[17]

Perhaps out of wishful thinking, Douglass never assigned blame to Lincoln. At least publicly, he never cast doubt on Lincoln's assurance to him that he would sign any commission Stanton sent him, although it was clear that Stanton had known of the idea from an exchange with Stearns a few days before meeting with Douglass, while Lincoln may have only learned about it during Douglass's visit. Douglass may have never blamed Lincoln because he did not want to publicly jeopardize the value of their developing relationship, but privately he suspected Lincoln's role in reneging on the commission. Ottilie Assing never forgave Lincoln for Douglass's not receiving the commission. Her strong feelings reflect the distress that she saw him suffer.[18]

As for the newspaper, it was embarrassing to have ended one of his great life's works for nothing. In his autobiography, *Life and Times*, this episode of his life bears the one-word title "Disappointment." Still, slavery was very much alive, and there was much work ahead of him. His mission would have to be fulfilled another way.[19]

Without a commission or a newspaper, Douglass took a brief break from his work, just to be a father and take on the new role of grandfather. Rosetta had abruptly given up her floundering teaching venture to marry a newly freed young man named Nathan Sprague. For a daughter so fixated on her father, it was not surprising that Sprague's background would be similar to that of Douglass. He was said to have descended from Maryland governor Samuel Sprigg and was free through a daring escape from slavery. Unfortunately for Rosetta, the similarities were too few. Nathan managed to fail at an extensive list of professional endeavors, many of which ended with a weary father-in-law parting with money. For now, the young couple moved into the Rochester property and

Rosetta gave birth to a child. After the heartbreaking loss of his youngest daughter, he was pleased to welcome a new child named Annie into his life. Julia Griffiths Crofts yearned to see the joy of a baby girl playing in the kind arms of Douglass among the old trees that surrounded his estate. She imagined "Grandpa Douglass" feeding the child his favorite "*Maryland biscuits.*"[20]

There was other news. Douglass's middle son, Charles, reported a rumor going around that Massachusetts Governor John Andrew might defy the War Department's resistance on black officers and commission Charles's older brother, Lewis, as a lieutenant. Charles found that "Lewis is highly spoken of in Boston and New Bedford . . . Everyone says that he will receive the first commission." As for what Charles heard of the regiment so brutalized at Fort Wagner, "the 54 boys have been worked hard but they are plucky yet and want to be in a fight." Lewis had been rewarded a furlough to return to New York because of his "good conduct in the field."[21]

But Lewis was falling deeper into an illness that would prevent his return to action. The water that he had been drinking in South Carolina was contaminated and many others in his regiment were experiencing its sickening effects. For three weeks in October, Douglass sat at his son's bedside, tending to his needs and talking of these past few chaotic months. He told Gerrit Smith that his battle-tested young man was mending slowly. Griffiths Crofts wrote, "Poor dear Lewis—I trust he will soon recover."[22]

As he nursed his son, Douglass imagined what would happen if the Union could just win this war. Fulfilling his duties as a father, the thought crossed his mind that if his great goal could somehow be achieved, it would please him to quietly retire with his growing family.[23] Douglass had already received an invitation from the Cooper Union Institute to speak early in the new year.[24] He knew that he would have to produce something significant for an address that would be nationally covered. Unfortunately, he only found himself depressed when he read the newspapers. In the eastern battlefields, there was no action and no progress as the Army of the Potomac awaited a new general to take over from George Meade. They would have to wait, for Grant had one last duty to fulfill in the west, righting the bloody Union loss at Chickamauga and raising the siege in Chattanooga.

Douglass composed one of his most important addresses, "The Mission of the War." On November 17, he tried out an early version of the speech at Corinthian Hall in Rochester, where he had given his first speeches defining the war. He had no trouble filling the hall and hundreds were turned away. Afterward, he felt very good about using this new message in travels around the country.[25]

He journeyed to Boston, where he spoke and spent time saying goodbye

Charles Douglass

to his son Charles, who had also endured sickness through the summer.
Charles was finally ready to ship off with two hundred other men to fill the
depleted ranks of the Massachusetts Fifty-fourth. He had been told a few
weeks before to be ready at a moment's notice to set out for Morris Island,
South Carolina. Having heard of the bloody engagements that Lewis had
been in, Charles retained little desire to experience war's glory firsthand.
Confusion over how long he rested from his illness led a commander to at
one point list him as a deserter. Charles assured his father, "I will never
desert, I will take a bullet first." That said, he was doing anything he could to
extend his time in Massachusetts. Charles asked for an autographed picture
of his father to give to a Swedish-born Lieutenant Wulff who, Charles believed, could request that Lewis be left in camp.[26]

While Lewis had been stationed in the Carolina islands, Charles had
been dealing with his own hardships. Falling sick soon after arriving at camp

in Massachusetts, Charles had a long stay in a makeshift hospital that left him thinking he would like to care for the others around him. For a young man who had grown up so far from suffering, it was a cruel baptism. His letters to Douglass in September convey disbelief at just how miserable the army allowed conditions to be for incapacitated black troops. Though he was a private, hardly a trained doctor or nurse, he spent many agonizingly long nights as the only man on duty in the sick ward. When men took a turn for the worse in darkness, Charles was helpless. He recounted, "I was up all night and stood over those that died and laid them out, wrote to their friends, and in fact done most all that was to do except doctor them." All he could do was ease their agony.

Away from the makeshift hospital until evening one day, upon returning he was told "that there had been no doctor there all that day and there is one man then that will die and others that are very sick." Before the regiment shipped out, the conditions improved, but there still seemed to be a lack of medical care at the camp. For those still here, Charles pronounced, "now they are treated worse than dogs."

Spending so many days and nights around the sick only worsened his own condition. Charles wondered if the government knew that it was nearly starving them to death. The army gave them tiny rations that were supposed to last a week. Charles boiled large pots of bland stew so their rations would last a little longer. No authorities were interested in his complaints. Charles objected that "hospital rations were small and that we could not draw full rations that is a funny way to starve a lot of men . . . we were used mean." When old friends ran into him, they hardly recognized the withered Charles. He told them that the transformation was not from sickness but from the lack of rations given to the sick. Begging his father to "think hard of me," he warned "a person will do most anything before they will starve" and he felt himself "falling away more and more."[27]

That illnesses struck Douglass's two fighting sons for a sizable portion of 1863 was no aberration. In the Civil War, disease killed more men than battle did; while the ratio for white soldiers of deaths by illness to deaths in combat was two to one, the rate for black soldiers was about ten to one. One in twelve white enlistees lost his life to infection, but a staggering one in five black soldiers met this fate. Poor prior health of many black men coming into the service from a life of bondage may explain part of the discrepancy, yet there were clearly critical elements of discrimination once they entered the service that proved to be fatal.

White commanders believed that black men could withstand more arduous work, especially in blistering sun and in lowland environments. They justified the dangerous work conditions because of their belief in physiological differences between the races. Many also assumed that the traditional slave diet ought to be replicated for the good of these men. This meant unremitting rations of pork and corn, with occasional variants of beef and wheat. Both of these assumptions created havoc with the health of free men and former slaves.

Whether or not Charles's commanders were correct in ordering him out of the hospital and off to South Carolina, many lives were also lost because white officers firmly believed that slaves were adept at faking illness to be spared severe toil. This proved to be a dire factor in pushing black soldiers back into action too quickly. As Charles discovered all too clearly, efforts to save black lives did not seem equal to those for white soldiers.[28]

Aside from the discrimination Charles witnessed in health matters, the continuing controversy over equal pay for black soldiers also infuriated him. He heard of Governor Andrew's solution, which was for Massachusetts to pay the three-dollar discrepancy between what the federal government paid white and black troops. He fumed whenever he thought of how they were denied "what was promised us." Of course, to many soldiers, the one who had passed on the faulty pledge had been his father. He hoped that "our boys wont except of any less than what they enlisted for."[29]

While in Boston saying goodbye to his second son headed into combat, Douglass gave his new speech again. He knew the speech well by now, having traveled from Rochester to Philadelphia to Boston, stopping at towns in between, spreading the word of this mission. He was back to the pace of travel he had been on for the better part of the war. Griffiths Crofts worried for him at his hectic pace, but added, "Never was a long-looked for letter more welcomed to anxious friend than yours . We are all thankful that you are still in Rochester [and] that the dangerous task of recruiting in the South is given up!" Her delight was palpable. Even so, she could not help but remind him how "the belief that you are gone to fight in the South" had hurt her fundraising efforts on his behalf in England. She continued to pray that he would "be preserved amidst all the danger around you [and] that your boys may escape the fire."[30]

Rosine Draz had thought that he was in the South "already and that you were exposed to most fearful dangers." When news reached her of what Douglass had decided, "I thanked God when I found my dear friend that you would not recklessly expose your precious life by going without the protection of Government in the midst of cruel enemies." Draz, an intensely religious woman, believed God had lifted up Douglass as his instrument to end slavery—and thus would never jeopardize his life in the South. She assured

Douglass that eventually he would see "the fruits of your noble devoted labors. Take courage, my believed friend. God is near to save his people."[31]

Douglass returned to Washington on December 7 to speak at Henry Highland Garnet's Fifteenth Street Presbyterian Church on behalf of the Contraband Relief Society. In saying farewell at their summer meeting, Lincoln had told Douglass to come and see him whenever he was in Washington; the two men did not meet to renew that conversation because Lincoln had returned home from the dedication of the Gettysburg cemetery with a mild case of smallpox and was confined to his room. Still, as the president recovered, Lincoln sent a letter to Henry C. Wright, head of the Massachusetts Anti-Slavery Society, saying, "I shall not attempt to retract or modify the emancipation proclamation; nor shall I return to slavery any person who is free by the terms of that proclamation, or by any of the acts of Congress." In reading these words, Douglass was indeed confirmed in his sense that, once having moved forward, this president did not go back.[32]

1864

CHAPTER 12

"An Abolition War"

The Cooper Union Institute was packed as Douglass stepped forward to the podium. This was Douglass's third time to speak from the nation's most prestigious lecture hall, and he was about to deliver a speech that he had been preparing for all his life. In the same place four years earlier, Lincoln had spoken in clear, cogent themes that defined and clarified the issue of slavery, propelling him to the presidency. Douglass needed to define the meaning of this war and to link his own life's mission to the larger mission of the war itself. The North was tired of this war and the toll of its dead soldiers, and without such a redefinition, everything might be for naught.

This night's sponsor was the Woman's Loyal League, a group advocating to amend the Constitution to end slavery. People arrived early to get good seats. Leaders of New York reform groups sat arrayed on the platform behind Douglass, and Oliver Johnson, the editor of the *National Anti-Slavery Standard*, introduced Douglass to the crowd's loud cheers and applause. His address lasted two hours, but they stayed with him through each peak and valley of his oratory, waving their hats, yelling "hear, hear," and rising to their feet in numerous ovations.[1]

This war, he said, would lead to either the nation's salvation or its ruin. The outcome was very much in doubt. It depended on whether the war "can teach a great nation respect for the long-despised claims of justice." Douglass called it cowardly to trust that God would intervene to fulfill the nation's charge. America's destiny was in their hands. He recounted the "desolation, ruin, shame, suffering and sorrow" of a war caused by slavery. They could now win a victory for all humanity in the epic struggle against human

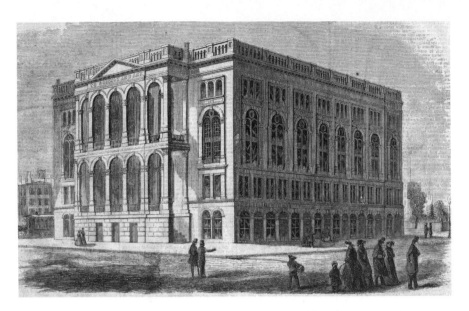

Cooper Union Institute, shown in *Harper's Weekly*, March 30, 1861

bondage. This nation would "have no business to mourn over our mission. We are writing the statutes of eternal justice and liberty in the blood of the worst of tyrants as a warning to all after-comers."[2]

In this speech, he tried not only to inspire a restless and war-weary people, he also tried to deal with the charge that he and other radical abolitionists were guilty of not wanting the war to end yet—not now, not with slavery untouched. That charge opened them up to bitter criticism and presented them as bloodthirsty and callous. Douglass was forthright in admitting that he was glad the war had not ended too quickly: "I say the longer the better if it must be so—in order to put an end to the hell black cause out of which the Rebellion has risen." But he answered quickly the deeper charge. "Say not that I am indifferent to the horrors and hardships of the war. In common with the American people generally, I feel the prolongation of the war a heavy calamity—private as well public. There are vacant spaces at my hearthstone which I shall rejoice to see filled again by the boys who once occupied them . . ." Then he asked all who mourned to reflect "upon the vastness and grandeur of its mission." The world had seen many wars, but not one like this: "The blow we strike is not merely to free a country and a continent—but the whole world from slavery—for when slavery fails here—it will fail everywhere. We have no business to mourn over our mission."

Douglass was glad to hear that Peace Democrats were proclaiming this war an "abolition war" and agreed with them emphatically. He restated that abolition was the "comprehensive and logical object of the war." Slavery—no other reason—had caused the South to disregard the ballot, republican institutions, and the Constitution.

The mission of the war had four components. First, this must be an abolition war. Second, no peace could be accepted if it was not an abolition peace. Third, as earned by their military service, America must regard black people as fellow citizens. Last, whether a soldier or citizen, blacks must be able to vote and live free of discrimination.

Douglass applauded the Emancipation Proclamation, but "excellent as that paper is—and much as it has accomplished temporarily—it settles nothing." For him, the problem was that Lincoln still spoke with moral indifference. He reminded them all that in Lincoln's annual message of 1863, he had painted emancipation as an emergency measure of wartime, believing that "the general government had no lawful power to effect emancipation in any State." Douglass thought Lincoln still had not shown he "understood and accepted its true mission." This lack of understanding was not necessary, for the Confederacy knew the conflict was over slavery, and John Brown had predicted it before a single cannon was fired.[3]

Lincoln had accepted a war to restore the old Union. He had been willing to "faithfully catch, hold and return runaway slaves," among other concessions to slaveholders. Despite the fondest wishes of the administration, the tide of events and great, almost mystical, forces were serving to propel this war toward the mission that Douglass articulated. He called it, "a growing war in every sense."

In his third Annual Message, Lincoln had also said of black soldiers, "So far as tested, it is difficult to say they are not as good soldiers as any."[4] As military operations extended into every corner of the land, the moral meaning of the war was also expanding. He recounted the proclamation, the recognition of Haiti and Liberia, the encouraging movement of border states turning away from slavery, and that black men now shouldered rifles. Yet the growing popularity of the Democrat Party's platform threatened all the progress that had come from the evolution of this conflict with an indifference to slavery's depravity. With an election looming in eight months, this was an hour of "hope as well as danger." Douglass ended the speech as he had begun:

> No war but an Abolition war; no peace but an Abolition peace; liberty for all, chains for none; the black man a soldier in war, a laborer in peace; a voter at the South as well as at the North; America his permanent home, and all Americans his fellow-countrymen. Such,

fellow-citizen, is my idea of the mission of the war. If accomplished, our glory as a nation will be complete, our peace will flow like a river, and our foundations will be the everlasting rocks.

This was Douglass's gospel. During February, he spread it through Portland, Maine; Trenton, New Jersey, and in Pennsylvania in Montgomery County, Newtown, Pineville, and Bucks County.[5]

Douglass's name was heard far and wide, and it turned up on Stanton's desk again in mid-February. General Benjamin Butler clipped an article from a Richmond newspaper, thinking the secretary of war would be interested in a glimpse into current Confederate psyche. The article had a rather distorted view of the prisoner exchange programs that would go on between the two sides: "If President Lincoln should signify that he is ready to permit a new negotiation to be entered upon, with a view to exchange, provided we send our commissioner to settle the terms with Frederick Douglass." Imploring the Confederate government to never negotiate with the hated black abolitionist, the writer waxed colorfully on the humiliation their soldiers would be subject to if an agreement influenced by Douglass determined their destiny. They wanted the Virginia legislature to introduce a measure forbidding them "to accept, as a federal agent of exchange . . . the mulatto Frederick."[6]

It was a puzzling piece detached from reality. Perhaps the South had heard of Lincoln and Douglass's meeting in which the protection of captured black soldiers was a principal issue. From there, it was quite a leap in imagination for Douglass to be representing the government's negotiations on the topic. It was a reminder of the fear and abhorrence Douglass brought to the minds of many in the South. The revolutionary nature of his meeting with the president was a powerful image.

At this time early in 1864, Lincoln asked Stanton for information and statistics about black citizens. He wanted to know how many men were enrolled in the military, how many had escaped from slavery since the Emancipation Proclamation, and how many were born free. The same day that Butler mailed to Stanton the southern fantasy of Douglass becoming Lincoln's personal negotiator, the president asked General Daniel Sickles to travel to New Orleans, through the Gulf region, and then north along the Atlantic coast in order to gather information on how black men were faring as soldiers, laborers, and most of all, as free people. Whether they were working for their old masters or for Union generals, placing them on abandoned plantations was of interest to Lincoln. In coming to grips with the sweeping new course he was setting for the nation, he wanted to understand whether life was better for them inside rebel lines or along the confused areas of northern occupation. He wanted to know what they were experiencing.[7]

On April 12, 1864, an incident on the muddy banks of the Mississippi River near Memphis showed the nation how real and dire the need to protect black soldiers from Confederate vengeance was becoming. Confederate General Nathan Bedford Forrest, a former slave trader, commanded the men who attacked Fort Pillow, a Union outpost in western Tennessee, that morning. Forrest's cavalry division surrounded a small fort defended by black and white regiments and demanded surrender. Acting Union commander William Bradford refused. The Confederates attacked, overrunning the fort and driving its occupants toward the bluffs along the river. Few of the black soldiers survived what followed.

One soldier remembered the fort becoming a "great slaughter pen," where "Blood—human blood—stood about in pools, and brains could have been gathered up in any quantity." Numerous accounts corroborate that it became an object of amusement among Forrest's men to shoot black soldiers in one leg, then make them stand and beg before murdering them. Rebels visited atrocities on Union white soldiers too, believing that they had betrayed Tennessee not only for remaining loyal to Lincoln but for fighting alongside black soldiers. Three women came across the seared body of Lieutenant John C. Akerstrom, who had been nailed to wood planks and burned alive.

Black women traveling with the army, along with their children, were shot and thrown into the Mississippi. When a Confederate officer saw one of his troops helping a black boy who looked about eight by putting him on his horse, he ordered the soldier to take him down and shoot him. The soldier objected, crying that he was "nothing more than a child."

The superior responded, "Damn the difference . . . Take him down and shoot him, or I'll shoot you instead." The soldier sadly lifted the youngster from his saddle, placed him on the ground and ended his life.[8]

Horrible as it was, Fort Pillow was not an isolated case. Six days later, black troops were not given the option of surrendering in Poison Spring, Arkansas; they were slaughtered. In Plymouth, North Carolina, eight days after Fort Pillow, white southern men took captured black soldiers; some were hung, others beaten to death with butt ends of muskets.[9]

It did not take long for these sickening stories to spread from the blood-soaked knolls around Fort Pillow throughout the nation. While northerners were largely indifferent to discrimination against black soldiers, Fort Pillow crossed a line of civilized behavior. The outraged cries of politicians and newspapers editors made this clear. In this new climate, Douglass did not want white Americans to believe that this was the inevitable result of whites and blacks fighting. Nor did he want them to suppose that the atrocities would necessarily deter black recruitment. His message was that it would only make black men more energized to enlist, as they would wish to avenge this atrocity.[10]

An address by Lincoln given at a Soldier's Relief gathering in Baltimore six days after the news of Fort Pillow touched on "A painful rumor, true I fear." Lincoln felt the massacre called into question his decision to allow black soldiers to fight in this war. He explained, "Upon a clear conviction of duty I resolved to turn that element of strength to account; and I am responsible for it to the American people, to the christian world, to history, and on my final account to God."

Lincoln said of the black recruit, "there is no way but to give him all the protection given to any other soldier. The difficulty is not in stating the principle, but in practically applying it." Lincoln wanted the country to know that the issue grieved him greatly and he was searching for a solution. His first priority was discovering what actually happened, because he dreaded executing anyone upon false reports. If men trying to surrender were killed in cold blood, "the retribution shall as surely come. It will be a matter of grave consideration in what exact course to apply the retribution; but in the supposed case, it must come."[11]

But it never did. Lincoln asked his cabinet for opinions in writing on what course he should take in the government's reaction.[12] In a meeting on May 6, some in his cabinet argued for the execution of the officers responsible if they were ever caught; others advocated the killing of an equal number of war prisoners if the Confederate government admitted the massacre. Lincoln never went forward with either course, being more interested in winning the war as the ultimate reprisal.

Lincoln did take action on one matter that concerned Fort Pillow, however. Mary Elizabeth Wayt Booth was the widow of Lionel Booth, the white commander of the fort, who had been killed by sharpshooters early in the battle. She had gone to the sight of the battle in its grisly aftermath and learned the plight of black widows. Slavery had prevented legal marriage contracts, so those widows were without the proof necessary to receive government pensions. The twenty-four-year-old Booth traveled from Ohio to Washington, determined to bring this issue to the attention of the president. Her case seems to have genuinely affected Lincoln, as on the same day as their meeting he wrote to Senator Charles Sumner saying she had asked for "widows and children *in fact*, of colored soldiers who fall in our service be placed in law, the same as if their marriages were legal." Lincoln wished Congress could ensure their having "the benefit of the provisions made the widows & orphans of white soldiers."

Six weeks later, a measure passed the House and Senate that included these black women. The widow pension was a redeeming moment in what is otherwise the darkest chapter in the history of black Civil War soldiers.[13]

On April 26, a beautiful Sunday morning, the Ninth, headed toward action in Virginia, paraded through Washington. It was a significant movement since the unit included black regiments recruited from Maryland, Pennsylvania, and Ohio, and the capital had never seen soldiers of color. They began their procession around eleven A.M., taking New York Avenue, a dusty road leading into the heart of the city. The troops halted at 14th Street, where the grand Willard's Hotel stood. Lincoln stood silently on the second floor balcony. Just two years ago, there had still been slavery in this city; now armed black men marched through it. When these men saw the president, military discipline gave way to euphoria. As they threw hats and screamed out his name, the president respectfully uncovered his head. His secretary, William Stoddard, asked what he thought of this remarkable sight. Lincoln tightened his lips and shut his eyes. He said, "It'll do, it'll do!"[14]

A letter he had written at the beginning of the month captured his quickly evolving views on the future of slavery. He spent the morning with three Kentuckians, including Governor Thomas Bramlette. Lincoln retained strong emotional ties to Kentucky, a state he believed he understood and certainly sympathized with. The delegation complained about the Union's recruitment of black men who might not yet be free, and Lincoln expressed a different opinion. Kentucky felt it should be exempt from the swift social changes from the Emancipation Proclamation since it had never seceded from the Union. One of the visitors, Albert G. Hodges, editor of the widely read *Frankfort Commonwealth*, suggested Lincoln record the contents of this "little speech" for a public letter.[15]

What Lincoln offered for many skeptical American eyes, not just his fellow Kentuckians, was the simple idea that if slavery was not wrong, "nothing is wrong." He added, "I can not remember when I did not so think, and feel." Yet, the presidency did not furnish him the right to act upon that which was not constitutional. He wondered, "Was it possible to lose the nation, and yet preserve the Constitution?" Recalling the incidents with his generals Frémont and Hunter, he had halted their military emancipation attempts because, at those points, "I did not yet think the indispensable necessity had come."[16] He reminded the nation about his many overtures to the border states for gradual, compensated emancipation. Those offers had been rebuffed and that helped set his course now—this moment of necessity had arrived.

By the end of 1863, Lincoln had faced a choice of "either surrendering the Union, and with it, the Constitution, or of laying strong hand upon the colored element. I chose the latter." A year later, the nation had not been marred; instead, it had gained thousands of soldiers. These were "palpable facts, about which, as facts, there can be no caviling. We have the men; and we could not have had them without the measure." Without those black troops, Lincoln did not see how winning the war was possible.

It is at this point in the letter (intended for the whole country to read) that Lincoln famously claimed "not to have controlled events, but confess plainly that events have controlled me." In defining controversial acts and defending a course of action that even he himself had not supported for two years, it is understandable that a politician would seek to portray himself as a vessel of fate, as a man subject to larger forces that he cannot control but must bow to. Lincoln contended that after three furious years, the state of affairs was not what any man or party intended or expected. "God alone can claim it." Yet, there is something more here, an emerging theme of Douglass's that would bear fruit in Lincoln's second inaugural address.

Frederick Douglass, in his January 1864 "Mission of the War" speech, said:

> Few men, however great their wisdom, are permitted to see the end from the beginning. Events are mightier than our rulers, and these Divine forces, with overpowering logic, have fixed upon this war, against the wishes of our Government, the comprehensive character and mission I have ascribed to it.[17]

In pivotal speeches, both Lincoln and Douglass grasped that powers beyond human comprehension were somehow guiding this war's end. Each man knew the power of their individual purposes, but humbly accepted that they were to be pieces contributing to a larger course determining the destiny of their country.

General Grant had taken command of the Union troops in the East in March, and the long-promised summer offensive was now under way. The prospects were promising, and the North finally felt it had a general who could confront the superior tactics of Robert E. Lee. They knew they had the numbers and the military matériel, and the advantage of technology and supply lines, and naval superiority. All they needed was a victory, and Grant looked like the man for the task—tough, tenacious, willing to dare.

If Grant's offensive worked, the Confederacy could well collapse, and a war-weary Union might then reelect Lincoln. If, however, Lee performed his usual magic—for even when he was checked, as he had been at Antietam and Gettysburg, he always managed to keep his army together and nimbly escape to fight again—the Democrats might nominate the controversial and retired general George McClellan on a peace platform. Then the South would achieve something that, for all their victories over befuddled Union generals, they had not as yet achieved on the battlefield. McClellan's policies promised in effect a draw, and for the beleaguered Confederate government, that meant victory—and certainly, survival of the institution of slavery.

Union victories during the early summer collapsed. Almost as if Lee could read Grant's mind, he effortlessly stifled and thwarted the Union advance. For soldiers under General Grant's command during May and June, the horror was unspeakable. The battles of the Wilderness where hundreds of men died each hour and then more died in fires sparked in the dense forest—Spotsylvania, and Cold Harbor were butcheries. But unlike previous failed federal offensives, Grant did not pull back. He was not daunted by Lee's superior performance and drove on, swinging south, wheeling around again and again, seeking some advantage.

During Cold Harbor, there were seven thousand Union casualties in twenty minutes, a battle with no advantage to show for this monumental forfeiture of life.

Charles Douglass, now a sergeant with the Fifth Massachusetts Cavalry, fought near Petersburg, Virginia. On the last day of May, Charles took a minute to write to his father from Virginia, but even as his pen glided over the paper, he expected "to be called into battle every moment." The reality was that they had "been fighting ever since our Regt came here." He was seven miles from Petersburg as Grant's great offensive was grinding down into what promised to be a long siege. As he wrote, he could hear bombs falling. Hinting at his fears of entering this carnage, he wrote his father, "I am not over anxious but willing to meet the devil at any moment." He added, "Fort Pillow will be the battle cry."[18]

In the previous week, he had faced this question of killing in cold blood. As he patrolled alone on picket duty, Charles had spotted a man in gray ducking behind a tree that was about twelve yards away from him. Startled, Charles ordered him to move slowly out from his position. The rebel reluctantly showed his face and then slowly moved into the open. When he was fully exposed, Charles nervously cocked his pistol. The subtle sound of a click seemed to reverberate throughout the still woods. Terror flashed over the white soldier's face and his body froze. The white man asked Charles if he intended to murder him. Charles aimed the gun at the Confederate's head. No one would ever know if he decided to take the life of a man fighting for an institution stealing the lives of his own family members. All he would have to do was squeeze his index finger.

The sensitive Charles could fight, but he could not murder.

With a harsh voice, Charles answered no. He ordered the petrified man forward and promised to shoot him if he dared pause. Charles took the prisoner to his commanders but kept the Confederate's revolver and fifty dollars he found on him. This man survived, but there are accounts of other black soldiers outside of Petersburg dispensing revenge for Fort Pillow. During a roundup of Confederate prisoners, a member of the 117th New York witnessed a United States Colored Troops private spotting an unarmed white man; the private, "came up to him . . . and ran his bayonet through his heart."[19]

Death nearly caught up with Charles in mid-June. On the evening of June 16, he packed two days' rations because his battalion had drawn a difficult assignment. He and about four hundred comrades left camp at two in the morning. Moving closer to the front lines, he saw ambulance trains heading the other way carrying men with appalling wounds. It went through his head, "some of us were not coming back again." They ended their march five miles from Petersburg, next to General Benjamin Butler's forces.

Alongside other black regiments, they started down a hill and into a wheat field, driving the enemy into woods. Moving on, Charles was under "a withering fire from the rebel batteries." Trying to push forward, he kept tripping on the underbrush. He was in the second line. His colonel ordered Charles's line to fix bayonets and take on the rebel defense that had turned back the first wave. The officer yelled, "Come on, brave boys of the Fifth!" as he was struck in the shoulder. Under this deadly fire, Charles charged forward through the Confederate breastworks. He not only lived, but also helped to capture a piece of artillery. As Charles looked around, he saw only about twenty of the men from his company with whom he had started this two-mile rush. The worst wound he had was the skin of his shoulder ground raw from his bag.[20]

His brother Lewis was not as lucky. Recovered, Lewis rejoined his company; they were supporting a Maine Heavy Artillery unit pounding the Confederate side of the Petersburg siege. In the confusion of the barrage, Lewis mistakenly walked next to the tremendous discharge of a hundred-pound Parrot gun. Lewis felt "as though something inside my head had burst." Though nothing hit him, his head was so close to the exploding cannon that the impact felt as if he had taken a piece of lead. All Lewis could hear was a deafening hum. A watery substance started dripping from his ears and did not stop for days. Friends moved him to his tent, where intense pain in his head continued. A rapidly rising fever soon accompanied it. Lewis would be lying there near the siege, battling for equilibrium, for months to come.[21]

CHAPTER 13

Revolutionary Dialogue

W hile moderates and conservatives all across the North, particularly in the Midwest, lamented the length and conduct of the war, radical abolitionists too had grievances against Abraham Lincoln. Treasury Secretary Salmon Chase had long coveted the presidency and was angling behind the scenes for the nomination. But Lincoln observed every move his officious cabinet member was making, and with finesse and infinite subtlety, laid the trap of overambition. Samuel Pomeroy, the Kansas senator who had shown Douglass around Washington when he had come to meet Lincoln, wrote a circular to promote Chase's candidacy. But this poorly executed and excessively derogatory pamphlet effectively killed his nomination before it had even begun, and the Republican Baltimore convention stuck with Lincoln.

In Rochester, Douglass observed police trying to deal with army deserters lingering around the city.[1] Their presence was a sign of a war dragging on and outlasting a public's will to fight it. With the tidal wave of summer's casualties and the evident blunting of Grant's advance, the North seemed to turn against the seemingly ill-fated president, and Frederick Douglass was no exception. Some abolitionists attached their hopes to General John Frémont, who had so audaciously defied Lincoln on emancipation in areas under his command in 1861. When the name of the failed general, but still beloved figure to abolitionists, arose as yet another challenger to Lincoln, Douglass did not dismiss the possibility he would support him. When those exasperated with Lincoln invited Douglass to attend a radical convention in Cleveland, Ohio, Douglass issued this signed public response:

I mean to complete abolition of every vestige, form and modification of Slavery in every part of the United States, perfect equality for the black man in every State before the law, in the jury-box and on the battle-field; ample and salutary retaliation for every instance of enslavement or slaughter of prisoners of any color. I mean that in the distribution of officers and honors under this Government no discrimination shall be made in favor of or against any class of citizens, whether black or white, of native or foreign birth. And supposed that the convention which is to meet at Cleveland means the same thing, I cheerfully give my name as one of the signers of the call.[2]

One reason Douglass opposed Lincoln only months after a historic meeting with him was the situation in Louisiana, the first southern state Lincoln could play an active role in reconstructing. For Douglass, this revealed much about Lincoln's vision for the nation if the Union were to win this war. This debate had roots in diverging opinions of the nature of this rebellion. Senator Charles Sumner believed in a concept he called "state suicide." He believed that states in rebellion had forfeited their previous status as democratic bodies within the country, and it would be Congress's duty to reconfigure them in ways that they determined to be best. This meant emancipation and black suffrage.

Lincoln, however, had never legally recognized the southern states' secession, believing this war was the work of certain misguided individuals who had seized control of these governments. When the government put down the rebellion, Lincoln expected states to adhere to the laws that governed them before. As this applied to Louisiana, Lincoln wanted a new state constitution drafted, to be approved by 10 percent of people in the state who would take an oath of loyalty to the Union. He saw this as reestablishing order and ending slavery as quickly as possible. Although Lincoln wished that black men with property or literacy would have the right to vote, "this was a question which they must decide for themselves." He did not think humanitarians should overrule states and constitutional rights.[3] Louisiana scheduled a constitutional convention for April 1864, with no indication that participants would incorporate equal suffrage for black men.

Leaders of the black community drew up a petition pleading for the right to vote based on their military service, their ownership of property, and the fact that many of them had been born free. The community selected Jean Baptiste Roudanez, a sugar plantation engineer, and Arnold Bertonneau, a wine merchant, to bring this document, signed by more than a thousand, to

President Lincoln. Both had called for black military service early in the war, and Bertonneau eventually served.

On March 3, they followed Douglass's example and met with the president. Lincoln was again polite but unable to fulfill their hopes. "I regret, gentlemen, that you are not able to secure all your rights," a journalist quoted Lincoln as saying, "and that circumstances will not permit the government to confer them upon you." Their voting rights would not be Lincoln's perquisite for Louisiana's readmission to the Union. He wished them the best, but their fate was up to loyal people of Louisiana. Lincoln spoke as if he had no power of influencing the result.[4]

They may have left the White House discouraged, but Lincoln did take some action to assist them. He wrote to Michael Hahn, governor of the new free state of Louisiana, with a suggestion in anticipation of this constitutional convention. Lincoln asked if some black people, especially intelligent ones and those who had fought for the Union, could be awarded the vote. This was "only a suggestion, not to the public, but to you alone."[5] Lincoln, by referencing the "intelligent," was endorsing what would later become a hallmark of the Jim Crow era, literacy poll tests. On the other hand, supporting any black voters at all was ahead of many Americans and many northern states, including his home state of Illinois. As tepid and moderate as it was, this suggestion was also a clear step forward from Lincoln's prewar beliefs.

But for Frederick Douglass, action was more important than sentiment. In this case, he did not believe Lincoln was doing all he could. Douglass met Roudanez and Bertonneau a few days after their meeting in Washington, when they traveled to Boston for a dinner in honor of their cause. He was for the radical remaking of southern states by any means. In his "Mission of the War" speech, he had outlined his vision: "The New England schoolhouse is bound to take the place of the Southern whipping-post. Not because we love the negro, but the nation." Douglass believed that anything short of creating this reality would represent Lincoln's abandonment of those he was emancipating.

Douglass had been writing about the reconstruction of Louisiana for more than a year. General Nathaniel Banks, commander of the Department of the Gulf, had issued rules in the wake of the emancipation regulating black people in the region. If the white people were loyal to the Union, Banks supported black people going back to their original plantation, provided the land owner reasonably compensated them. He forbid the wandering about of those without employment, making it necessary for blacks not on a plantation to carry a pass. Douglass found this edict far too close to slavery and asked, "What is freedom? It is the right to choose one's own employment."

Controlling all the factors of a person's work and punishing them when they do not obey was slavery. Douglass thought, "It defeats the beneficent intentions of the government, if it has beneficent intentions, in regard to the freedom of our people."[6]

Lincoln made no effort to amend this new—though strangely familiar—order. Half a year later, however, he did write to Banks: "Education for young blacks should be included in the plan." Without many other objections, he approved of Banks's work. Yet, by calling it "sufficient for this probationary period," Lincoln suggested that he might not endorse this as a permanent arrangement. For the moment, he was more concerned that Louisiana reentered the Union without slavery in its constitution, as the Emancipation Proclamation in fact did not apply to much of the state.[7] For Douglass, rules like these and the prevailing passivity on voting rights might, despite Union victory, pave the way for a perpetual slavery-like society.

In July, Congress passed the Wade-Davis Bill, which would have required 50 percent (instead of Lincoln's low percentage of 10) of a state's population to take an oath to the Union, slowing the process that Lincoln wanted to expedite. The Wade-Davis Bill also required immediate emancipation in these places. Lincoln pocket-vetoed it, fearing the damage it would do to his ongoing work in Louisiana and other states. Abolitionist anger soared.

Frederick Douglass's passionate speeches were heard or read by thousands every month, but made a particular impact on John Eaton, a young chaplain. General Ulysses Grant had plucked Eaton from an obscure regimental post in late 1862 to organize the dispossessed black people around the Union lines in Tennessee and extending into Mississippi. The thirty-five-year-old from quiet New Hampshire farmland had light brown hair, soft, boyish eyes, and a sharp mind. His reputation had grown out of following the battle action so closely that rebels captured the young minister, though they soon released him. With Grant's new assignment, he was faced with "men, women, and children in every stage of disease or decrepitude, often barely naked, with flesh torn by the terrible experiences of their escapes." Eaton had to keep them alive. Yet, he wanted to tackle a bigger question, that of self-sufficiency and ultimately citizenship. For Eaton, this boiled down to, "How was the slave to be transformed into a freeman?" This meant everything from organizing the labor of these thousands to more personal aspects of life. He loved seeing the eager former slave couples marry legally; a colleague once had presided over 119 weddings in an hour.[8]

Around the time of Douglass's first visit to the White House, Eaton had also sought an interview, believing Lincoln should know what he was learning about these freedmen. Lincoln was keenly interested in questions such as, "How far did they understand the changes that were coming to them, and what were they able to do for themselves?" He clearly wanted to absorb every detail of what Eaton knew, even asking him to come back the next morning.[9]

In late July 1864, almost exactly a year later, Eaton returned to the White House with more information. On his way east, he stopped in Toledo, Ohio, to see his brother. During his brief stay, he heard Douglass speak. He was so captivated that he sought Douglass out afterward to talk more about the abolitionist's views. By the time he reached Washington, Douglass was still on his mind.

At Lincoln's request, Eaton would be staying for a week so he could have more time to discuss the issue of newly freed black people, usually after Lincoln had finished his daily work. In their conversations, Lincoln once brought up John Brown and the ill-fated raid to liberate slaves. Lincoln admitted that he was revolted by the bloodshed at the time, but now he was ruminating on "every possible means by which the Negro could be secured in his freedom, and at the same time provide a source of strength to the Union." He wondered what sort of "grapevine telegraph" there was to inform enslaved people that freedom lay at Union lines. If such a system of communication could be developed or strengthened, the Confederacy would lose labor and the Union would gain soldiers. He asked Eaton what he thought, but the chaplain did not know enough about the slave community to say.

The tired president told the younger man that he knew there was an unforgiving torrent of criticism swirling outside his gates. Eaton agreed and recounted what he could remember from the Douglass speech. Though he had been talking about this issue for over a year, Douglass had been particularly dismayed that "The Confederates had threatened not to treat as prisoners of war any captured colored soldiers or their officers." The point hit home for Eaton because "I was one of those officers." He elaborated, "The Negro orator felt keenly that our measures of retaliation against cruelty to Negro soldiers were not sharp enough." It was four months since Fort Pillow, and no Confederate executions had ensued from Lincoln's harsh order. Eaton continued, "My heart was heavy with the mistreatment and suffering of the Negroes in the conquered territory over which my supervision extended." This was an issue where Eaton and Douglass could learn from each other. Douglass went far enough to decry that summer "the swindle by which our (the Federal) Government claims the respect of mankind for abolishing slavery— at the same time that it is practically re-establishing that hateful system in Louisiana."[10]

In a powerful letter sent to an English friend at this time, Douglass made one of the harshest statements he would ever make about Lincoln: "The President has virtually laid down this as the rule of his statesmen: *Do evil by choice, right from necessity.*" He had asked why the black man was good enough to die for the government but not to elect it. When peace would come, Douglass believed, the plan was to "hand the negro back to the political power of the master, without a single element of strength to shield himself from the vindictive spirit sure to be roused against the whole colored race." Douglass's opinions that Eaton related to the president were similar in nature.[11]

Lincoln, only moments before comfortably accepting critiques of himself, seemed taken aback. Eaton perceived Lincoln to be hurt to an extent that surprised the minister. He asked if Douglass knew what he had written to the new governor of Louisiana about black suffrage. Eaton could only say that Douglass had not mentioned this letter. Lincoln rose from his chair as he spoke. He went over to his desk, picked up a copy of the letter and read,

> I congratulate you on having fixed your name in history as the first Free State Governor of Louisiana. Now you are about to have a convention, which among other things, will probably define the elective franchise, I barely suggest for your private consideration whether some of the colored people may not be let in—as for instance, the very intelligent, and *especially those who have fought gallantly in our ranks.* They would probably help, in some trying time to come, to keep the jewel of liberty within the family of freedom.[12]

Lincoln was proud of lending support for black voting rights. The letter showed the effect black soldiers had upon him—he believed that they had earned the ballot.

The Louisiana Constitutional Convention, however, had not chosen to include black people in the franchise. Had Lincoln made black voting a requirement instead of a suggestion, maybe that would not have been the case. Lincoln knew the result, and a day before had written to General Banks, "I have just seen the new Constitution adopted by the Convention of Louisiana, and I am anxious that it shall be ratified by the people."[13]

After reading his letter, Eaton recalled, "The President of the United States and the greatest man of his time asked me, with that curious modesty characteristic of him, if I thought Mr. Douglass could be induced to come to see him." Eaton replied that he thought Douglass could.

Why was Lincoln so concerned about what this one man thought of him? In abolitionist circles, and particularly within the black community, Douglass's views would have sway in a time when Lincoln would be needing every vote he could muster. Still, no black man in 1864 could be considered terribly important politically. However, Lincoln said something else suggesting a more personal quality to why he valued Douglass's assessments. Lincoln said to Eaton, in his only considered comment about Frederick Douglass that we have, that there was some tie between them, and "considering the condition from which he had arisen and the obstacles that he had overcome, and the position to which he had attained he regarded him one of the most meritorious men, if not the most meritorious man in the United States."[14]

Douglass had clearly made quite an impression on the president. It was now Lincoln himself prompting a second meeting. In thinking about the ease and evident lack of prejudice that marked his meetings with Lincoln, Douglass maintained that this connection was forged in their both being self-made men. Though it might seem audacious to compare a president's early days with his own, Douglass was well aware of the grinding poverty of Lincoln's childhood, and he later pondered that this commonality was a source of their ease with one another. Douglass concluded, "I account partially for his kindness to me because of the similarity with which I had fought my way up, we both starting at the lowest rung of the ladder." So when receiving the invitation, Douglass resolved to go "most gladly."[15]

With the promise of victory and emancipation, not to mention Douglass's faith in Lincoln, in grave condition, the stakes could not have been higher.

It was August and Douglass was again in Washington. The temperature was pitched to its usual ferocity. Reporter Noah Brooks, friend of the beleaguered president, wrote "those days will appear to be the darkest of the many dark days through which passed the friends and lovers of the Federal Union." Grant's arrival in the East raised expectations that were now dashed, with the only movement in Virginia from the lengthening lists of the dead; "a deadly calm prevailed where so lately resounded the shouts of victory."[16]

Washington had experienced a shock three weeks before, when Confederate general Jubal Early and a force of under twenty thousand snuck away from the action in Virginia to head toward the Union capital. Maneuvering all the way to Silver Spring, Maryland, the rebels were close but never really threatened the city. It was another discouraging factor in the North's doldrums. At Fort Stevens, Lincoln became the only sitting U.S. president to come under enemy fire, as sniper bullets killed a man near Lincoln when he stood to observe the action.

Things had hardly been ideal when Douglass made his first visit, but the optimism that the victories at Gettysburg and Vicksburg had produced then had now vanished. Confederate leadership, facing their own dire prospects, knew the key to their independence might well lie in a Lincoln defeat in November. If the year continued at this rate of attrition, it was virtually assured the president would not be reelected.

Every aspect about Douglass and Lincoln's second meeting must be considered relative to the fact that Lincoln and much of the nation believed there would be a new president in a few months, and that the war might end in compromise. Lincoln remarked that summer, "You think I don't know I am going to be beaten, *but I do* and unless some great change takes place, *badly beaten*." Thurlow Weed, the ultimate political insider, told Lincoln "his re-election was an impossibity [*sic*]." He felt, "The People are wild for Peace." *New York Times* editor Henry Raymond informed Lincoln, "The tide is strongly against us," and Lincoln would at this point even lose his home state. He recommended that Lincoln start negotiating with the Confederate government now, lest the next administration garner terms less favorable to their aims.[17]

No president had served a second term since Andrew Jackson in 1832, more than thirty years before. Regardless of Lincoln's situation, the nation was not accustomed to the idea of a president being in office more than four years, and there was a widespread sense that if any administration needed retirement, this was the one.

It was all the more gut-wrenchingly fitting that if Lincoln followed this trend, the man who would be replacing him was the recalcitrant general who had cost Lincoln so much valuable time. A week before, New York City, never a Lincoln stronghold, had witnessed a massive rally in support of George McClellan's candidacy. As many as hundred thousand people in Union Square celebrated with speakers, music, fireworks, cannon, and anti-Lincoln cheers. Without a dramatic change in the war itself, it would be McClellan facing Jefferson Davis next March.

One of the biggest stories of the summer also came from that city. It was a seventy-two-page pamphlet, available for twenty-five cents, entitled *Miscegenation: The Theory of the Blending of the Races, Applied to the White Man and the Negro*. Seemingly written from the perspective of an overzealous abolitionist, it was actually the scheme of two New York Democrat newspapermen. The document advocated racial mixing, attesting, "All that is needed to make us the finest race on earth is to engraft upon our stock the negro element which providence has placed by our side on this continent." They linked this concept to the current war, asserting that the government was nobly fighting this war for racial amalgamation. The last piece of the rancid political ploy was that the paper then reported how much support this document enjoyed from Republicans and abolitionists. The Democrats struggled to shift the focus of the election to exploit racial feelings. If nothing else, they were riling their base.[18]

While his party tried to cope with racial demagoguery, Lincoln was showing his own signs of progress on racial matters. There were indications that he had abandoned his old belief in colonization; in relief, his secretary John Hay wrote in his diary on the first day of July, "I am glad the President has sloughed off that idea of colonization." Lincoln wrote to Governor Andrew of his hope that Massachusetts could "afford a permanent home within her borders, for all, or even a large number of colored persons who will come to her."[19]

Lincoln was also asking Edwin Stanton for more statistics on the increasing tide of black troops and how many had come straight from enslavement. Stanton reported there were 71,976 at the time, 58,433 who were estimated to have come directly out of bondage. Lincoln told Josiah B. Grinnell, an Iowa congressman, "When you give the Negro these rights, when you put a gun in his hands, it prophesies something more." Lincoln was reflecting changes that other white people were going through around the country, prompted by the performance of black troops. Military commanders made their opinions clear. In west Tennessee, Colonel Frank A. Kendrick reported on commanding these soldiers, "The majority of the men were for the first time under fire, but their conduct did not disappoint my most sanguine anticipation, as, after the first few rounds, they received and returned the enemy's fire with the steadiness and deliberation of veterans." Assessments like this meant, as Samuel Denison in New Orleans wrote to Secretary of the Treasury Chase, that "the whole army, from colonels down, is thoroughly abolitionized. They have seen the negros drill and fight, and they want to give them a chance and put down slavery. I have not seen a soldier who has not this feeling."[20]

Earlier in the summer Lincoln had allowed black Washingtonians to use the White House grounds for an after-church outdoor lunch and fundraiser. It was a simple gesture, but a first for an American president.[21] By calling Douglass to the White House to advise him, Lincoln achieved another milestone in American history. On Thursday, August 18, he received a note informing him that Douglass was expected on a train getting into Washington at eleven o'clock in the morning. They would meet the following day.[22]

Also on Thursday, Leonard Swett, a particularly close Illinois friend, and Lincoln met to discuss the election at this juncture, after his Baltimore renomination. Swett expressed in a letter to his wife that "Lincoln's election is beyond any possible hope. It is probably clean gone now." Swett added that Lincoln should withdraw his name for the good of the party.[23]

But if Lincoln was going to be defeated, he had a radical notion of a task Frederick Douglass might do before the election.

That evening Douglass gave a speech at the Fifteenth Street Presbyterian Church. The church was packed from the pews to the gallery and a reporter guessed that the audience in the traditionally black church was about a third white. Douglass kept them waiting with a late arrival, but after an introduction from Reverend Henry Garnet, he spoke without either a prepared address or any notes. He thrilled the audience with his praise of the black soldiers. While celebrating them, he struck a different note with regard to Lincoln, declaring that he would not decide whether to vote for him until he knew if a more radical abolitionist candidate was entering the race. If slavery was to be killed, Douglass said that he did not expect to be "invited to the President's table," but hoped just to be treated as a citizen. It was an interesting comment because the next day he would be at the president's residence.[24]

Douglass sat waiting to be called in to see the president. Sitting near Douglass, anticipating their own visit with Lincoln, were two Wisconsin men, Alexander Randall, a former governor and diplomat to the Vatican, and Joseph Mills, a judge on the fifth judicial district.[25]

The room was dark as Mills caught sight of Douglass, silently reading in the corner of the room. They were fascinated by the black man waiting there. Mills recorded that this man "possessed a remarkable physiognomy," another way of saying they were mildly shocked to see a black waiting to meet with the president. Douglass so riveted Mills that he stood up to get a better look. As he stared unabashedly, Douglass felt the glare of this stranger's fixed gaze. Douglass swiftly lifted his focus from his book and forcefully met Mills's stare. Mills was taken aback by the power of one glance from Douglass. Caught off guard, he quipped, "Are you the president?" He pretended he had mistaken Douglass for Abraham Lincoln.

Douglass would be the subject of no man's ridicule. His response typified the manner in which Douglass carried himself through his entire life. With immeasurable dignity he answered, "I am Frederick Douglass."[26]

Douglass got in to see the president before the Wisconsin men did. The Lincoln he found shocked him. Lincoln had been a serious man before, but now he was in an "alarmed condition." To Douglass, "The dimmed light in his eye, and the deep lines in his strong American face, told plainly the story of the

Abraham Lincoln, 1864. Photograph by Anthony Berger
at Brady's Studio.

heavy burden of care that weighed upon his spirit." Douglass later remarked that he felt as if it would have been easier to dance at a funeral than to make a joke in front of the burdened Lincoln he met with. Of course, there was, famously, a more jovial and storytelling side to Lincoln, but they did not have a chance to know each other intimately enough for that. As Douglass concluded, "it was never my lot to find him in such a mood."[27]

Lincoln had always impressed his contemporaries as being a man with an intensely melancholy aspect in the best of times, but now a flood of events burdened his frayed spirits. Francis Carpenter, an artist who knew Lincoln's face well, said that summer that "his care-worn, troubled appearance was enough to bring tears of sympathy into the eyes of his most bitter opponents." The black wells under his eyes were marked and heavy. That Lincoln's emotional suffering intersected with a physical deterioration was evident to anyone who sat down with him. In December, another man who had known Lincoln before the war was stunned to find a Lincoln who "looked like death," with "pale, haggard features, furrowed with wrinkles, his sunken eyes."[28]

Lincoln also was encountering a man whose sadness was deep and enduring. At the end of May, Rosine Draz wrote to Douglass of his "poor crushed heart." She worried when he was hesitant to "speak of its grief even to your own friends." A month later, she wrote to him, "at last you will sink under the heavy burdens you are perpetually bearing." The war was a crushing burden for both Lincoln and Douglass, yet neither was about to lay their burden down, so they got down to business.[29]

Douglass wrote that at the time, "Everybody was thinking and dreaming of peace." The *Daily National Intelligencer* that morning prominently featured an article entitled "How to Make Peace" that referred to peace missions. This would be the first matter of their meeting, for the issue of peace negotiations had been plaguing Lincoln all summer. Horace Greeley, who had been using the pages of his widely read paper to urge negotiations with the South, implored Lincoln to send representatives to Niagara Falls in order to meet with a group of men Greeley believed represented the Confederate government. Lincoln correctly suspected these men were not interested in brokering a peace, but just in damaging Lincoln's reelection prospects by fostering peace sentiments. While Greeley waited on the Canadian-American border for Lincoln's representative, he instead received a letter from Lincoln that clearly stated, "Any proposition which embraces the restoration of peace, the integrity of the whole Union, and the abandonment of slavery, and which comes by and with an authority that can control the armies now at war against the United States will be received and considered."[30]

Lincoln's letter may have rendered Greeley's plan a fiasco, but Lincoln was soon the one in trouble when his letter became public. Earlier in the war, Lincoln had promised to save the Union. This letter made emancipation sound like a new prerequisite for peace. The *Cincinnati Enquirer* interpreted the letter as saying every boy who died "will lose his life not for the Union, the Stars and Stripes, but for the negro." Many Americans were not willing to pay that cost for slavery as a condition for peace. Public opinion against Lincoln continued to plummet as the perception of emancipation as a war aim gained force.[31]

Frustrated with Lincoln's letter to Greeley, Charles Robinson, editor of the *Green Bay Advocate*, wrote a letter that he wanted personally delivered to Lincoln. The Wisconsin men whom Douglass had encountered minutes before he entered Lincoln's office had given this letter to the president three days before. It was a significant situation for Lincoln, because Robinson was a Democrat who had faithfully supported the war effort over the last four years but was now at his breaking point. With the election three months away, there were thousands like Robinson around the country—and if Lincoln lost him, the same would probably hold true of them. Robinson told Lincoln that he was used to "taking some hard knocks with some of my party" because he had defended Lincoln, even upholding "the freeing of the negroes as sound war policy." However, he found Lincoln's statement to be thoroughly disturbing. He believed, "This puts the whole war question on a new basis, and takes us War Democrats clear off our feet, leaving us no ground to stand upon." The point of his letter was to ask Lincoln to "suggest some interpretation of it" that would allow him and like-minded people to continue to support Lincoln. Otherwise, Lincoln was in even worse political trouble.[32]

The day after receiving the note, August 17, Lincoln drafted a reply but held it to give it more consideration. Before he discussed it with Mills and Randall, or even handed over the letter, Lincoln decided to discuss it with Frederick Douglass.

Lincoln was attempting to walk a fine line of pacifying anti-emancipation moderate voters without losing his abolitionist support. Almost no one's words carried more weight with this bloc around the country than Douglass's, so Lincoln was in effect testing whether he could retain his support while bringing the Robinsons of the world back into his camp.

From the start of the meeting, Lincoln seemed to Douglass deeply troubled by the attitude of Greeley and all his former supporters now calling for peace. Lincoln explained to Douglass that he was "accused of protracting the war beyond its legitimate object and of failing to make peace." What impressed Douglass in these first few minutes was how Lincoln seemed to have learned the hard lesson Douglass had been pressing all over the country from the very start of war: The Union should never accept peace under these circumstances. Lincoln asserted to Douglass "the danger of premature peace." Thus, he assured his guest of how little credence he put in "futile conferences with unauthorized persons, at Niagara Falls, or elsewhere." Douglass felt an immense relief.[33]

Lincoln still had the problem of convincing the American people to let him continue this conflict. He said that the country thought he was driving an abolition war (the very phrase Douglass championed) instead of still trying to save the Union. It looked like he might not be able to accomplish either, but he had drafted a letter that he believed could help. Lincoln then handed Douglass the letter he had been working on to respond to Robinson.

The paper Douglass held in his hands began with an equivocation, "To me it seems plain that saying re-union and abandonment of slavery would be considered, if offered, is not saying that nothing else or less would be considered, if offered." This set the tone for a letter trying to appease those against abolition without saying he was ready to abandon emancipation. Lincoln quoted what he had written to Greeley two years before, a passage that still made Douglass shudder: "What I do about slavery and the colored race, I do because I believe it helps to save the Union." Lincoln confirmed that he had written that sincerely, and that he had later authorized black soldiers because it greatly benefited the Union.

He also quoted himself in this provisional letter claiming that the pledge of freedom motivated black men to fight, "And the promise, being made, must be kept." If he was to forsake that oath, Lincoln asked his critics, "As matter of morals, could such treachery by any possibility, escape the curses of Heaven, or of any good man?" On a more practical level, discarding emancipation would mean, as Douglass well knew, "All recruiting of colored men would instantly cease, and all colored men now in our service, would instantly desert us. And rightfully too. Why should they give their lives for us, with full notice of our purpose to betray them?"

Lincoln was arguing to Robinson that he could not end the war without negro freedom because it would cost thousands of soldiers he could not re-place. In fact, the election of any president who did not support emancipation would certainly lose the war even before they began negotiating for peace—because the Union army badly needed these black soldiers. Lincoln added lines that are quite revealing of his typical cast of mind, in his deep-set belief in reason and order: "It is not a question of sentiment or taste, but one of physical force, which may be measured, and estimated as horsepower, and steam power, are measured and estimated."

Lincoln's letter also finished with a phrase disconcerting to Douglass: "If Jefferson Davis wishes, for himself, or for the benefit of his friends at the North, to know what I would do if he were to offer peace and re-union, saying nothing about slavery, let him try me."[34]

Douglass had mere seconds to collect his thoughts, as the president asked him a crucial, but simple question: "Shall I send forth this letter?"[35]

Douglass sorted through his feelings. He did not mind the idea that Lincoln "stood ready to listen to any such propositions," in that it painted Lincoln as never standing in the way of peace. Lincoln had not taken back what he said in the Greeley letter, but his passivity bothered Douglass. Lincoln was saying that he could not take back emancipation even if he wished to. Douglass badly wanted a moral declaration from Lincoln on why they must all fight to end slavery, not a disingenuous pronouncement of Lincoln's power-lessness in the larger war equation.

Considering the message at the heart of the letter, Lincoln may have been expecting Douglass to like it more than he did. But Douglass saw something dangerous to the Union in the first and last line, as well as in the implicit message of issuing this at all. When he asked whether he should make it public, Douglass retorted, "Certainly not."

Explaining his answer, he contended that, "It could be given a broader meaning than you intend to convey—it would be taken as a complete surrender of your antislavery policy—and do you serious damage." Douglass thought that the previous letter had been clear in its stipulations for peace—and that by issuing this document, especially with the first and last lines seeming to be open to new peace conditions, he was in effect repudiating the earlier, stronger statement.

Douglass wanted Lincoln to weather this onslaught of criticism and stand committed to what he had previously said. Douglass had faith that it would not end the hope of winning this war. He did not ignore the practical realities of politics, however, suggesting to Lincoln, "In answer to your copperhead accusers—your friends can make this argument of your want of power—but you cannot wisely say a word on that point." If politicians around the country wanted to tell their constituents that Lincoln was powerless to annul the Emancipation Proclamation because of the effect it would have on the army, so be it. But for Lincoln himself to concede this rendered a serious blow to the moral case for abolition that Douglass was hoping to build into a permanent reality.

Douglass offered strength to the president on a decision that could have huge ramifications for Douglass's abolition war. When the war began Douglass offered ideas in the public arena, hoping against hope that they would somehow work their way to Lincoln. Now he had the chance to influence a Lincoln decision directly, and he did so with clarity and force.

At some point during Douglass's zealous advice not to release this letter, a secretary of Lincoln's announced "Governor Buckingham of Connecticut." Lincoln ignored the message and Douglass, puzzled, continued making his point. A few minutes later, the attendant made the same pronouncement.

Douglass arose from his seat and said, "I must not stay to prevent your interview with Governor Buckingham." Douglass knew immediately that this was not just any state governor, but one he viewed as noble and patriotic. William A. Buckingham was also someone for whom Lincoln held personal affection. While visiting his son Robert at Exeter in 1860, Lincoln had spoken around New England to raise his national profile. During a number of speeches in Connecticut, Lincoln had shared the podium with Buckingham. Lincoln knew he could count on Buckingham to be a reliable supplier of troops and support.

Douglass exclaimed, "Mr. Lincoln, I will retire."

Lincoln cut him off, "Oh, no, no, you shall not, I want Governor Buckingham to wait." He called out in a voice Douglass always found surprisingly high, "Tell Governor Buckingham to wait, for I want to have a long talk with my friend Frederick Douglass."

Douglass would later record, "This was probably the first time in the history of this Republic when its chief magistrate had found an occasion or shown a disposition to exercise such an act of impartiality between persons so widely different in their positions and supposed claims upon his attention." Douglass was being modest in describing his national importance, as Lincoln knew exactly what he was doing.

Lincoln had a shocking proposal to make, and Frederick Douglass was the only person he wanted for the assignment.

All of what they had discussed before, the opposition to the war, the fury at emancipation aims, the cries for peace, the North's abandonment of Lincoln—all this boiled down to a grim prospect that both men well understood: Lincoln would not be reelected, and the war would end in a peace that left the majority of slaves still in bondage. After all, Swett had given him this very fact the day before. If this was the real situation, what must be done? Lincoln had a solution that would need Douglass's expertise and effort.

Every day the war went on, the Emancipation Proclamation and the Confiscation Acts made it possible for women and men to find freedom when they reached Union army lines, or when these lines reached them. But Lincoln was not satisfied. He wanted to make the proclamation much more effective in these precious few remaining weeks. The war after all, might end in six months or less. In what Douglass described as a regretful tone, Lincoln lamented, "The slaves are not coming so rapidly and so numerously to us as I had hoped."

Douglass did his best to explain to Lincoln how skilled slaveholders were at keeping information from their laborers. For all he had thought about slavery, Lincoln had little practical experience of it. Douglass attempted to convey just how cut off from the world, from information that others took for granted, an enslaved person truly was. Douglass estimated that most did not actually know of the president's proclamation.

"Well," Lincoln pronounced, "I want you to set about devising some means of making them acquainted with it, and for bringing them into our lines." Douglass listened as Lincoln told him that he wanted a plan "by which we could get more of the slaves within our lines."

Lincoln sincerely wanted to know the best way they could induce blacks out of their situation in the South, for McClellan would surely not care. Lincoln related, with urgent words underlined by Douglass in a letter, "Now was there time—and <u>that such only of them as succeeded in getting within our</u> <u>lines would be free after the war is over.</u>"

Douglass found Lincoln's words spoken with "great earnestness and much solicitude" while he listened with concentrated interest. Douglass immediately replied that it would take organizing a group of black scouts, following a plan owing much to John Brown's ideas, to venture beyond Union lines—despite the dangers of the war and capture—to spread word of the Emancipation Proclamation and lead whoever they could find toward freedom.

Lincoln asked Douglass to submit a written plan on how to implement this task. As Douglass left, Governor Buckingham strolled into Lincoln's office. He was a markedly handsome, white-haired man with chiseled cheekbones and a sharply angled nose. Douglass still feared that he might have been rankled by having to wait, but this was far from the case as Buckingham's manner was jovial.

Never was the revolutionary nature of the Civil War clearer. In two months, it would be the fifth anniversary of John Brown's raid on Harpers Ferry. At the time, Lincoln, ever the cautious politician, recovering from his senatorial loss and unsure of what role, if any, politics would play in his future, had denounced this type of zealous, violent exploit. Now, as president of the United States, he proposed a mission that bore Brown's stamp. The man to whom he was making this overture had been wanted for treason in connection with Brown and once might have been on the very same Virginia gallows with Brown.[36]

Douglass would not turn down Lincoln's proposal. At the time of their meeting, it is estimated that less than 5 percent of the enslaved population were freed because of the Emancipation Proclamation. Despite all the thousands in conscript camps, the progress of slaves finding emancipation was going slowly. Douglass had written in the November 1862 *Monthly* that he expected a slave insurrection to follow the proclamation. Yet that had not happened, and Lincoln was right to wonder if something could be done to hasten the process.[37]

Acute southern fears of a slave rebellion existed before and after Nat Turner, Denmark Vesey, and the onset of war. Incidents like the hanging of seventeen black men in Culpeper County, Virginia, in October 1862 under the accusation of insurrection were common across the Confederacy. What really chilled the slaveholder's spine was the fear that the North would use covert agents as catalysts to start slave uprisings, especially after the Emancipation Proclamation. Until Lincoln's meeting with Douglass, this had only been paranoia.[38]

Lincoln's idea did not come out of nowhere. In May 1863, James Gilmore of the *New York Tribune* furnished Lincoln with a copy of a proposal from Augustus Montgomery, a Tennessee Unionist, to General William Rosecrans that outlined a plan to induce black people throughout the South to rebel on the night of August 1. Lincoln would not publicly endorse the scheme, but there is no evidence that he objected to it.[39] However, nothing would come of it other than an anxious Jefferson Davis, who sent a copy that he obtained to all rebel governors. Clearly these ideas had been developing for a long time. That Lincoln had included in the Emancipation Proclamation a provision prohibiting Union army interference with any effort among black people to attain their freedom suggests how far back these ideas about slave insurrection went in his mind, though he was now inclined to contradict his earlier thinking. During the meeting with John Eaton that had prompted Douglass's second visit to Washington, Lincoln wondered aloud about what sort of communication system they needed to free more black people, by any means. Eaton did not have an answer, but Douglass did.

CHAPTER 14

Going Home

Douglass's mind was racing after this second meeting with Lincoln. There was much to digest. He had entered the meeting still thinking of the politician who said he would save the Union with or without slavery. Instead, what he found in Lincoln on that August day was a "deeper moral conviction against slavery than I had ever seen before in anything spoken or written by him."[1]

While gaining a newfound admiration for the president was encouraging, it did not outweigh a general distress Douglass felt because the country was unlikely to reelect Lincoln. He and the president must somehow free as many enslaved people as they could before November. Once Lincoln was out of office, there was little hope for the millions still in chains. Douglass was keenly aware of the current political climate, but something about hearing Lincoln's acknowledgment of it drove home this crushing reality like never before. In addition, Douglass feared Lincoln might not take his advice and might release his response to Charles Robinson's letter that would retreat from emancipationist aims.[2]

After seeing Douglass, Lincoln told his Wisconsin visitors, Judge Joseph Mills and former governor Alexander Randall, that he could not go back on his previous stipulations for the end to the war, no matter how it might affect his own political prospects. He could not live with himself by, in effect, turning back to bondage the men who had fought so hard: "I should be damned in time and eternity for so doing . . . The world shall know that I will keep my faith to friends and enemies, come what will." He never sent the letter.[3]

Later that afternoon, John Eaton encountered Douglass, who seemed a nervous wreck. During the trip, the orator was staying with William Lee, one of the most prominent black men in Washington. The strong presence of slavery in Washington until two years before existed alongside a tradition of black enterprise in the city. Lee's father, Alfred, had started a business selling feed in 1830. Having grown up around the store, William carried on and expanded its operation when his father died. Now William Lee was a wealthy man.[4]

Eaton called on Douglass at Lee's house on Bridge Street in Georgetown. The energetic chaplain was eager to hear how the meeting with the president had gone. Referring to Lincoln's queries on spreading word of the Emancipation Proclamation through the South, Douglass explained, "He asked me a number of questions, which I am preparing to answer in writing."[5]

Over the next ten days, Douglass consulted with as many black leaders as he could, attempting to formulate an effective plan. All whom he spoke with thought it was an inspired notion, and most thought he could actually accomplish this difficult goal. Ten days after the meeting, Douglass composed a letter to Lincoln with a detailed ten-page plan. Lincoln would appoint a general agent to employ twenty-five loyal men (whether the general agent might be Douglass himself, the letter did not say). This leader would assign the group to various areas near Union lines where they could maximize their effectiveness by reaching the most slaves. Once in position, they would find one or more local residents intimately familiar with the terrain they would be moving in. They would train as many local "conductors" as possible on how to run missions to steer people out of bondage and toward the army. These agents, paid two dollars a day, would clandestinely move behind enemy lines, keeping meticulous records of the locations of plantations they visited. They would also record the names of any people led from these places.

Douglass was adamant that they would have to possess the support of Union commanding officers on the ground to maximize the protection they would have during this dangerous work. Douglass also insisted that "provision be made that the slaves or Freed men thus brought within our lines shall receive subsistence until such of them as are fit shall enter the service of the Country or be otherwise employed and provided for." Every two weeks, an agent would send on a written report, with up-to-date numbers, to the general agent, who would then prepare an overall report for Lincoln's eyes. The general agent would work out of Washington with one clerk, along with a roving commission that would visit the various patrols to provide additional oversight on the progress and faithfulness of the agents. Douglass closed his description of what such an operation would look like saying, "I think it enough to give your Excellency an Idea of how the desirable work shall be executed."[6]

Douglass drew extensively on some of the plans that John Brown had written in Douglass's Rochester home when his children were young. But these plans also owed much to Underground Railroad conductors such as Harriet Tubman, who had perfected daring raids of escape in the South over the last ten years. Douglass was simply providing a national infrastructure to coordinate as many escapees as possible before the Emancipation Proclamation was annulled. When he wrote this letter to the White House on August 29, they did not have a day to waste.

Meanwhile at the White House, the same despondency on the fate of his re-election that caused Lincoln to ask Douglass for help prompted the president to write a remarkable memorandum. It read, "This morning, as for some days past, it seems exceedingly probable that this Administration will not be re-elected. Then it will be my duty to so co-operate with the President elect, as to save the Union between the Election and the inauguration; as he will have secured his election on such ground that he cannot possibly save it afterwards." Lincoln asked his cabinet members to sign the back of the folded and sealed paper, without knowledge of its contents.[7]

George McClellan's Democratic nomination became official in Chicago on August 29. McClellan's nomination cemented for Douglass as well as for many wavering and previously harshly critical radical abolitionists the idea that they must at last support Lincoln. Douglass sincerely wanted a more strongly antislavery candidate, but in the face of McClellan, Lincoln would do.

Charles Douglass, struggling to survive Grant's brutal offensive campaign in Virginia, received wonderful (possibly lifesaving) news in the summer of 1864. His unit was to leave the area around Petersburg, Virginia, and report to the vastly safer Point Lookout, Maryland. Although now safe from battle, his sicknesses returned and his body weakened; respiratory problems and high fevers were soon a major concern.

Lewis, recovering on Morris Island in South Carolina from his own health problems, worried about his brother's fever. Would they both make it out of this war? Lewis had had enough of fighting and the southern climate, and wished he could go home to help recruit black troops in New York and to see his beloved Amelia as well.[8]

Douglass was seemingly powerless to help Charles, as he desperately waited for news of his son. During his first bout with illness in 1863, when he had been on the outskirts of Boston, Charles had often written of the poor treatment a black soldier received. The chance of Charles enduring a second bout was dangerously uncertain—and even more precarious as he was now in a very different environment. Point Lookout was on a desolate, sandy, windswept peninsula where the Potomac River meets the Chesapeake Bay. In close proximity to thousands of suffering Confederate soldiers in an over-flowing prison camp in Point Lookout, Charles and these soldiers were bearing up to excessive heat and unsanitary water while living on sandy and soggy ground.

It occurred to Douglass that there was one man who could do something about Charles's fate. For a man as proud as Douglass, it would not have been easy to turn to Lincoln for help, especially regarding favored treatment for his son. But Charles's life was at stake, so on the same day that he sent Lincoln his plan, Douglass sent a second letter. This one was labeled "Private." In it, he confessed, "I hope I shall not presume too much upon your kindness—but I have a very great favor to ask." Thinking that Lincoln might assume this had to do with the other letter he would be receiving simultaneously, Douglass made it clear, "It is not that you will appoint me General Agent to carry out the Plan now proposed—though I would not shrink from that duty." The purpose of this letter was "that you will cause my son Charles R. Douglass. 1st Sergeant of Company I—5th Massachusetts Dismounted Cavalry—now stationed at 'Point Lookout' to be discharged."

It was a rare instance when Douglass took off the mask of national race leader to reveal a father, loving and afraid. Douglass pleaded his case, "He is now sick—He was the first colored volunteer from the State of New York—having enlisted with his Older Brother in the Mass-54th partly to encourage enlistments—He was but 18, when he enlisted—and has been in the service 18 Months. If your Excellency can confer this favor—you will lay me under many obligations."[9]

Douglass trusted Lincoln enough to open himself and lay bare his fears. Lincoln had disappointed Douglass on many occasions when it had come to the war, but in doing this very personal action, Lincoln gave Douglass an immeasurable gift. Lincoln wrote a simple note, "Let this boy be discharged," and sent it on to the War Department.[10]

It took less than half a month for Charles to receive word that, thanks to Lincoln, he was being honorably discharged. Though he had spent the majority of his service being quite ill, he had done his duty in battle bravely and endured almost all a body could bear. Charles headed to Washington, D.C., to recover in better conditions as well as to deal with his discharge paper-work, ensuring the government would pay all they owed him. Now he could sign the correspondence to his father, "Charles Douglass civilian."[11]

Once again, Lincoln did not follow up on all he had discussed with Douglass. Before, it had been the missing commission; now it was the emancipation plan. The reasons were the events of September 2, when the electric news arrived that General William Sherman had taken Atlanta. That long-delayed victory changed everything. For the Union cause, the prior four months had seemed caught in a morass of despair, but now this significant strategic success suddenly revealed that victory was not only possible, but likely. The loss of the great city of Atlanta in the heart of the South doomed the Confederacy in a way that the loss at Gettysburg had not. Sherman's army had battled from Tennessee through Georgia over more than four months, with Atlanta in their sights. The *Chicago Tribune* read, "The dark days are over. We see our way out . . . The Republic is safe!"[12] For the first time in months, it seemed as if the man in the White House was not leading the country to ruin.

As the tide turned in September, things worsened for Lincoln's political opponents. McClellan released a public letter on September 8 that expressed his belief that he could not look into the eyes of his old troops and tell them their sacrifices to save the Union had been in vain.[13] He felt obligated to re-pudiate the peace platform of his party, which threw the Democrats into dis-array. In the Shenandoah Valley, General Philip Sheridan burned a path of victory against Jubal Early, eliminating the Confederate threat to the capital. Another perception of the war had shifted dramatically. It was not certain that Lincoln would carry the election, but the political and military terrain had changed—making the radical and dangerous plan to reach deep into Southern lines no longer necessary.

Though the plan Douglass and Lincoln had formulated was looking less likely, many around the country were learning of Douglass's visits to the White House. Democrats were eager to use this as ammunition against Lincoln. In 1858, Stephen Douglas had used an imagined relationship between Lincoln and Frederick Douglass to bait the voters. Six years later, an actual relationship was an inviting target, and Democrats used it for racial demagoguery. One campaign pamphlet issued by the party reprinted Douglass's quote, ". . . the President of the United States received a black man at the White House just as one gentleman received another." Democrats used the visit to the White House by a figure as reviled as Frederick Douglass as appalling proof that Abraham

Lincoln was too radical for the American people, and worse, that this war was being carried on for abolition purposes Americans would not endorse.[14]

However, Douglass's relationship with the president was a source of pride in the black community, some of whom saw the Democrats' ire over this connection as somewhere between distressing and amusing. James Rapier, a black army surgeon, wrote sarcastically to a friend, "Did you ever see such nonsense!" Mocking racists, he continued, "The President of the United States sending for a 'Nigger' to confer with him on the state of the country!"[15]

Because Democrats were so eager to exploit these types of racist reactions to Douglass's presence, Douglass found that he could not play the type of public role in the Republican campaign he might have wished, because Republican candidates did not want to be labeled as the Negro party. He bitterly described it as being like a child "put out of the room when company comes." He wanted to speak on this injustice but, not wanting to hurt a party whose victory was necessary for the possibility of emancipation, decided it would be best to do so after the election.[16]

Douglass was shocked to discover that William Lloyd Garrison, his bitter former mentor, ran a letter in the *Liberator* that Douglass had written in haste to an English friend earlier in the year, when his frustration with Lincoln had been at its highest and before their White House meeting. The unfortunate publication revealed his wish that a more fervent antislavery candidate might replace Lincoln. When Douglass wrote it, he was supporting John Frémont, who had now dropped out of the presidential race, and the Democratic party had not yet nominated George McClellan.

After the unauthorized publication of his letter, Douglass wrote to Garrison and said he did not deny having wanted a man with "a firmer faith in the immediate necessity and practicability of justice and equality for all men, than have been exhibited in the policy of the present administration." He added that he made no secret that, "I, like many other radical men, freely criticized, in private and public, the actions and utterances of Mr. Lincoln, and withheld from him my support." Things were different now, and the choice was clear to Douglass between Lincoln and McClellan. Now, "all hesitation ought to cease and every man who wishes well to the slave and to the country should at once rally with all the warmth and earnestness of his nature to the support of Abraham Lincoln." Douglass believed that the platform the Democrats had set out would be the "heaviest calamity of all these wards of war and blood" because it would "sacrifice and wantonly cast off everything valuable purchased so deeply with the precious blood of our brave sons."[17]

Douglass, like many other black leaders, fervently believed that the issues most central to the black community needed to be injected into the presidential campaign and heeded by the American public—and that the Republicans' determined silence on slavery and voting rights had to end.

Sixteen South Carolinians, four of whom were black, had shown up at the Republican convention in Baltimore. One was the renowned hero Robert Smalls. Born a slave in South Carolina, Smalls had been working on a 147-foot vessel in Charleston. When the white crew went ashore to sleep for the night, Smalls and a small group of allies took over and set sail for freedom, picking up his family and a number of other enslaved people along with way. By both escaping slavery and robbing the Confederacy of a gunboat, he warranted praise from black and white northerners alike at a crucial time, when men like Douglass were asserting that black men did have the courage to fight in the war.

Yet Smalls's remarkable exploit was not enough to earn official recognition from the Republican convention. The party's platform did endorse the immediate end to slavery by a constitutional amendment as well as the protection of black soldiers; but while the anti-Lincoln radicals gathering in Cleveland had approved of measures offering political equality to black citizens, the Republicans meeting in Baltimore rebuffed the measures and Robert Smalls. The Republicans were making it clear that they would not risk losing this election for any reason.

The National Convention of Colored Men in Syracuse demanded that the rest of the country hear them during this election. The call went out from the Reverend Henry Highland Garnet, a longtime black leader who had lost a leg to a circulatory problem as a young man, but had not let that dull his zealous work for equality. Like Douglass, he was born a slave in the countryside of eastern Maryland. When Garnet was nine, his father, Joseph—a proud man who taught Henry that he was descended from the chiefs of western Africa—packed up the family for a relative's funeral, but that was not their real destination. Through the woods and swamps, they headed on a long, perilous trip to freedom in New York City, the same place that Douglass's journey ended twelve years later.[18]

Garnet advocated a radical form of black nationalism, and he often found himself clashing with the more charismatic Douglass on a variety of issues, particularly Garnet's support of voluntary colonization projects in Africa and the Caribbean. Their rift was also personal, as Garnet saw Douglass as an opportunistic and vacillating leader, while Douglass saw Garnet as arrogant and wrong for the future of their people. They often battled for leadership at black abolitionist conventions.

Henry Highland Garnet, circa 1881. Photograph by James U. Stead.

Garnet was then serving Washington's Fifteenth Street Presbyterian Church. He had come close to powerful men but was reminded of Douglass's ascendancy: The minister repeatedly called on Lincoln but had never been invited in. Garnet told fellow emigration sympathizer Martin R. Delany that because black people who had tried to get into the White House were "expecting something and coming away dissatisfied," so the president had resolved to "receive no more black visitors."[19]

The National Convention of Colored Men convened at seven P.M. on October 4 in the Wesleyan Methodist Church. There had been national conventions of black leaders in the antebellum period but none in nine years. About 150 men attended, from eighteen states, including slaveholding states such as Mississippi and North Carolina. Some of these men had fought in the war, some had been enslaved, and many had led free black communities in activism for years. To Garnet's dismay, the convention elected Douglass its president, offering another reminder of his preeminence. That night, as Garnet was walking alone through the streets of Syracuse, a group of Irish-Americans leaving a tavern noticed the disabled black man and knocked him to the ground. They took his silver-plated cane and degraded this dignified man by forcing him to crawl through mud.[20]

The convention continued the next day in Wieting Hall. When word of Garnet's ordeal filtered through the hall, a collection was raised for him to re-place the cane. Rivalries aside, to have one of their own humiliated like this, especially during a conference at which they were asserting full citizenship, was horrifying. It made their business at hand more pressing.

On the platform was the flag of the First Louisiana Native Guards, who had so bravely proved the merit of black soldiers at Port Hudson and else-where. This battle flag was a deliberate reminder of the sacrifices that had been made so that the demands the speakers asked for would be heeded. Douglass spoke again on the second night. He discussed the recent disturbing speech by Secretary of State William Seward in Auburn, New York, in which Seward mentioned the possibility that if the war were to end in the autumn (which the fall of Atlanta in September had made possible), the issue of eman-cipation would end up in the courts. Everyone knew that was not a prospect to be accepted. They needed a constitutional amendment to end slavery forever. It was clear that the Emancipation Proclamation was not enough.

Equal rights through the elective franchise were now firmly on the black agenda. Douglass's address forcefully made this argument, asking, "Are we good enough to use bullets, and not good enough to use ballots?" Delegates thought the speech so effectively conveyed their case that they ordered ten thousand copies printed. After more speakers, the night ended with the singing of "Battle Cry of Freedom."[21]

Over the course of the next two days, they passed resolutions that were to be sent to the president and Congress affirming their patriotism; thanking them for the gains of the past four years; appealing for equal rights, equal treatment of their soldiers in pay, labor, and promotion; requesting the cre-ation of opportunities and safety for freedmen; and protesting any regenera-tion of the Union with slavery. John Rock, a remarkable Bostonian who was both a doctor and a lawyer, articulated the feeling of the men in the hall when he proclaimed, "We ask the same for the black man that is asked for the white man; nothing more, and nothing less."

As for the choice in the election, that was clear. There was Lincoln's party "for Freedom and the Republic; and the other, by McClellan, is for Despotism and Slavery . . . The fate of this Republic will be settled in this contest." Some radical abolitionists never came around to supporting Lincoln because of his reconstruction plans, but the black leaders of this convention did not share this opinion. They were lending their support to Lincoln while making their demands of him unambiguous. Douglass was at the helm of a landmark moment in the formulation and advancement of a black political agenda in a presidential election.[22]

Some black soldiers experienced the same dilemma and ultimate conclusion when it came to the election of Lincoln. Charles W. Singer, stationed in Louisville at the time, wrote, "though we abhor him when we consider the many injustices he has allowed to be practiced on colored men, we cannot but think him a better object than George B. McClellan." Singer referenced discrimination against his comrades in arms, Lincoln's proposal for compensated emancipation in the border states, and colonization as matters that gave him pause, yet these did not outweigh his belief that no man on the continent other than McClellan was "more desirous of seeing the South achieve her independence with human slavery."[23]

When Election Day came, Douglass felt he had "certainly exerted myself to the uttermost in my small way to secure his reelection . . . by speeches, letters, or other electioneering appliances."[24] He had been confident since mid-October, after Sherman's and Sheridan's military successes had remade the political equation, that Lincoln would win. Even if Grant was still mired in a great siege outside of Petersburg, the Union would now press on to victory, which meant he had no reason to press Lincoln further on their plan. Once that siege was lifted (something Grant had demonstrated he could do at Vicksburg), then the vastly superior federal troops could smash on to Richmond to seek the final destruction of Robert E. Lee's army.

All over the country, the majority of black men who could vote, and many who could not, supported Lincoln. Though the nation had yet to bestow suffrage on the black community of Nashville, they held their own election in a protest. It would not affect the official tally but it did reveal the depth of support for Lincoln: He finished with 3,193 votes, while McClellan garnered only one.[25]

It was a glum, rainy day in Washington as the future of the country was decided at polling stations around the country. The White House was quieter than usual, with cabinet members attending to election duties elsewhere and Stanton sick with chills. Journalist Noah Brooks quoted Lincoln as saying, "I am just enough of a politician to know that there was not much doubt about the result of the Baltimore Convention, but about this thing I am far from being certain; I wish I were certain." At seven o'clock, Lincoln went to the War Department to begin receiving telegraphs communicating the results around the country, though it would take another two hours before anything meaningful came into his hands. Positive word came from Maryland, Massachusetts, then Pennsylvania, usually a decisive indicator. But a long wait drew out more suspense before the rest of New England, Ohio, Indiana, Michigan, and Wisconsin came in. Thankfully for Lincoln, Illinois was still faithful. It was clear to Lincoln by midnight that the country had decided it had not given up on him, or on the hope that the country would find deliverance from this violent tempest. Lincoln was subdued when he received the final tally, too worn to be anything but relieved and comforted.[26]

The institution of slavery in Maryland had come to an end when a revision of the state constitution was ratified on November 1, 1864. Less than a week before the election, a group of black people left their triumphant church service and descended on the White House to pay tribute to this momentous occurrence. Following a torchlight parade and band music, the crowd arrived outside the building and cheered for the president, who eventually appeared. Lincoln called out, "I have to guess, my friends, the object of this call, which has taken me quite by surprise this evening."

A leader of the gathering answered, "The emancipation of Maryland."

Lincoln told the jubilant crowd, "It is no secret that I have wished, and still do wish, mankind everywhere to be free." The crowd applauded, as Lincoln speculated that it would be as much of a good for his race as for theirs. He desired that all would now move forward; "Who have been emancipated, will use this great boon which has been given you to improve yourselves, both morally and intellectually; and now, good night." Lincoln retreated back into White House to shouts of approval.[27]

It took Douglass only sixteen days after the Maryland emancipation to return to Baltimore for the first time since he had left as a fugitive.

From roughly age eight to thirteen—when his owner sent him back to the fields of the Eastern Shore for the worst years of his life—and then from sixteen to eighteen, Douglass had lived in the labyrinth of cobblestone streets known as Fells Point. It had not been part of the original Baltimore Town and that separateness, a world unto itself, remained in Douglass's memory. Its essence was the water—every inch of the place smelled of it. The land hooked into the harbor, the streets fed into the shipyards, and upbringings led to sailing, caulking, fitting, chandlery, or carpentry on the ships. He had learned to write by copying the names of the ships docked there. Douglass's owners, the Aulds, lived on a road where brick row homes and one-and-a-half-story frame houses stood in a line. But that was only half of Fells Point. The poorer folks lived in the alley houses that packed an elaborate web of dirty back streets, with one water pump for several struggling families.

Walking through the Baltimore streets, Douglass was filled with nostalgia.

Despite the pain of his childhood, he had never stopped loving Maryland, and he was always searching to reconnect to or redeem the past. He spoke six times over the next two weeks in Baltimore, but there was one place where he fit in perfectly. Radicalism was part of the fiber of the Bethel AME Church, and their first minister, Daniel Coker, had been born to a white indentured servant mother and slave father in 1780. He had escaped to New York, but after converting to Methodism, had returned to his home state. Coker led a group to form the first independent black congregation and became one of the first African-American antislavery writers with his book, *A Dialogue between a Virginian and an African Minister*. Bethel's influence and popularity grew in the antebellum period. The congregation's action on slavery was aggressive and their worship style was unrepentantly lively.

Bethel had played a huge role in Douglass's life. His relationship with organized religion become thornier as his life went on, but his early years formed his understanding of black Christianity. Douglass also was reunited with the now elderly Charles Lawson, who had told the strikingly gifted boy he was destined to do great work for the Lord.[28]

Within the church, Douglass now found congregants packing the room with many guests in the pews, including some white Marylanders, in anticipation of his return. A distinguished-looking Douglass walked down the isle of the church hand in hand with his sister, Eliza Bailey Mitchell. Word about the famous orator Frederick Douglass coming to Baltimore had reached all the way to Talbot County, where she heard the good news. She left home and traveled sixty miles in the hope of reconnecting with a brother whose life had taken a radically different course. Douglass had not seen his sister in almost thirty years. Slavery's rules forbid any correspondence, and he had not known if she was even alive. He wrote, "Our meeting can be better imagined than described."[29]

After recovering from the shock and emotion of the reunion, he was gratified to find both vigor and warmth left in the fifty-two-year-old woman who was a maternal figure to the whole community around St. Michaels. Douglass knew how effectively slavery could extinguish a person's spirit. That had not happened to Eliza. She was illiterate but had managed to follow his ascending career, naming a daughter, Mary Douglass Mitchell, after him in 1856. Before the recent emancipation, she had been free because earlier her owner Thomas Auld had agreed to sell her and her two children to her husband, Peter Mitchell, for one hundred dollars. This had been a costly manumission in sweat and toil, since she did domestic work for five dollars a month and Mitchell was a field hand, making less than fifteen. They were also raising nine children. But in time, enough had been saved. After emancipation, their children worked in the same menial careers, the sons doing farm labor and the daughters serving households.

This was better news than what had become of Douglass and Eliza's own generation. The siblings talked of family members Douglass remembered, though this was a painful exercise. Story after story ended with a sale into a Deep South slave state, at which point Eliza's knowledge of a loved one ceased. Their family had been thoroughly scattered in a way no one could ever reconstruct.[30]

The choir sang "Home, Sweet Home!" as the brother and sister stepped forward together. There was magnificent, lengthy, and affecting applause as Douglass reached the dais and surveyed this remarkable scene. Behind him was a "Welcome Home" sign. He was overwhelmed, confessing, "I could not anticipate the extent and depth of this welcome." He reminisced about those who had been at this church more than thirty years before. Many were deceased but they were very alive in Douglass's memory. He saw familiar faces all over the audience and rejoiced not just that they were meeting again, but "especially that we are permitted to meet here on the soil of our birth," for it was a land he loved and wished he had never had to leave. Two days above all others marked a lifetime for him: the day he left Maryland and the day he returned. "No speaker, I think, ever appeared before a public assembly, in circumstances more unusual and striking than I do this evening."

Though there was plenty to say, he did not talk just about the past. The Maryland constitution now ended slavery, but he pressed his audience to ensure there would now be equal rights. Those against it were seeing black people as threats to white people, but Douglass framed this argument as disparaging the ability of white people. He thought that they were fully capable of succeeding while others had full rights, explaining, "I would defend you from yourselves." In his opinion, "The more men you make free, the more freedom is strengthened, and the more men you give an interest in the welfare and safety of the State, the greater is the security of the State." Unfortunately, the vote would not come to Maryland blacks until the Fifteenth Amendment.[31]

He exhorted the crowd to save, to buy land, and to create strong schools for their children. "You have now the opportunity, and I trust you will improve it." Douglass for nearly three hours invested his address with more emotion than any he had ever given.[32]

He made speeches at two more Baltimore churches, then at three additional events, before returning to Washington for an oration at the Israel Baptist Church. There he found a message from President Lincoln, inviting him to come to the Soldiers' Home to take tea with him that night.

Douglass was in a bind. It was not every day the president requested one's company, and he understood the power of having access to that man's ear. With Reconstruction looming, there were many more battles to wage, either as allies or contestants. More than that, his later writings about Lincoln make clear that however frustrated this president made him politically, Douglass did feel a personal connection to him and would have enjoyed having tea with him. On the other hand, Douglass respected his audiences and chose never to break a speaking engagement, not wanting to disappoint people desiring to hear him.

The president's invitation was an honor and Douglass gave it considerable thought that afternoon before deciding not to go. His relationship with Lincoln was growing, and Douglass concluded there would be ample time for more conversations in the coming years.

1865

CHAPTER 15

Sacred Efforts

D ouglass needed this war to end. Emotionally and physically, his last reserves of energy were close to being exhausted. The constant traveling from place to place began to wear on his iron constitution. He lagged in responding to letters of old friends, obsessed with only his work. Mary Carpenter in England still wrote to him "in the hope of extracting a reply from you." Looking about him, he could see that most of the long-standing antislavery orators were no longer on the road.[1]

After all the years of travel, he dreamed of a quiet, bucolic farm, where he would set down roots and stay. His fatigue in the latter part of the war was such that when he spoke of the future, he believed he wanted no part of a public life in its aftermath.

However tired his body felt, Douglass knew that this was no time to let up if the abolition war was to result in an abolition peace. In the North, everyone could feel that the war was about to end. In the South, that chilling realization was about to descend upon a hard-pressed populace. For any Confederate who imagined the war could still be won, William Sherman's relentless March to the Sea and capture of Savannah on Christmas put a resounding end to the argument. As Sherman turned his army northward to link up with the stalemated Army of the Potomac outside of Petersburg, the end would not be long in coming.

So Douglass pressed on, spreading this hope in the early part of 1865 from Troy to Albany, New York; Salem to Worcester, Massachusetts; Philadelphia, Pennsylvania; Wilmington, Delaware; and Hoboken, New Jersey (which he used often as a place of winter rest at Ottilie Assing's home) along the way. When he spoke again at the Cooper Union Institute to around two thousand people, a quarter of them black, he told them of his recent emotional return to Maryland. It had taken nearly four years of war for Maryland, although yoked to the Union as it had been, to finally outlaw slavery. He wanted to share what that return had meant to him personally and in relation to all that this war was about.

His return had been sentimental, but he realized it represented changes that were also historic and world-changing. The Boston address, given when the brutal northeastern weather seemed to miraculously give way to a beautiful night, was entitled, "What the Black Man Wants." Men like Wendell Phillips and William Lloyd Garrison were at the time debating whether their old antislavery organizations should be disbanded at the end of the war or should press on for civil rights. Garrison, who had mostly supported the president during the war, believed his life's work was over when the war was over. Douglass sided with Phillips on the issue of advocating for full suffrage, telling the crowd, "if Abolitionists fail to press it now, we may not see, for centuries to come, the same disposition that exists at this moment." In a time that could have been celebratory, Douglass never underestimated the risks at hand.[2]

Douglass asked, "Shall we be citizens in war, and aliens in peace? Would that be just?"[3] He was acting as a conscience to his nation, refusing to let them forget what black people had achieved. Like Garrison, he was nearly at the end of his mission to kill slavery. He was beginning to sense that slavery would not completely die if the war's conclusion meant that blacks could not vote, serve on a jury, hold political office, or in any sense be a full citizen.

People could be free and yet not equal.

Douglass's mission now included a vision of a nation healed—not just the wounds of North and South, but a new reality of citizens truly part of one nation. This was the only end to the war that could possibly justify the horrific deaths so many had suffered. All had paid the heavy price of the Founding Fathers' failure to end slavery when they could have, before the South began to fully, and fatally, identify its essence with a flawed system of enforced labor.

While Douglass's speaking schedule kept him moving, it was an exciting time in Washington, and his son Charles was taking it all in. He was working in a Freedman's Hospital, as Washington had huge encampments of black people fleeing the South and waiting for the opportunities that were supposed to come with freedom. Charles had not been born in bondage, but he too saw more hope for the days ahead than he had ever felt before. He was thinking about going South with a friend interested in the cotton business around Savannah or Nashville. He was sensitive to being reliant on his wealthy father, proclaiming, "I will not return home a beggar," but the sentiment was as much about the optimism he and many other black people felt with the war drawing to a close. The dreams Douglass had for the America his children would live in must have felt near when Charles wrote to him, "I can see that a black man can be something now . . . all he has to do is make a start."[4]

But with the war not yet over, Charles was still pursuing justice for the black soldier. He and Lewis, along with eight other men, had written a petition asking the government to create black regiments with exclusively black officers. He was frustrated by Lewis's lack of responses to his letters, grumbling to his father, "I never do any of the boys that way." Lewis was now back home in Rochester where Anna and Rosetta could take care of him and the baby Annie. Rosetta reported, "He still has his sick times though not as violent as in the early part of winter." She anxiously hoped he would go back to his regiment in South Carolina, which he said he was willing to do. Even without his brother's affirmation by mail, Charles wished to move this project forward. He and his colleagues had obtained signatures from senators, congressmen, generals, men such as Sumner, Greeley, James Garfield, Nathaniel Banks, and, of course, his father. Charles hoped to follow his father's example by meeting with President Lincoln to present the document, though there is no evidence that he succeeded.[5]

The efforts of Douglass and so many others had not been in vain. Policies regarding black men in the military were finally improving. In June of 1864 President Lincoln had asked Attorney General Edward Bates his opinion on what the government legally owed these men in terms of equal payment. That same summer, a House and Senate conference had hammered out language that assured equal payment for black soldiers who had been free men at the start of the war. Senators such as Sumner were indignant that while it was fully retroactive for those who were free at the start of the war, it would only compensate back to the start of 1864 for those who had fled slavery for a Union uniform. Nonetheless, men in the field found a clever solution in the "Quaker oath."[6]

When asked to swear if they had been free on April 19, 1861, they appealed to a law higher than the government. Those who had been enslaved were asked, "You do solemnly swear that you owed no man unrequited labor on or before the 19th day of April, 1861. So help you God." Former slaves felt justified in simply testifying that they were never anyone else's property, which in their heart, they knew they never were. As men in Lewis's old 54th Massachusetts Regiment stepped out of the paymaster's office with the desperately needed money so long denied to them, they shouted in the air and sang joyous songs.[7]

These important changes were represented by the experience of Martin Delany, a doctor and writer (and briefly, assistant editor of Douglass's *North Star*), who had become one of the most prominent black leaders in the country. A strong advocate of black emigration from America, he and Douglass had both collaborated and clashed in the years before the war. Delany met with Lincoln in early February to propose that a group of black men should go into the South to proclaim emancipation and to arm the former slaves, enlarging this black army with black officers. Ironically, Delany's account of the meeting presents Lincoln as never having heard of such an idea when, in fact, he himself had proposed a strikingly similar one to Douglass.[8]

If some of the details of the meeting, which Delany described to a biographer three years later, may be puzzling, the essence of the meeting corroborates Lincoln's support of the kind of plan he discussed with Douglass. It also shows that Douglass had opened the door of Lincoln's office for other black leaders. Perhaps Delany's open interest in emigration made him a voice in the black community that the Lincoln administration was open to cultivating. He was appointed an officer in the Union army, but by the time he was in the field and actively putting together his regiment, the war had ended.

Change was definitely in the air in Washington. Most notable was the intense lobbying to fulfill the Baltimore convention's stated goal of a Thirteenth Amendment that would finally and completely eradicate slavery. This effort to sway Congress was drawing the newly reelected president's full attention and effort.[9] The amendment had already passed the Senate easily the previous spring, but the two-thirds majority needed in the House was going to be a challenge. This effort was in line with other evidence of profound growth in Lincoln's views on race as the war neared closure. He signed bills allowing black people to testify in federal courts, to end discrimination in the capital's streetcars, and to raise the pay of black troops, finally settling an issue that had first brought Douglass to his office. When General Sherman issued Special Field Order Number 15, giving freedmen "possessory" rights to forty acres for each family inland stretching from Charleston to Jacksonville, Lincoln did not raise a finger to undo this radical redistribution of land.[10]

On January 31, the House would try to make this the day to approve the amendment. In the gallery was Ottilie Assing, who described the scene:

"From the very start, the visitor galleries are filled, and unusual excitement and tension are in the air." Last-minute converts to the effort and those still holding out for the amendment's defeat gave speeches that Assing found agonizingly boring. Men had been debating slavery in this room for years and she thought the time for this had now passed. Yet, for three long hours, it continued. Assing watched senators enter the hall, along with Supreme Court justices, government officials, and free blacks, who, of course, had the most invested in what was about to happen. The press of prominent citizens pushing their way in and journalists fiercely defending seats they were in danger of losing gave the occasion an unusual intensity.

There was a movement on the floor to table the measure, but Republicans blocked the attempt. Democrats tried to move the vote to the next day, hoping to buy time, to no avail. Finally, Speaker Schuyler Colfax called the vote, reading, "Neither slavery nor involuntary servitude, except as punishment for crime whereof the party shall have been duly convicted, shall exist within the United States, or any place subject to their jurisdiction."

The House clerk called the roll, name by name. For Democrats with the courage to vote in favor of passage, a special applause went up from the crowd. Then, above the anxious silence, Colfax announced the amendment had passed 119 to 56. With the three-fourths approval in the states not in doubt, the meaning of the moment was unmistakable. Thunderous applause erupted. The elated room was full of clapping, hugging, handkerchiefs waving, crying, and shouting.[11]

From outside came the sound of a hundred cannons. Charles Douglass heard these batteries giving their endorsement of what had occurred, echoes of the battles that had been fought to make this day even conceivable. The animated reactions of white people wholeheartedly in support of the amendment shocked Charles. Writing to the father he wished was there to share the moment, he saw "such rejoicing I never before witnessed." He thought, "if they will only give us the elective franchise and shoulder straps which is only simple justice, that will be all I ask."[12]

At the start of this war, Congress had debated a thirteenth amendment to preserve slavery forever. Four years later, this Thirteenth Amendment could not have been more different. This was the distance the United States had traveled in the crucible of four years of conflict. From England, Rosine Draz wrote in disbelief to Douglass, "your people are free, forever free!"[13]

Douglass was not in Washington for the amendment's passage, but he would not miss Lincoln's second inauguration in March, as it was sure to be a day to remember. The night before Lincoln would be sworn in, Douglass had tea with a man suffering from decidedly mixed feelings. Salmon Chase was the new chief justice of the Supreme Court, but the next morning he would swear in Lincoln to the job he had really wanted.

Chase's life had been one of political triumph (excluding the presidency) and stunning personal tragedy. He had had the excruciating fate to bury three wives and four children along his rise to power. Only his daughter Kate survived. Douglass had known him for years, as Chase had "welcomed me to his home and his table when to do so was a strange thing in Washington, and the fact was by no means an insignificant one."[14]

Chase's creditability in the abolitionist movement began with his life-threatening defense of a Cincinnati antislavery publication. The mob of slavery's advocates he faced down while clinging to the doorway of the printer's building would be the first of many who would not make Chase back down. He defended fugitives in court, advocated civil rights in Ohio, and opposed slavery as a national leader. In the Senate, he and Charles Sumner were the black citizens' eloquent defenders. His consistent and noble stances are often undervalued because he was stiff, slightly pompous, and lacking in the charisma and personal grace of a Lincoln. Chase's greatness and contribution to the success of the war have been obscured by comparison to Lincoln, but Douglass knew well the power of Chase's actions through the years and held him in great respect.

Chase and his daughter Kate had plotted his ascent to the presidency for years, and as Lincoln's secretary of the Treasury, he had never been closer to the seat of power. Though Chase had done a laudable job with the nation's finances, his blatant and easily blunted political ambition finally caused Lincoln to accept his resignation. Chase was not unemployed for long, for Chief Justice Roger Taney passed away on October 12, 1864. New York Republican George Templeton Strong remarked, "The Hon. Old Roger B. Taney has earned the gratitude of his country by dying at last. Better late than never." Pressure from abolitionists immediately descended upon Lincoln to appoint the one man who could be counted on to secure gains to be made on slavery and civil rights in this period. As Lincoln proved many times, personal animus did not distract him from appointing the best person for the job, even if he would rather have "swallowed his buckhorn chair than to have nominated Chase."[15]

Douglass sat in the living room of Chase's three-story red-brick house, on the corner of Sixth and E Streets in downtown Washington. With a devastating mix of intelligence and beauty, Kate was the belle of Washington and thus the object of Mrs. Lincoln's fierce jealousy. Kate's wedding to the wealthy William Sprague—rumored to be motivated by her wish to use his money for her father's political career—had been the social event of the pre-vious year. Chase could not deny the great opportunities in his new role on the court, but this was far less true of a dejected Kate.[16]

Yet, in their evening with Douglass, they did their best to focus on what Chase could do as the most powerful man in America's court system. The highlight of the evening for Douglass was helping Kate place Chase's new robe on his broad shoulders. Douglass wrote, "There was a dignity and grandeur about the Chief Justice which marked him as one born great."[17]

Although the war was drawing to a close, it was not over and there was more death to come. The president weighed this oppressive fact as he prepared his inaugural address, which, to the surprise of many, would be cast in a far from triumphant mode. The war could be won, but after the death of nearly one in ten of the young men who had fought it, *victory* was a hard word to employ.

As the morning broke on Saturday, the threatening clouds burst open. After this terrible war, Noah Brooks wrote that the rain fell from "tearful skies." Special trains dashed down the Baltimore & Ohio tracks, and Willard's Hotel packed people in the hallways to accommodate the thou-sands of visitors for the inaugural. At midmorning, Lincoln began the trip down Pennsylvania Avenue, riding alone with the top of his carriage folded down. Douglass maneuvered to walk as close as he could to Lincoln's car-riage. Every wink or nod between individuals he saw lining the vast avenue sent Douglass's mind spinning through nightmarish assassination scenarios. He felt a visceral sense of dread, a foreboding in his gut.[18]

As the wheels of the president's barouche sank into the thick mud along the way to the outdoor ceremony, police ordered the crowds to stay back. This made it easy for Douglass to keep pace with Lincoln's horses. When they reached the Capitol, Douglass felt the president was safe. However, it was later established, and confirmed by a close inspection of photographs taken of the moment of the inaugural address, that John Wilkes Booth was stand-ing close to Lincoln, on a high balcony above the speaker's stand.

Douglass found a place in front of the east portico. Hard winds whipped through the restless crowd. What many noticed about this inauguration day was the large number of black people in the crowd. Washington residents claimed to have never seen so many in the city before. An English correspon-dent estimated that half the crowd was black.[19]

Lincoln entered the Capitol and attended Vice President Andrew John-son's swearing-in ceremony in the white rotunda. The morning had been an inauspicious start to Johnson's tenure. After consuming three full glasses of whiskey straight while awaiting the ceremony, the Tennessean had taken his official oath in an incoherent ramble before horrified members of the administration in the Senate chamber. Before heading back outside, Lincoln made it clear that under no circumstances should they allow Johnson to address the crowd.[20]

Douglass was close enough to catch Lincoln's eye as the president walked outside to the platform built over the Capitol steps. Lincoln even took a moment to point out the orator to Johnson. As Lincoln pointed to him, Douglass got a glimpse into Johnson's soul he would never forget. The drunken Johnson shot Lincoln an irritated look and gesture. He seemed contemptuous that Lincoln would call his attention to him; Douglass knew well the signals of racial enmity when he saw them. The vice president realized Douglass was gazing right back at him, and Johnson immediately stiffened up into a rigid face of forced affability. The damage was done. Leaning over to a man next to him, Douglass said Johnson "was no friend to my people."[21]

Douglass found the ceremony "quiet, earnest and solemn," though he also noted "a leaden stillness about the crowd." As Lincoln stepped forward and began his address, the sun broke through the clouds. It was a startling phenomenon, flooding the scene with light as the president's distinctive midwestern twang, high pitched and able to reach out surprisingly far above the crowd, began the shortest inaugural address in our history. There was an emotional poignancy to his voice, and its power grew with conviction. Douglass found it firm and yet inconsolably sad. Lincoln's subject was tragic, but his voice would not quite break.[22]

The president was an unusual speaker for the times because he rarely gestured or moved on the platform. He did not move his hands in placing emphasis but held them firmly behind his back, the left holding the right. His feet never moved. On this day, the famously awkward Lincoln seemed possessed of a solemn gravitas.[23]

Lincoln prepared the crowd for a short address, letting them know he would offer neither a forecast for the end of the war, nor congratulatory sentiments over its increasingly evident outcome. He simply hoped that people found the war's progress "satisfactory and encouraging to all," then reminded the crowd of the dire situation that accompanied his first inauguration speech. Lincoln asked his listeners to remember the nation's situation at that time. "Neither party expected for the war the magnitude or the duration which it has already attained," nor that it would end up eradicating slavery.

Lincoln said, "Both read the same Bible and pray to the same God, and each invokes His aid against the other. It may seem strange that any men

Lincoln speaking at the presidential inaugural ceremony, March 4, 1865. (He is standing in the front row on the wooden stage, behind a short white baluster at the center of this photograph.)

should dare to ask a just God's assistance in wringing their bread from the sweat of other men's faces; but let us judge not that we be not judged." On other occasions, Lincoln had conjured harsher words for those defending slavery through their Bibles, but that was not his message this day.

The unavoidable truth was that God could not grant two opposing wishes, yet this did not mean that either one would be fully fulfilled. Lincoln surmised, "The Almighty has His own purposes." The president supposed that "American slavery" had been an offense that God was ready to see destroyed. It was no accidental choice of words, for Lincoln defined slavery throughout the speech and throughout his career as a vast national sin owned by the whole nation, refusing to reprimand the South through moral superiority. He said God "gives to both North and South, this terrible war, as the woe due to those by whom the offence came."

He declared, as he closed a speech that likely lasted no more than seven minutes, that a great price had been paid for the burden of slavery, and now was a time of relief and release from the past:

Fondly do we hope, fervently do we pray, that this mighty scourge of war may speedily pass away. Yet, if God wills that it continue until all the wealth piled by the bond-man's two hundred and fifty years of unrequited toil shall be sunk, and until every drop of blood drawn with the lash shall be paid by another drawn with the sword, as was said three thousand years ago, so still it must be said "the judgments of the Lord are true and righteous altogether."

With malice toward none; with charity for all; with firmness in the right, as God gives us to see the right, let us strive on to finish the work we are in; to bind up the nation's wounds; to care for him who shall have borne the battle, and for his widow, and his orphan—to do all which may achieve and cherish a first, and a lasting peace, among ourselves, and with all nations.

As he listened, Douglass was overwhelmed. Even in his highest expectations, he had not imagined Lincoln's speech having this kind of power. As he remembered, "such a sentence I never heard from the lips of any man in his position before." He thought the authority of these words "rang out over that throng" more like a sermon and less like a state paper. Hardly a hero-worshiper, especially of Lincoln, Douglass immediately recognized an element of the ancient prophet in the man in front of him.[24]

The second inaugural speech, in its essence, was a melding of Lincoln's and Douglass's visions of the Civil War, which had been so long so divergent. Douglass's impact was evident. Still, like so many others who had strived to influence Lincoln, Douglass had been more witness than persuader. The greatest influence by far had been the powerful flood of events washing over them all; as Douglass had said of this war, there were "mighty currents" shifting everything in its path, no single person or voice. Lincoln was an intensely private and inner-directed man, and those who knew him best had long concluded that no one really swayed him—though his reading of his people's mood could do the trick. Yet, this speech did not materialize from a void; it was a realization and culmination of themes that had been emerging in Lincoln's mind for months, even years. Here was their final eloquent expression, and its commonalities with Douglass's messages are unmistakable.

One need only go back to the October 1861 issue of the *Douglass Monthly* to find the concept of national sin that was at the core of Lincoln's speech. At the time, Lincoln was fighting to keep slavery out of the war, but Douglass said the Americans were failing "to recognize the great and all-comprehensive National Sin to which the calamities deplored owe their existence." Douglass also quoted scripture, "Be not deceived. Whatsoever a man soweth, that shall he reap."[25]

Lincoln's speech confronted a question that had long tormented him: Was there meaning in the taking of so many lives? Douglass had wrestled with the same question, asking, "Why does the cold and greedy earth now drink up the warm red blood of our patriot sons, brothers, husbands and fathers—carrying sorrow and agony into every household?" The path to the nation's healing was captured in the president's closing entreaty to the people: "With malice toward none; with charity for all; with firmness in the right, as God gives us to see the right, let us strive on to finish the work we are in; to bind up the nation's wounds . . ."[26]

The inauguration reception was fully open to the public and Douglass resolved that he would be there that evening. To his knowledge, no black person had ever presented himself at such an occasion other than as a servant or waiter. Douglass did not realize that four black men had attended the president's annual New Year's Day reception three months before. He believed that a black man congratulating the president seemed a modest and appropriate thing to do; yet he also knew that in reality, it might not be a light matter "to break in upon the established usage of the country, and run the risk of being repulsed."[27]

Among black friends Douglass saw after the ceremony, he floated the idea of them joining him at the reception. All were wholeheartedly in favor of Douglass going and breaking this barrier, though they declined to do so. Douglass thought back to days when he had risked his life to desegregate Massachusetts trains, sitting in and absorbing beatings until he was thrown off the train. Other men had praised the undertaking, leaving it to Douglass to carry it out. Someone had to lead. He decided it was his right to see President Lincoln during this illustrious event.

Standing in the vast line, Douglass took in the elite nature of the individuals surrounding him. Douglass felt "a man among men," but harsh reality intruded as the line moved forward, and Douglass reached the door. Two brawny policemen guarding the White House entrance forcibly grabbed his arms and told him to stand back, pushing him hard in that direction. They were to admit no person of color, an order they appeared enthusiastic to obey.[28]

Douglass had come this far and did not intend to turn back. Ignoring the embarrassment of being singled out in front of so many distinguished people, Douglass told the guards that there must have been some mistake, for "no such order could have emanated from President Lincoln." Douglass boldly predicted, "If he knew I was at the door he would desire my admission."

The officers were now uncomfortable, expecting this issue to have been easily settled instead of resulting in a loud dispute with an indignant black man. Furthermore, Douglass was obstructing the doorway. One security man then spoke in a more polite tone, telling Douglass that a third officer would conduct him in. A satisfied Douglass followed the red-faced, burly man into the White House as he called back to him, "Oh, yes; come this way!" It did not take Douglass long to realize there was something wrong about the path they were taking. The guide was escorting him to a makeshift plank headed into an outside window, a temporary passageway for the White House's extra visitors that evening. Douglass had been led in to be led right out.[29]

More enraged than ever, Douglass cried, "You have deceived me. I shall not go out of this building till I see President Lincoln." Suddenly, a gentleman moving through the corridor recognized Douglass. Douglass called to him, "Be so kind as to say to Mr. Lincoln that Frederick Douglass is detained by officers at the door." This man rushed in to Lincoln.[30]

Less than a minute later, Douglass walked into the East Room and beheld a "bewildering sea of beauty and elegance . . . such as my poor eyes had never before seen in any one room at home or abroad." It was a scene of jewelry, gold, silks, and elegance. He later learned that no such order to keep out black people had ever come from Lincoln's White House. The officers were just acting on old customs. But it was no matter to Douglass now, as cabinet members and generals in their finest uniforms mingled while the Marine band played patriotic numbers. Douglass browsed through this immense crowd of guests and saw Lincoln standing with "grand simplicity, and *home-like beauty*." Douglass thought he looked like a mountain pine above them.[31]

He started to move toward the president, but before he was near, Lincoln's eyes caught his, and in a voice loud enough for all near him to hear, Lincoln exclaimed, "Here comes my friend Douglass." Douglass weaved through people to reach the president's side.

Lincoln took his hand and told him, "I am glad to see you. I saw you in the crowd today, listening to my inaugural address; how did you like it?" He had already shaken hands with thousands of well-wishers from eight o'clock on, and Douglass could see a long line of impatient faces craving a minute with their leader, and he was embarrassed.[32]

He responded, "Mr. Lincoln, I must not detain you with my poor opinion, when there are thousands waiting to shake hands with you."

Lincoln replied, "No, no." He added, "You must stop a little, Douglass; there is no man in the country whose opinion I value more than yours." He then asked again of his speech, "I want to know what you think of it?"

Douglass related exactly what he felt: "Mr. Lincoln, that was a sacred effort."

Lincoln's smile was warm, with a sincere sense of affirmation for his efforts. He told Douglass, "I am glad you liked it!"[33]

Tonight the president did not hide his relationship with a man who had once been political poison. He seemed proud to welcome this controversial man into his home, even to call him friend. It took Douglass's boldness to force his way in, and Lincoln's equal courage to proclaim their bond.

Two nights later, Elizabeth Keckley, whose remarkable life had taken her from slavery to being Mrs. Lincoln's dressmaker (and closest friend in Washington), was dressing her employer. She told the first lady of how she ran into the famous Frederick Douglass at a mutual friend's house after he had left the White House. As she described to Mary Lincoln how delighted Douglass appeared after his exchange with Lincoln, the president walked into his wife's room. She immediately asked him, "Father, why was not Mr. Douglass introduced to me?" Mary Lincoln was from a slaveholding family, but her many days and nights with Keckley were a major factor in her emerging sympathy for and interest in black people.

Lincoln replied, "I do not know, I thought he was presented."

This was not an acceptable answer for his sharp and demanding spouse. She retorted, "But he was not."

All Lincoln could say was, "It must have been an oversight then, Mother, I am sorry you did not meet him."[34]

The words of encouragement that Douglass gave to Lincoln regarding his speech would have been comforting to him due to the weight he gave Douglass's views and because others around him clearly failed to grasp the greatness of the speech. Former secretary of war Simon Cameron received a letter from his home state of Pennsylvania that called the address "one of the most awkwardly expressed documents I have ever read."[35]

Lincoln knew what people were saying and that it was not a popular work, at the time. He wrote to Thurlow Weed, "Men are not flattered by being shown that there has been a difference of purpose between the Almighty and them."[36] Even if it cost him humiliation, he believed it a truth that demanded telling.

CHAPTER 16

"It Made Us Kin"

That spring, as a war that stained the land was closing and a country was readying to begin anew, spring rains fell unrelentingly in upstate New York. In Rochester, this precipitation loosened the deep snow banks that remained. The Genesee River was rising near the town, and on the morning of March 17, the waters rushed past the riverbanks, over the dam and through the town. By the afternoon, muddy water was coming through Front, State, and Buffalo Streets, overtaking the business district, coming through the floors and ruining expensive houses downtown. Those wishing to reach the center of Rochester for the next few days did so by rowboat. The debris would take weeks to clear.[1]

While the residents of Douglass's city were trying to put their lives back together, Lincoln and his son Tad stepped ashore in the captured Confederate capital of Richmond after its fall. The first black man to see the president walking the largely deserted streets recognized him from pictures and fell to his knees, crying that the messiah was before him. Lincoln was clearly embarrassed and asked him and others to only praise God, but a crowd delirious with joy was already forming. From the waterfront, Lincoln then walked through the former Confederate capital with a mass of the formerly enslaved that only grew in size and ecstasy. Seeing how the residents responded to Lincoln, one soldier wrote, "To see the colored people, one would think they had all gone crazy."[2]

Black troops proudly had been the first to enter the city and these men patrolled the streets during Lincoln's crowded walk. The adulation of Richmond blacks aside, the city was a hotbed of animosity toward him, and any window could harbor a sniper. Soon Lincoln was safely back on board a Union steamboat and returned to military meetings that were now more about how to deal with the shattered pieces of the Confederacy than how to defeat it.

After Union forces took the Confederate capital, Douglass told a jubilant Boston audience in Faneuil Hall, a crucial site of the first American revolution, "I, for the first time in my life, have the assurance, not only of a country redeemed, of a country regenerated, but of my race free and having a future in this land." There were times when he had been close to giving up hope, casting his eyes toward Haiti for a moment, but he had elected to keep trust in America. The theme of regeneration he had spoken of in future terms, he now discussed in the present tense. He made a special point of noting that it had been black troops who first entered Richmond, and how the cherished vision he had nurtured seemed so close to completion. Douglass closed by saying his people were the Lazarus of the South: "Here came North, clothed in silk and in satin, and shining with gold, and his breast sparkling with diamonds—his table loaded with the good things of this world. And a certain Lazarus sat at his gate, desiring the crumbs that fell from his table." A change had taken place, for much to the rich man's chagrin, Lazarus was up and in Abraham's bosom: "But Father Abraham says, 'If they hear not Grant nor Sherman, neither will they be persuaded though I send Lazarus unto them.'" The crowd roared with laughter and approval. They cheered for Douglass to go on, but he resisted the urge, knowing he ended on a perfect moment.[3]

On April 10, only six days later, even better news reached Rochester. In the evening, word that General Lee had surrendered the Army of Northern Virginia filtered through the city. Most people had turned in for a quiet Sunday night, but Mayor Daniel Moore decided this was cause enough to wake them. At eleven, firefighters sounded City Hall's bell and continued ringing it until two in the morning. Others who owned bells contributed their own chimes of joy, victory, and peace. Residents jumped out of their beds and it was not long until the intersection of Buffalo and State Streets was flooded with celebrating residents. Cheer after cheer went up. People lit rockets that blazed through the sky while their excitement drowned out Mayor Moore's attempts to speak from the steps of Power's Banking Office. Others started bonfires in the street and a cannon was hauled out for a more powerful blast. Only daylight dawning broke up the relieved celebration.[4]

The next night, another happy throng gathered, this time on the lawn of the White House, demanding that the president address them. The president spoke on the process that Louisiana was experiencing to restore proper relations with the federal government. The new state constitution did not give the black man the vote, and Lincoln commented, "I would myself prefer that it were now conferred on the very intelligent, and on those who serve our cause as soldiers." However, he felt, "The question is, 'Will it be wiser to take it as it is, and help to improve it; or to reject, and disperse it?' " He asserted that it was better to readmit a former Confederate state going through chaos with a constitution ending slavery, and then look to their legislature to settle these voting questions. He asked whether black men would attain the vote sooner "by saving the already advanced steps toward it, than by running backward over them?" Lincoln seemed to be taking his usual cautious and moderate path, one that was likely to set him in conflict with the Radical Republicans and Douglass, but this time he said explicitly that he had a faith in progress and the compassion of people of these states. As he concluded, he made it clear that this was not just a speech about Louisiana, but one that would impact what many more states would undergo during the reconstruction of the nation.[5]

Had Douglass been among the assembly hearing Lincoln that night, he would have profoundly disagreed with his approach. There were grounds for another critical and forceful debate developing between Douglass and Lincoln. The warmth of their last encounter would not diminish this likely clash. Still, no American president had ever publicly spoken in favor of any black people having the right to vote.

There were people in the crowd that evening listening to Lincoln who were horrified that the president would voice support for black civil rights under any conditions. One such listener was Confederate sympathizer John Wilkes Booth, who despised the second inaugural address he had also witnessed, and he loathed this one more. Lincoln had said nothing on Inauguration Day of whether the black man would vote. Tonight he had crossed that line. A seething Booth uttered to his cohorts, "Now, by God, I'll put him through. That is the last speech he will ever make."[6]

Three nights later, on April 14, Booth entered the back of the president's viewing box in Ford's Theater and shot him. Lincoln had said just weeks before that God's will would prevail "until every drop of blood drawn with the lash shall be paid by another drawn with the sword." Slumping toward his wife with a bullet through the back of his head, Lincoln too was held under that harsh fate. Under his own conception of the Civil War, Lincoln was one more casualty.

Douglass was in a daze.

He wandered into Rochester's City Hall and sat alone near the back. After the unthinkable news reached their city, Mayor Moore called a meeting for three in the afternoon. Bells tolled in a very different mood than they had a week before. Hundreds of citizens lined up to stand clamoring for a seat inside the memorial gathering. Douglass was here to mourn with others, to process this devastating shock and find solace in common grief.

From Washington to New York City and beyond to California, businesses closed and adults wept like children. There was a sense of deep pain, not just in America but soon enough on the other side of the ocean. From England, Julia Griffiths Crofts and Rosine Draz dashed off letters to Douglass urging him to be careful, to stay in New York, and not to go anywhere near Washington.[7] Black Americans felt this loss in an exceptionally deep way, as if Lincoln had been a family member or more. One soldier wrote, "God has willed it, that he has taken our beloved father, Abraham Lincoln, from us."[8] Douglass did not view Lincoln's death in these terms. Lincoln was no father figure to him or any kind of savior. He had not known him deeply, but well enough. Lincoln was no abstraction, no symbol. Their disagreements, the excruciating caution Douglass sensed in him, made Lincoln real, a man like any other—except fate had propelled this man from the people to being the pivot about which turned one of the greatest wars in history. Lincoln called Douglass a friend, and whether or not Douglass would use the same word, Lincoln was certainly a man with whom Douglass felt a keen bond of experience. Douglass felt a genuine personal loss as he sat stupefied in the back of the room.

No one volunteered to speak at first. The room was filled with mourners too stunned to muster words. Eventually, two ministers and a prominent judge said their piece; then Douglass's name went up from the assembly. It carried to every side and filled the room until Douglass had no choice but to rise.

Looking out into the anguish in so many faces he knew, Douglass confessed that he had not expected to speak and found this an almost impossible task. "This is not an occasion for speech making, but for silence." But a lifetime of experience drew him on, and he spoke of encountering friends all this day, who took his hands and asked for words, and how he had found himself wordless. All he could relate now was what he was experiencing: "I feel it as a personal as well as national calamity; on account of the race to which I belong and the deep interest which that good man ever took in its elevation."

As so many leaders and ministers were saying across the nation this day, he wondered if there was some underlying meaning to this death and its strange and disorienting timing, coming as the war was ended. He pondered, "It may be in the inscrutable wisdom of Him who controls the destinies of Nations, that this drawing of the Nation's most precious heart's blood was necessary to bring us back to that equilibrium which we must maintain if the Republic was to be permanently redeemed."

Douglass granted them a glance into his heart when he said, "How I have to-day mourned for our noble President, I dare not attempt to tell. It was only a few weeks ago that I shook his brave, honest hand, and looked into his gentle eye and heard his kindly voice uttering those memorable words." Douglass then quoted a long passage of the second inaugural from memory. As Douglass tried to unite the crowd, to translate sorrow into hope, he would once more return to the theme of national regeneration through brutal sacrifice that he had used for the last four years. If there was a lesson here, Douglass believed it to be "that the blood of our beloved martyred President will be the salvation of our country."

Their president had been killed not just by Booth, but by a society still infected with slavery. Redemption, not just reconstruction, meant, "wherever there is a patriot in the North or South, white or black, helping on the good cause, hail him as a citizen, a kinsman, a clansman, a brother beloved!" In this moment, Douglass's plea was "Let us not remember our enemies and disenfranchise our friends." He asked, "For the safety of all, let justice be done to each." As Douglass stepped down, he had gone from struggling for words to making one of his greatest speeches. "I have heard Webster and Clay in their best moments," one witness wrote, "Channing and Beecher in their highest inspirations; I never heard truer eloquence! I never saw profounder impression. When he finished, the meeting was done."[9]

Douglass had made many astonishing speeches, touched the hearts of hundreds of audiences, but he had never felt more connected to one. Through the cheers, the complete reversal of mood in the room, from shock and deep pain to a hopeful determination, he had taken a journey with them. Douglass remembered, "We shared in common a terrible calamity, and this 'touch of nature' made us more than countrymen, it made us 'kin.' "[10]

After the armies had spiked the cannons, staked their arms, and held their last Grand Processions, the Civil War truly ended on December 18, when—despite Delaware, Kentucky, New Jersey, and Mississippi's rejection—twenty-seven states approved the Thirteenth Amendment. The ratification outlawed slavery forever.

America's Stepchildren

A few weeks after the assassination, Mary Lincoln, although prostrate with grief, gathered herself enough to send a few mementos of her husband to several people who had been important to him. She remembered him saying that he wanted to extend to Douglass some token of his regard. A long package arrived in Rochester addressed to Frederick Douglass, and when he opened it, he saw that the widow had sent him Lincoln's "favorite walking staff." Douglass wrote back to her, "this inestimable memento of his Excellency will be retained in my possession while I live—an object of Sacred interest—a token not merely of the kind consideration in which I have reason to know that the President was pleased to hold me personally, but as an indication of this human interest in the welfare of my whole race."[1]

Years later, when Mrs. Lincoln's financial problems worsened, Douglass offered to lecture to raise money for her, but Mrs. Lincoln was too proud to accept this offer. He took genuine concern in her welfare, writing to Mrs. Lincoln's seamstress Elizabeth Keckley in 1867, "I would gladly see Mrs. Lincoln, if this could be done in a quiet way without the reporters getting hold of it, and using it in some way to the prejudice of that already much-abused lady." Mrs. Lincoln wrote back to Keckley that when Douglass was in Chicago, "Tell him, for me, he must call and see me; give him my number." For his efforts to see that she lived a dignified life, Mrs. Lincoln wrote that Douglass would "always have my most grateful thanks."[2]

Abraham Lincoln would often be in the thoughts of Douglass in the remaining thirty-seven years of his life, and in hundreds of speeches, articles, interviews, and one final autobiography. However, Douglass's relationship with Lincoln's successor was problematic. On February 7, 1866, Douglass joined a delegation of black men, including his son Lewis, to greet the new president. As Douglass stepped inside the White House for the fourth time, the building had not changed, just the man occupying it. Less than a year earlier, Douglass had walked into this house to be treated by its resident with esteem and respect. He was about to find out how much had changed in that year.

President Andrew Johnson was a man who took great pride in having risen in society from being a tailor and former Tennessee slaveholder to being part of a Union party ticket with Lincoln, and he now presided over a nation at peace. Andrew Johnson slouched in his chair, waiting for the delegates. He did not seem pleased to be greeting them into his office.[3]

George Downing of Rhode Island spoke first, asking Johnson to see them as friends. Then he appealed for better enforcement of the Thirteenth Amendment, as oppressive Black Codes were cropping up all over the South and new measures were needed to ensure that all could vote.

Douglass spoke next and immediately invoked Lincoln. He reminded Johnson, "Your noble and humane predecessor placed in our hands the sword to assist in saving the Union." Now Johnson had the power to put the ballot in their hands. Douglass declared, "The fact that we are the subjects of the Government and subject to bear the burdens of the State, makes it not improper that we should ask to share in the privileges of this condition."

Johnson began a meandering tirade, speaking of his days as a slaveholder, calling himself a friend to their people because he had never sold a slave, only acquired them. Johnson did little that day to mask his pride at having risen high enough in southern society to be a slaveholder. He told the delegation that he had treated his slaves well before and after emancipation. For this reason, Johnson took as an affront that they would question him on these matters. As he spoke, he moved toward Douglass, standing close to him, laying out each insult. That look of loathing in Johnson's eye that Douglass thought he had seen during the inauguration was now blatant.

The president said he did not like "to be arraigned by some who can get up handsomely-rounded periods and deal in rhetoric, and talk about abstract ideas of liberty, who never periled life, liberty or property. This kind of theoretical, hollow, unpractical friendship amounts to very little." Johnson pronounced that he would not support their efforts toward the voting booth because this would only lead to a race war resulting "in the extermination of one or the other. God forbid that I should be engaged in such a work!" He was pleased that he could call himself a "Moses" to their people, but what he did for them would not be at the expense of the poor whites who resented them.

Johnson accused blacks of being ungrateful for the freedoms the Civil War had brought, especially since it had been poor white southerners who had truly suffered. The president believed that if more was to be given, meaning the ballot, it should come from these new state governments. For him to force anything more would be a catalyst for racial wars of unprecedented bloodshed.

With that, Johnson tried to end the meeting with his visitors by thanking them for their presence, but Douglass would not be bullied out of the White House. He would not leave without some kind of dialogue.

"If you will allow me," Douglass persisted, "I would like to say one or two words in reply." He wanted Johnson to understand "enfranchisement of the blacks as a means of preventing the very thing which your Excellency appears to apprehend—that is a conflict of races."

"I repeat," Johnson curtly spoke, "I merely wanted to indicate my views in reply to your address, and not to enter into any general controversy." Johnson reiterated his belief that "the colored people can live and advance in civilization to better advantage elsewhere than crowded right down there in the South."

Douglass could not let these assertions go unquestioned by a man with such power over their future. He pushed back again, pointing to the former masters writing harsh Black Codes, which when enacted meant "we cannot get away from the plantation."

Johnson feigned ignorance, "What prevents you?"

"We have not the simple right of locomotion through the southern states now."

"Why not?" Johnson claimed the government "furnishes you with every facility."

Douglass tried to convey the present realities of the South, where "his master then decides for him where he shall go, where he shall work, how much he shall work—in fact, he is divested of all political power. He is in the hands of those men."

Johnson conceded nothing and retreated to a familiar idea: "There is this conflict, and hence I suggest emigration. If he cannot get employment in the South, he has it in his power to go where he can get it." After a war in which his own sons had fought to save a nation, Douglass was back to having a president tell a black delegation that they could leave the country.

All Douglass could do was wearily thank Johnson for his time. But before he and his entourage left the room, he issued a subtle challenge, "The President sends us to the people, and we go to the people."

"Yes sir," President Johnson remarked, "I have great faith in the people. I believe they will do what is right."[4]

Once they were gone, Johnson showed that his emotions for Douglass and his people were even rawer. No doubt, Johnson's mind had centered on Douglass, whom he deemed a man who "would sooner cut a white man's throat as not."[5]

Since President Johnson had not been open to their thoughts, the delegation drafted a public document in answer to him, deeming "the views and opinions you expressed . . . entirely unsound and prejudicial to the highest interest of our race as well as to the country at large." They rejected the idea that southern prejudices against black people were grounds to not push for enfranchisement. They advised, "Peace between the races is not to be secured by degrading one race and exalting another; by giving power to one race and withholding it from another; but by maintaining a state of equal justice between all classes." The anger in their letter in reply to Johnson is clear: After having fought a war, they believed that they had earned the right to be citizens.[6]

This ill-fated call to the White House put into perspective the amazing promise of Douglass's three Lincoln visits, as well as capturing the disappointment that Douglass would become greatly familiar with in the years to come. Though the visit with President Johnson was exceptional in its intolerance, subsequent presidents never listened to Douglass in the respectful way that Lincoln had. President Ulysses Grant appointed Douglass secretary of the Santo Domingo Commission, charged with evaluating whether the United States should annex the Dominican Republic. On the ship traveling home, however, Douglass, barred from the dining room, was forced to take his meals in his cabin. Grant knew of this and did nothing. When Grant invited the commission to dine at the White House, Douglass was not allowed to attend.

President Rutherford Hayes effectively ended Reconstruction by removing troops protecting black rights in the South, and he would not hear Douglass's anguished advice. Then President Grover Cleveland asked for Douglass's resignation as Recorder of Deeds of Washington, D.C., in 1886, a symbolic end to a largely symbolic position that finished Douglass's government career. It was a muted culmination to the way that Lincoln's successors took for granted Douglass and the counsel he could have given.[7]

Thus Lincoln, imperfections and all, continued to hold a special place in Douglass's life. A mark of his continued respect for Lincoln was displayed not only in his popular lectures on his relationship with the Civil War president, but in the prominent placement on his parlor wall in his Anacostia home, Cedar Hill, of a portrait of Abraham Lincoln. At times, the Lincoln-Douglass relationship was remembered; as the *Rochester Union and Advertiser* wrote in 1886, "Mr. Douglass held the most intimate and friendly relations with the late President, having been specifically invited to the White House by Mr. Lincoln."[8]

More often, however, this rare and unusual relationship was a bothersome and neglected fact for a nation erasing the reality and memory of black progress in the Civil War and immediately after. The attitude President Johnson demonstrated to Douglass's delegation was indicative of attitudes exhibited by both North and South during Reconstruction, in which old patterns reasserted themselves and the revolutionary aspects of the late war were muted and often reversed. Through new Black Codes, voting restrictions, and the advent of the Ku Klux Klan, black lives were restricted and hemmed in. Slavery was gone, but the old structures found creative and inventive ways to bind the future of black citizens.

Yet, these profound reversals and disappointments did not make the Civil War any less of a transformation in American life. Extraordinary times of hope and change are often followed by countermovements pushing against what has been achieved. These reactions can be strong, as the harsh close of Reconstruction moving into a long Jim Crow era certainly proved. Sometimes a people can almost forget just how much they have accomplished, but not quite and not forever. As much damage as Andrew Johnson did during the crucial months and years after the war, he did not and could not halt all the progress of the Civil War era.

At the end of the war, black troops numbered almost two hundred thousand, roughly a fourth of the entire army, and a tenth of all those who served; thirty-eight thousand black men gave their lives, a mortality rate that was 35 percent higher than white soldiers, an extraordinary number considering that they began to fight only in the latter half of the war.[9]

Even with the considerable setbacks felt by black America with the rise of Jim Crow laws, the war's impact on black America has often been underestimated. Illiteracy among black Americans stood at 90 percent when the war ended, but was down to 70 percent by 1880 and 50 percent by the turn of the century. Half of all blacks did not experience the minimal social changes Douglass had wished for, but it was an undeniable change from a dire situation. Black land-owning in the South went from almost nothing in 1865 to a quarter of all black farmers owning land in 1910. Numerous black men, some of whom were born slaves, served in Congress and the highest state offices in that era, and although these black politicians were largely forgotten within a hundred years, the black men and women who hold political office today carry on their tradition.[10]

What was written into the Constitution after the Civil War would be footing upon which future freedom fighters could stand and proclaim justice. In the immediate aftermath of the war, the Thirteenth Amendment's ratification abolished slavery. Congress approved the Fourteenth Amendment in 1866, which made all people born in the country full citizens and promised that the government would protect their rights equally. Ratified in 1868, though its pledge was often betrayed, the amendment would be tested in the twentieth century and beyond for civil rights advancement. Finally, the Fifteenth Amendment of 1869, ratified in 1870, was a further attempt to ensure citizens would not be barred from voting because of their race.

On April 14, 1876, with a great ceremony attended by all of official Washington, the Freedman's Monument was dedicated as a memorial to the martyred president. For more than a decade, a freed black woman named Charlotte Scott had collected money, starting with her own hard-earned contribution of five dollars. Thousands of black citizens contributed small amounts in order to erect a twelve-foot-high bronze statue of Lincoln.

Near Seventh and K Streets, spectators leaned out of windows and packed the square and streets radiating into it to observe the ceremony. Flags were at half-mast in honor of Lincoln. A procession of mounted police, politicians, black soldiers and bands traveled down Pennsylvania Avenue and along East Capital Street to Lincoln Park. President Ulysses Grant sat on the stand in front of his cabinet, Supreme Court justices, and scores of senators and congressmen. As the president officially unveiled the monument, a loud combination of gasps and claps went up from the crowd.[11]

The famed sculptor Thomas Ball had been commissioned to make a bronze Lincoln standing over a kneeling black man. The man whose picture was used for the black figure, Archer Alexander, had actually escaped slavery in Missouri during the war, bringing vital information to Union lines. Alexander's former owner had pursued him, but Alexander found safety in Alton, Illinois. His son Tom would give his life to the Union cause. Alexander certainly represented the best of the roles his people had assumed during the war.[12]

Only one man had been considered to deliver the dedicatory address. As Frederick Douglass climbed the platform, he looked over a park packed with bands and banners. No black speaker had ever commanded such an audience, and the profound effects of the war could hardly have been better symbolized. The irony is that Douglass had severe misgivings about the Freedman's Monument itself, with its depiction of a serene president clutching the Emancipation Proclamation in one hand and reaching toward a

Freedman's monument (*Emancipation* by Thomas Ball, Lincoln Park, Washington, D.C., 1876)

black slave crouched before him. Douglass hated seeing his people portrayed on their knees.

For Frederick Douglass, the Civil War had been the central event of his life. Douglass had been forty-eight when the war ended. Though the annihilation of slavery had been triumphant, Douglass had felt a strange melancholy concerning what his purpose in the world would be, as abolition had defined his life for as long as he could remember. Douglass wrote, "I felt that I had reached the end of the noblest and best part of my life." He had rejected his dream of bucolic retirement, however, and soon was back on the road. Nothing in his later years would match the impact of this day's speech. It was no surprise that it largely dealt with the enigmatic and inscrutable politician who had so unexpectedly affected his life.

He commenced an hour-long oration upon Lincoln, the man he had long pondered, sometimes praised, often condemned. Douglass first lulled his listeners with a noble setting of the scene, reminding them that this would not have been possible under "The spirit of slavery and barbarism, which still lingers to blight and destroy . . ." He employed his considerable skills as a powerful public speaker to relax the crowd with a sense that Union triumphalism would be praised this day, but then came words that his esteemed audience did not expect.

"It must be admitted, truth compels me to admit, even here in the presence of the monument we have erected to his memory, that Abraham Lincoln was not, in the fullest sense of the word, either our man or our model. In his interests, in his associations, in his habits of thought and in his prejudices, he was a white man." Douglass was now entering uncharted social territory, with the wounds of war so fresh, with the nation's acute need to transform Lincoln into a figure nearly Christ-like in humble saintliness—for had not the president been killed on a Good Friday?

Douglass went on: "He was preeminently the white man's President, entirely devoted to the welfare of white men. He was ready and willing at any time during the first years of his administration to deny, postpone and sacrifice the rights of humanity in the colored people in order to promote the welfare of the white people of this country. In all his education and feeling he was an American of the Americas."

He then stated what was obvious but seldom said about the execution of the Civil War. "The race to which we belong were not the special objects of his affection . . . First, midst, and last, you and yours were the objects of his deepest affection and his most earnest solicitude. You were the children of Abraham Lincoln. We are at best only his step-children; children by adoption, children by force of circumstances and necessity." When it came to the enslaved, Douglass reminded the crowd that Lincoln had been ready to recapture those escaping and put down those rebelling. Lincoln had told them they should leave the country, then discouraged their military service. Douglass told his listeners, "Our faith in him was often taxed and strained to the uttermost, but it never failed."

Douglass was taking the chance to speak his truth, and he dared those in attendance to hear things they did not want to consider. Reconstruction was failing precisely because they would not. Douglass began to talk about the vast historical forces that the president had transformed through his grim determination to save the Union. Lincoln had eventually enrolled near two hundred thousand of them in the armed services and played the essential role in outlawing slavery in the capital and then in every inch of the country. Douglass recounted, "His great mission was to accomplish two things; first, to save his country from dismemberment and ruin, and second, to free his country from the great crime of slavery."

The first was true, but the second was more a reflection of Douglass's initial mission, one that was taken up over time by Lincoln. In the most incisive estimation of Lincoln that Douglass was ever to make, the speaker reminded his audience that at the time of the beginning of the war, abolitionists (including Douglass) had seen him as "tardy, cold, dull, and indifferent," but when Douglass measured him against the rest of the country at the time, Lincoln was "swift, zealous, radical, and determined." Douglass now fully understood what Lincoln had gone through, balancing public opinion and justice.

In the end, Douglass's people had come to love this president, and for a simple reason: "We came to the conclusion that the hour and the man of our redemption had somehow met in the person of Abraham Lincoln."[13]

This vital address was skilled and subtle in what it conveyed. Douglass, in emphasizing Lincoln's racist attitudes, actions, and propensities, did not do so in a tone of accusation, blame, or even regret. In the end, Douglass wanted the crowd to know that Lincoln was, in fact, not different from them; even in his evident greatness, he was one of them, sharing the limited views and blindness born of the nation's burden of race—and yet he had done marvelous acts to move this country forward and to give justice to African-Americans. They could do the same.

Everyone in the crowd knew that Lincoln had invited Douglass to the White House to speak with him. He had not given Douglass all he wanted, or all his people deserved, but he had listened. He even did Douglass the courtesy to disagree, to gently argue, to treat him simply as a man. Douglass told white America that their instinctual prejudices were forgivable if their actions reflected an openness to listen and to grow, as Lincoln had. W. E. B. Du Bois took the same meaning from Lincoln's life that this speech reflects: "I love him not because he was perfect, but because he was not and yet triumphed . . . The world is full of folk whose taste was educated in the gutter. The world is full of people born hating and despising their fellows. To these I love to say: See this man. He was one of you and yet became Abraham Lincoln."[14]

In the meetings of black activists and our presidents, there has more often than not been an edge of conflict and distrust. Theodore Roosevelt invited Booker T. Washington to dinner in the first month of his presidency, though he argued, "As a race and in the mass they are altogether inferior to the whites."[15] When Woodrow Wilson met with William Monroe Trotter in the White House, they fell into a heated forty-five-minute argument in which the Virginian informed the civil rights leader, "Your tone, sir, offends me."[16] John F. Kennedy, who refused to appear in person at the famed March on Washington, met with Martin Luther King Jr. and other black leaders at the White House later in the day, after the speeches at the Lincoln Memorial. He had been reluctant to make a national observance of the anniversary of the emancipation, which may be one reason why King made a special point to use Lincoln's proclamation as a theme in his great speech that day. As usual with Kennedy, he was polite but cool to King; within a week, his brother, Attorney General Robert F. Kennedy, would approve the FBI's secret tapings of the civil rights leader. Yet, this kind of pained dynamic, despite all the hard and harsh words Douglass had poured on Lincoln, had been singularly absent when Douglass decided he should confront the president face-to-face about "complaints of my people."

Across our long racial chasm, Lincoln and Douglass courageously talked. Douglass's Civil War mission was predicated on white and black realizing that they needed each other. Lincoln could not win the Civil War without utilizing the whole country, which meant calling on the bravery of black people, but these men could not fight without Lincoln's approval and his actions curbing discrimination against them. Lincoln and Douglass offered an example that a rebuilding nation could heed.

Indeed, no matter what shortcomings Lincoln possessed as a reformer, Douglass felt that thankfulness toward the president was well earned: he had been "the first American President who . . . rose above the prejudice of his times." Lincoln had shared in much of this prejudice, but had not, in the end, been paralyzed by it. He had entered the war not intending to free the slaves, but he had not stepped away from the challenge or the opportunity when the tide of war demanded it. And he had done so with wisdom and sure political skill. A lesser man in Lincoln's position could never have accomplished the imposing and unlikely task of freeing the slaves in the midst of four years of total war. Certainly, a less skilled and astute politician might have been swamped by the conflicting painful demands of that war, and a headstrong radical would never have survived those whipsaw currents.

He never intended to end slavery—this was something Lincoln stated plainly many times. Still, Lincoln's innate distaste for slavery created an equally clear reality: He never regretted for a moment ending slavery, or having become by circumstance an active agent in its demise. Lincoln never saw any conflict in having been thrust by history into ending an institution he abhorred, even as he was frank in admitting that he had never harbored any intention to be that agent of world-historic change.

A hundred years on, Martin Luther King Jr. stood before Washington's immense memorial to Lincoln and directly referred to the Emancipation Proclamation as a "bad check," a promissory note still not delivered upon.[17] What remains for us is a pervasive racial divide so great that black and white still hesitate to become friends, to live alongside one another, and to educate their children together. The nation's laws have changed, but the heart's willingness to live out a reasonable common life has not shifted much.

We are still enslaved by distrust. The three meetings of Lincoln and Douglass were, admittedly, small moments in the centuries-old unfolding of the trial of race in America. Their relationship, in its complexity and honesty, still offers an example of engagement, argument, and honesty. There is no need to sentimentalize the relationship, to claim they were friends, or to falsely claim that Douglass somehow made Lincoln into "the Great Emancipator."

They met not as friends but as men able to talk. This relationship, exactly in its twists and even its frustrations, ought not be left behind, but remembered, instructive for a divided America today. The greatness of Lincoln is that he did, through patience, skill, and unwavering firmness, accomplish his mission—to save our country from fragmenting. Disunion not only would have left behind in that resulting chaos a legacy of racial brutality, it would have made our nation's experiment in democracy an irrelevance in the world. He saved the nation, and freed nearly four million people as a necessary condition in doing so. In saving the Union, Lincoln preserved the soul of democracy.

Near the end of his life, Douglass said "my special mission in the world . . . was the emancipation and enfranchisement of the Negro. Mine was a great cause."[18] Douglass's greatness lies in accomplishing two of his three great missions—the end of slavery and the arming of his people in the fight for their own emancipation. An even more impressive greatness may be seen in his third mission, which he did not achieve in his lifetime but worked and yearned for—full citizenship and simple equality. He hands on to us, for however long it takes, this last mission. The Civil War, in fact, will not be over until it is accomplished. During the centennial of the Civil War, John F. Kennedy said that the agitator was part of the legend of America. He wrote: "As a successful fighter for freedom a century ago, he [Douglass] can give inspiration to people all around the world who are still struggling to secure their full human rights. That struggle must go on until those rights are everywhere secured. By advancing that cause through law, democratic methods and peaceful action, we in America can give an example of the freedom which Frederick Douglass symbolizes."[19]

Douglass's mission still has not been fully realized. In an 1862 speech, Douglass told the country that Americans cannot escape from each other, as much as we might try. We only damage each other when we succumb to the seduction of believing our destinies are not intertwined, inextricably. We have to acknowledge and engage each other to create equality. It was through excruciating sacrifice that we must learn "lessons of wisdom, power, and goodness," because "Over the bleeding back of the American bondman we shall learn mercy." Douglass summarized his country's situation: "My friends, the destiny of the colored American, however this mighty war shall terminate, is the destiny of America."[20]

Appendix: Aftermath—The Douglass Family

In the optimism at the close of the Civil War and the frustration in years afterward, the Douglass family reflected much of what black America would experience. The war itself was an anxious and dangerous time for them, with two sons laying their lives on the line, but it could also be seen as their most triumphant years, or at least ones they emerged from with hard-won grounds for optimism. Their father had helped achieve a goal once deemed impossible, the boys had done their duty bravely, and they and Rosetta were starting new families.

Times would not always remain this encouraging. Rosetta's choice of a husband would set the stage for so much of her misfortune. Nathan Sprague failed at every pursuit he tried, putting them into such deep debt in Rochester that they were forced to sell beloved belongings. She watched as her piano was dragged away in the pouring rain. With options exhausted in Rochester, they followed Douglass to Washington. One afternoon when Douglass went to Salmon Chase's daughter's house to play croquet, he found his son-in-law working as their stableman. To make matters worse, Nathan would later cheat Kate Chase on a horse. Tragedy would overshadow embarrassment when the Douglass family lost their second Annie to illness, this time Rosetta's dearly loved daughter at age twenty-eight. And it was not until 2003 that a volunteer archivist in Rochester, Jean Czerkas, discovered Rosetta's own long-obscured grave.[1]

As for his sons, Douglass biographers have unduly emphasized their lack of achievement; this may be rooted in unfair comparisons to a truly exceptional man who happened to be their father. Douglass had made incredible advances in society, but few around him could achieve similar triumphs. Lewis, Charles, and Frederick Jr. were attempting to compete in an era when the United States, North and South, was building new and more subtle racial barriers. For instance, Lewis spent time in Rochester trying repeatedly to join the Typographical Union so he could find work in the printing industry but was rejected because of his skin color. Douglass had employed countless young white men to help him print his newspaper but watched a depressed son return home day after day when he was turned away from jobs. Though Lewis, Charles, and Frederick Jr. never received college degrees and often relied financially on their father as they shifted from various pursuits in the years following the war, they all eventually found respectable positions, primarily government related, to sustain them and their families through the rest of their days.

The American social upheaval at the close of the war prompted Lewis to explore the Talbot County region where in childhood his father had been in bondage. Lewis met relatives he might have grown up knowing had slavery not severed these contacts. Though separated by education and life experiences, Lewis was trying to reconstruct a family.

When Douglass's sister Eliza saw Lewis, she recognized him as her nephew immediately. She introduced him around town and to the black community of St. Michaels, and they treated him like royalty. He heard stories of his father's youth, scars he earned, remarkably daring feats that were still legendary in these parts. His letters to Douglass were filled with names of people who wanted to convey their regards to a long-lost friend.

Frederick Bailey had attempted to teach people to read the Bible here, but had nearly been killed by angry white residents who broke up the school. Thirty years later, Lewis revived his father's work in the St. Michaels neighborhood. Some of the men that Douglass had tried to teach, now in their fifties, showed up, hoping to finally learn how to read. Thirty young offspring of the generation Douglass had known learned to read from Lewis.[2]

The Eastern Shore was a microcosm of what was happening around the nation—the human reconnections that were possible but also, sadly, what could go wrong. It remained dangerous territory; as Lewis learned, "The white people will do any thing they can to keep the blacks from buying land." Many of the men earned their money through harvesting oysters, and those who had enough saved to purchase land were thwarted.

Douglass knew quickly what was beginning all over the nation. By December of 1865, Douglass was already feeling that the war had ended too soon—too much of the Confederate spirit had persisted, and was threatening black people in the South.[3] Rosine Draz wrote to him in August, "I understand you when you say you cannot yet rejoice and I clearly see with you that until the colored people get the franchise they cannot be said to be free."

Emancipation Proclamation by F. G. Renesch, Chicago, 1919

Douglass told another friend, "The negro needs justice more than pity." This meant his quest went on; as he expressed it, "My mission, for the present is, to ask for equal citizenship for the negro—in the State: and equal admission into the state schools. Of course till we get this, we shall be a crippled people."[4]

Though Frederick Douglass may have never again captured the rhetorical power of the abolitionist era in his life, he would recover his voice as a much-needed advocate of civil rights. He ended his days as an agitator with speeches on black lynching as strong and stirring as any he had ever given, as if recapturing his old verve and profound anger at his country's wayward ways.

Still, at the end of his long and eventful life, he admitted to friends that to the world he was still nothing more than a witness to servitude: "It is too late now to do much to improve my relation to the public. I shall never get beyond Frederick Douglass the self-educated fugitive slave."[5] Long before W. E. B. Du Bois's searing self-assessment that to live as a black man in America was to exist as a "double soul," as "two souls, two thoughts, two unreconciled strivings; warring ideals in one dark body, whose dogged strength alone keeps it from being torn asunder,"[6] Douglass lived this persona to the hilt—half white and half black, half freed man and half trapped in a representative symbol of the iniquity of slavery, half devoted family man and half free agent in his sexual relationships, half an American and half a man attracted to the ideal of a Pan-Atlantic black world transcending national borders and boundaries.

Douglass would serve as U.S. marshal and later Recorder of Deeds for the District of Columbia, and Minister Resident and Consul General to Haiti. He was president of the Freedman's Savings and Trust Company, though it was in fatal trouble when he inherited it and he could do nothing to save it. The final years of his life were spent in a beautiful Anacostia home where he could look over the capital. In Douglass's voluminous writings, his marriage to Anna is a cipher and his role as father to his five children is largely passed over with the exception of his sons' service in the war. As could be expected, his close relationships with white women supporters and admirers over forty years is hidden away. Never abandoning Anna in forty-four years of marriage, despite extreme emotional distance and tension as well as extended periods of separation, Douglass offered her continued respect and an odd kind of devotion, contentiously caring for her, their bedrooms across the hall from one another. When Anna died in 1882, Douglass's friend of thirty years, Ottilie Assing, thought they would finally be together. Instead, he married another white woman two years later, his dedicated, loyal, and younger secretary Helen Pitts, with whom he would travel the world. Assing later took her own life. The family schisms that his bold freedom created only became clear after his marriage to Helen, when his children rose up in what appears to have been long-repressed resentments.

Douglass would die five years before the twentieth century began.

Acknowledgments

In researching this book, we embarked on a trip to several important Lincoln museums and libraries that culminated in poring over the voluminous Frederick Douglass Papers Project in Indianapolis, Indiana. At every step of our pilgrimage, one truth presented itself: The figure of Frederick Douglass is growing increasingly linked in popular culture with that of Lincoln. At our first stop, Fort Wayne's Abraham Lincoln Museum, the story of Douglass as a young slave introduces the section on slavery, and later in the exhibition a wax figure of the adult Douglass stiffly stands next to Lincoln in the slide-show theater, spotlit out of darkness, to illuminate the Emancipation Proclamation.

Dramatic presentations were heightened in the newly opened Abraham Lincoln Presidential Museum and Library in Springfield, Illinois, which is an innovative, high-tech rendering of the Lincoln story. Wax figures at the entrance include Lincoln, John Wilkes Booth, Generals McClellan and Grant drinking tea, and Sojourner Truth and Frederick Douglass (partnered although the two did not much like one another). In publicity photos marking the day of the museum's opening, Douglass looms over the president's shoulder. Douglass also appears in the Emancipation Proclamation section as part of a large cacophonic throng of holographic heads giving advice to the president, and in the next room a projected shadow figure of Douglass further lectures a distressed Lincoln.

It felt as though we were part of Steve Almond's recent short story "Lincoln, Arisen" (found in his *The Evil B. B. Chow and Other Stories*, Chapel Hill: Algonquin Books, 2005), in which the black abolitionist becomes increasingly part of a troubled Lincoln's dreams. From fairly historically accurate depictions of their meetings, Almond presents the president's night visions growing increasingly disturbed to the point when, like Huck and Jim, Abe and Fred Douglass are floating on a flatboat on the great river to New Orleans, free of all constraints:

> "You will understand," Lincoln says. "You are the one man among all of them who must, by needs, understand." He stares at Douglass and Douglass stares back. Each man can hear the other's breath. They are so close they might embrace. Instead, Lincoln takes up his long pole and pushes off from the bank. Douglass stands on the shore, watching, until the figure is but a gangly figment, dead to duty, dead to memoranda, dead to the human struggle and to the wickedness of blood . . .

Douglass researcher Mark Emerson gave us his time and knowledge at the Frederick Douglass Papers Project at Indiana University–Purdue University Indianapolis (IUPUI). We thank him for that invaluable contribution to our book. The continued publication of the *Collected Writings of Frederick Douglass*, an epic historical editing saga begun at Yale and continuing today at IUPUI under the leadership of John R. McKivigan, will serve to make the voice of this great figure more central to our self-understanding as a nation as the years go by. This monumental publishing effort is increasing awareness of the significance of the relationship of Frederick Douglass and Abraham Lincoln, itself a remarkable shift in how we view the twisting and tormented saga of race in American life. Previous generations gave little importance to Douglass's role in the Civil War, much less his ongoing battle with Lincoln over the mission of the war, and this book is our addition to the work of previous historians who were part of and contributed to that great shift. *Douglass and Lincoln*, while telling a story long obscured, draws on the groundbreaking work of historians such as David Blight, James McPherson, Eric Foner, Benjamin Quarles, Maria Diedrich, and, most especially, Philip Foner.

A special mention, and sincere thanks, go to our friend Donald Yacovone, research manager of the W. E. B. Du Bois Institute at Harvard University and an editor of the magisterial *Black Abolitionists' Papers* project. Donald generously read the manuscript and offered wise insight into this era and the often enigmatic characters of Lincoln and Douglass.

The longer odyssey that was the creation of this book began, as always, with the work of our remarkable agent Flip Brophy. Jacqueline Johnson, our editor, adroitly shaped, shortened, and sculpted the manuscript. Recognition and appreciation also goes to Roberta Scheer for her perceptive and careful editing of the manuscript. George Gibson of Walker & Company was a marvelous guide on our path, full of insight, vision and, most of all, faith in this story. They all deserve great thanks, and we appreciate the unique contributions of each to the realization of this book.

Much of the book was written at the Boston Athenaeum, where Michael Murray generously provided access to dozens of valuable research materials. Gracious help and inventive thinking was offered by Kathryn Harris, director of library services at the Abraham Lincoln Presidential Library and Museum; we also offer thanks to Jan Perrone of the microfilm division there for access to Illinois newspapers. Cathy Ingram, curator of the Frederick Douglass Historic Site of the National Park Service, helped find important images for the book, and we could not have proceeded on the pictorial front without essential and timely assistance from Cindy VanHorn at the library of the Lincoln Museum in Fort Wayne, Indiana.

Thanks as well go to the First Church of Boston, the George Washington Williams House, Young People for the American Way, and Kid Power DC. Tiffany Cruz Gonzales and Donald Peters braved a record snowstorm in a show of support. David Reno offered enthusiastic interest along the way. Maytal Selzer was a loving part of this project every step of the way and is simply sunshine on a cloudy day. We thank Liz, Anna, and Elizabeth Kendrick for editing, moral support, and walks on the Boston Common that mean more than we can express. Finally, those taken too soon, during the writing of this book—Ardyce Hogan, Imette St. Guillen, and Carl Anderson.

Notes

ABBREVIATIONS FOR FREQUENTLY CITED TITLES AND COLLECTIONS

AL   Abraham Lincoln

ALP   Abraham Lincoln Papers at the Library of Congress

CW   Roy Basler, ed., *Collected Works of Abraham Lincoln* (New Brunswick, N.J.: Rutgers University Press, 1953)

DM   *Douglass Monthly*

FD   Frederick Douglass

FDA   Frederick Douglass, *Autobiographies: Narrative of the Life, My Bondage and My Freedom, Life and Times* (1845, 1855, 1893; rpr. New York: Library of America, 1994)

FDP   John W. Blassingame and John McKivigan, eds., *The Frederick Douglass Papers,* 5 vols. (New Haven: Yale University Press, 1979)

FDS   Philip Foner and Yuval Taylor, eds., *Frederick Douglass, Selected Speeches and Writings* (Chicago: Lawrence Hill Books, 1999)

LLA   Library of America, *Lincoln: Speeches and Letters* (New York: Library of America Press, 1989), two vols.

LC   Frederick Douglass Papers, Library of Congress

PROLOGUE: THE MISSION

1. *Illinois State Journal,* 4/4/66.
2. *Springfield Register,* 4/4/66.
3. Douglass as quoted in *Illinois State Journal,* 4/4/66.
4. LLA, vol. 2, 585.
5. *Illinois State Journal,* 4/4/66.
6. LLA, vol. 2, 699.
7. Philip Foner, ed., *The Life and Writings of Frederick Douglass* (New York: International, 1950), vol. 3, 197.
8. FDS, intro, xiii–xiv.

9. James Washington, ed., *A Testament of Hope: Essential Writings of Martin Luther King, Jr.* (San Francisco: Harper & Row, 1986), 279.

10. FDS, 559.

11. Ibid., 560.

12. Foner, ed., *Life and Writings of Frederick Douglass*, vol. 5, 541.

13. FDS, 435.

14. Ibid., 511.

15. Foner, ed., *Life and Writings of Frederick Douglass*, vol. 3, 424.

16. FDS, 619.

17. LC, vol. 4, 434.

18. John Winthrop, "The Model of Christian Charity," in Alden T. Vaughan, ed., *The Puritan Tradition in America, 1620–1720* (revised) (Hanover: University Press of New England, 1972), 146.

19. Edward McNall Burns, *The American Idea of Mission* (New Brunswick: Rutgers University Press, 1957), 7.

20. CW, 5:53.

CHAPTER 1: BLACK REPUBLICANS

1. Don E. Fehrenbacher, *Prelude to Greatness* (Stanford: Stanford University Press, 1962), 101.

2. Robert W. Johannsen, *Stephen A. Douglas* (Urbana: University of Illinois Press, 1997), 641.

3. Douglas Wilson and Rodney O. Davis, eds., *Herndon's Informants*, (Urbana: University of Illinois Press, 1998), 731.

4. CW, 2:383.

5. CW, 2:467.

6. James Simon, *Lincoln and Chief Justice Taney* (New York: Simon & Schuster, 2006), 122.

7. Robert W. Johannsen, ed., *The Lincoln-Douglas Debates of 1858* (New York: Oxford University Press, 1965), 39.

8. Ibid., 46.

9. CW, 3:15.

10. Johannsen, ed., *Lincoln-Douglas Debates of 1858*, 51.

11. Ibid., 52.

12. Ibid., 52–53.

13. Ibid., 81.

14. Richard Carwardine, *Lincoln, Profile in Power* (London: Pearson, 2003), 83.

15. William Herndon to Truman Bartlett, July 19, 1887, Massachusetts Historical Society, Boston.

16. Johannsen, ed., *Lincoln-Douglas Debates of 1858*, 92.

17. Ibid., 161–62.

18. Ibid., 189–90.

19. FDP, III, 214.

20. Ibid., 233.

21. Ibid., 237.

22. Johannsen, ed., *Lincoln-Douglas Debates of 1858*, 319.
23. Benjamin Quarles, *Lincoln and the Negro* (Oxford: Oxford University Press, 1962), 39.
24. *Illinois Daily Journal*, 11/3/53.
25. *Illinois Daily Journal*, 11/23/57.
26. Ibid.
27. *Rochester Democrat and American*, 9/1/58.
28. *Freeport Journal*, 2/17/59, *Dixon Republican and Telegraph*, 2/17/59, *Mendota Press Observer*, 2/18/59, *Belvidere Standard*, 2/15/59.
29. *Galesburg Democrat*, 2/27/59.
30. *Belvidere Standard*, 2/15/59.
31. CW, 4:45.

CHAPTER 2: A SELF-MADE MAN

1. David Blight, ed., *Narrative of the Life of Frederick Douglass* (Boston: Bedford Press, 1993), 39.
2. FDA, 172, 477.
3. FD to James Hall, 6/10/59, Maryland Historical Society, Maryland Colonization Society MSS.
4. Blight, *Narrative of the Life of Frederick Douglass*, 2.
5. Ibid., 57.
6. FDA, 41, 225.
7. Ibid., 74.
8. FDA, 59.
9. FDA, 60–65.
10. George P. Lampe, *Frederick Douglass: Freedom's Voice, 1818–1845* (East Lansing: Michigan State University Press, 1998), 108.
11. FDA, 367.
12. FDP, 1:27.
13. FDP, 2:50.
14. Alan J. Rice and Martin Crawford, "Triumphant Exile," in *Liberating Sojourn: FD and Transatlantic Reform*, ed. Rice and Crawford (Athens: University of Georgia, 1999), 5.
15. FDP, 3:365.
16. Blake McKelvey, *Rochester on the Genesee: The Growth of a City* (Syracuse: Syracuse University Press, 1973), xi.
17. McKelvey, *Rochester on the Genesee*, 33.
18. FDA, 710.
19. Blake McKelvey, "Lights and Shadows in Local Negro History," *Rochester History* XXI, 4 (October 1959), 4.
20. FDA, 706–9; Horace McGuire, "Two Episodes of Anti-Slavery History," paper read at the Rochester Historical Society, 10/27/1916, 218.
21. Thomas Paine, *Common Sense* (Mineola: Dover, 1997), 51.
22. "Self-Made Men," FDP, 5;566.
23. Ibid., 5:550–56.
24. Ibid., 5:574–75.

CHAPTER 3: TO THE BRINK

1. Maria Diedrich, *Love Across Color Lines: Ottilie Assing & Frederick Douglass* (New York: Hill & Wang, 1999), 216.
2. *Frederick Douglass' Paper,* 12/16/59.
3. CW, 3:541.
4. FDA, 716.
5. FD to William A. White, 7/30/46, LC.
6. *Frederick Douglass' Paper,* 12/16/59.
7. Benjamin Quarles, ed., *Frederick Douglass: Great Lives Observed* (Englewood Cliffs, N.J.: Prentice-Hall, 1968), 122–23; William S. McFeely, *Frederick Douglass* (New York: W.W. Norton, 1991), 163.
8. Quarles, *Frederick Douglass: Great Lives Observed,* 102.
9. Annie Douglass to FD, 12/7/59, LC.
10. William Lloyd Garrison to Samuel J. May, 9/28/60, Garrison Papers, Boston Public Library.
11. FDP, 3:365.
12. Amy Hanmer-Croughton, "Anti-Slavery Days in Rochester," *Publications of the Rochester Historical Society* XVI (1936), 113–55, 145; Rosetta Douglass to FD, 4/20/60, LC; DM, 1/60.
13. FDS, 391.
14. DM, 6/60; Amy Hanmer-Croughton, *"Anti-Slavery Days in Rochester,"* 145.
15. Rosetta Douglass to FD, 4/20/60, LC; FDA, 763.
16. FDS, 391.
17. DM, 1/60; Benjamin Quarles, *Frederick Douglass* (1948; rpr. New York: Da Capo Press, 1997), 109.
18. FDA, 763.
19. Philip S. Foner, *Frederick Douglass: A Biography* (New York: Citadel Press, 1964), 85; FDA, 706.
20. FD to Gerrit Smith, 7/2/60, Gerrit Smith Papers, Syracuse University.
21. Diedrich, *Love Across Color Lines,* 15.
22. Diedrich, *Love Across Color Lines,* 175, 150.
23. McFeely, *Frederick Douglass,* 136.
24. Rosetta Douglass Sprague, *Anna Murray Douglass: My Mother As I Recall Her.* Delivered Before the Anna Murray Douglass Union W.C.T.U., Washington, D.C., May 10, 1900. Rpt. Washington, D.C., 1923, LC, 21.
25. Sprague, *Anna Murray Douglass,* 13–14, 16, 27.
26. Diedrich, *Love Across Color Lines,* 192.
27. DM, 6/60.
28. DM, 6/60.
29. FDS, 394.
30. LC, 10/9/60.
31. DM, 8/60.
32. DM, 8/60, 7/60.
33. FDA, 767.
34. DM, 9/60.

35. DM, 10/60.
36. Stephen Myers to Frederick Douglass, 3/1/59, in *Frederick Douglass' Paper*, 3/4/59.
37. DM, 6/60; DM, 9/60.
38. Foner, *Frederick Douglass*, 187.
39. CW, 4:139.
40. CW, 4:149.
41. DM, 12/60.
42. DM, 12/60.

CHAPTER 4: "I USED TO BE A SLAVE . . ."

1. Paul Zall, *Lincoln on Lincoln* (Lexington: University of Kentucky Press, 1999), 1.
2. Douglas Wilson and Rodney O. Davis, eds., *Herndon's Informants* (Urbana: University of Illinois Press, 1998), 348.
3. David Herbert Donald, *Lincoln Reconsidered* (New York: Alfred A. Knopf, 1956), 67.
4. CW, 3:511.
5. Stephen B. Oates, *With Malice Towards None: The Life of Abraham Lincoln* (New York: Harper & Row, 1977, repr. 1994), 4.
6. Michael Burlingame, *The Inner World of Abraham Lincoln* (Urbana: University of Illinois Press, 1994), 36.
7. CW, 1:368.
8. Benjamin Quarles, *Lincoln and the Negro* (Oxford: Oxford University Press, 1962), 16.
9. CW, 1:412.
10. Gabor Boritt, *Lincoln and the Economics of the American Dream* (Urbana: University of Illinois Press, 1994), 285.
11. CW, 1:75.
12. CW, 1:260
13. CW, 2:323.
14. CW, 2:255.
15. David Herbert Donald, *Lincoln* (New York: Simon & Schuster, 1995), 103.
16. CW, 2:246.
17. Quarles, *Lincoln and the Negro*, 15.
18. Ibid., 26–27.
19. LAA, 1, 268–71.
20. CW, 3:243.
21. Michael P. Johnson, ed., *Abraham Lincoln, Slavery, and the Civil War: Selected Writings and Speeches* (Boston: Bedford-St. Martin's, 2001), 78; LLA, 2:29.
22. William K. Klingaman, *Abraham Lincoln and the Road to Emancipation, 1861–1865* (New York: Viking, 2001), 8.
23. FDA, 765.
24. Tremont Temple incident: *New York Tribune*, 12/3/60, quoted in DM, 1/61; FDP, 3:387–412.
25. FDP, 3:413.
26. FDS, 414–15.
27. CW, 4:160.

CHAPTER 5: MIGHTY CURRENTS

1. DM, 2/61.
2. DM, 2/61.
3. DM, 3/61.
4. DM, 3/61.
5. CW, 4:204.
6. CW, 4:215.
7. CW, 4:226.
8. DM, 3/61.
9. Rufus Rockwell Wilson, ed., *Lincoln Among His Friends: A Sheaf of Intimate Memories* (Caldwell, Id.: Caxton Printers, 1942), 308.
10. CW, 4:271.
11. CW, 4:263.
12. FDS, 433.
13. CW, 4:270.
14. DM, 4/61.
15. Richard Striner, *Father Abraham: Lincoln's Relentless Struggle to End Slavery* (Oxford: Oxford University Press, 2006), 132.
16. Kenneth Stamp, ed., *The Causes of the Civil War* (New York: Simon & Schuster, 1986), 116.
17. FDP, 3:427.
18. DM, 4/61.
19. *Rochester Democrat and Chronicle*, 4/16/61.
20. DM, 5/61.
21. FDP, 3:424.
22. FD to James Redpath, *Liberator*, 7/27/60.
23. Blake McKelvey, *Rochester, The Flower City: 1855–1890* (Cambridge: Harvard University Press, 1949), 64–65; FDP, 3:429.
24. FDP, 3:427; DM, 5/61.
25. FDP, 3:427.
26. FDP, 3:435.
27. DM, 5/61.
28. FDP, 3:425; FDP, 3:427; FDP, 3:431.
29. DM, 5/61.
30. DM, 5/61.
31. DM, 5/61.
32. DM, 1/61.
33. DM, 7/61, 5/61.
34. FD to William B. Sprague, 5/1/61, Princeton University Library.

CHAPTER 6: REMORSELESS STRUGGLE

1. DM, 5/61.
2. DM, 5/61.
3. Benjamin Quarles, *Lincoln and the Negro* (Oxford: Oxford University Press, 1962), 67–68.

4. Dudley Taylor Cornish, *The Sable Arm: Black Troops in the Union Army, 1861–1865* (Lawrence: University of Kansas Press, 1956), 16.

5. DM, 6/61.

6. DM, 9/61.

7. DM, 5/61.

8. DM, 7/61.

9. DM, 7/61.

10. DM, 5/61.

11. FDP, 3:487.

12. Cornish, *The Sable Arm*, 4.

13. Cornish, *The Sable Arm*, 8.

14. FDP, 3:447; CW, 2:255.

15. DM, 9/61.

16. CW, 4:240.

17. DM, 8/61.

18. *Congressional Globe*, 37 Congress, 2 Session, 82–87; Hans L. Trefousse, *The Radical Republicans: Lincoln's Vanguard for Racial Justice* (New York: Knopf, 1969), 30.

19. FDP, 3:371.

20. John Hope Franklin, *The Emancipation Proclamation* (Garden City: Doubleday, 1963), 24; T. Harry Williams, *Lincoln and the Radicals* (Madison: University of Wisconsin Press, 1941), 61.

21. DM, 8/61.

22. DM, 10/61.

23. FD to Rev. Samuel J. May, 8/30/06, in Philip Foner, ed., *Life and Writings of Frederick Douglass* (New York: International Publishers, 1950), 3:158–59.

24. DM, 10/61.

25. AL to John Frémont, 9/2/61, ALP; John Frémont to AL, 9/8/61, ALP.

26. Tom Chaffin, *Pathfinder: John Charles Frémont and the Course of American Empire* (New York: Hill & Wang, 2002), 467.

27. DM, 11/61.

28. DM, 12/62.

29. DM, 9/61.

30. *Syracuse Journal*, 11/14/61.

31. *Syracuse Daily Courier and Union*, 11/18/61; *Syracuse Journal*, 11/18/61.

32. *Syracuse Daily Courier and Union*, 11/15/61, 11/18/61.

33. Rosine Draz to FD, 8/10/61, LC; Rosine Draz to FD, 11/13/61, LC.

34. DM, 12/61.

35. *Boston Daily Journal*, 12/4/61; *National Anti-Slavery Standard*, 12/14/61; DM, 1/62; FDP, 3:452–73.

36. FD to Gerrit Smith, 12/22/61, GSP.

37. CW, 5:48.

38. CW, 5:49.

39. *New York Times*, 12/3/61.

CHAPTER 7: DIFFERENT AMERICAN DESTINIES

1. FDP, 3:488.
2. FDP, 3:492–93.
3. FDP, 3:479; DM, 2/62; Philip S. Foner, *Frederick Douglass: A Biography* (New York: Citadel Press, 1964), 126–27.
4. Rosetta Douglass Sprague to FD, 3/15/69, LC; Benjamin Quarles, *Frederick Douglass* (New York: DaCapo Press, rpr. 1997), 107–8.
5. FDA, 712.
6. Rosetta Douglass to FD, 4/4/62, LC.
7. DM, 2/62.
8. DM, 2/62, 3/62.
9. Moncure Daniel Conway, *Autobiography, Memories and Experiences* (New York: Houghton Mifflin, 1904), I, 345–46.
10. AL to James A. McDougall, March 14, 1862, ALP.
11. FDP, 3:518.
12. *London Inquirer*, 3/29/62.
13. FDP, 3:518.
14. Benjamin Quarles, *Lincoln and the Negro* (Oxford: Oxford University Press, 1962), 95.
15. Christoph Lohmann, ed., *Radical Passion: Ottilie Assing's Reports from America and Letters to Frederick Douglass* (New York: Peter Lang, 2000), 235.
16. Quarles, *Lincoln and the Negro*, 100.
17. DM, 3/62.
18. Ernest B. Furgurson, *Freedom Rising: Washington in the Civil War* (New York: Alfred A. Knopf, 2004), 171.
19. Quarles, *Lincoln and the Negro*, 104.
20. Daniel Alexander Payne, *Recollections of Seventy Years* (Nashville: A. M. E. Sunday School Union, 1888), 146–49.
21. AL to Congress, 4/16/62, ALP.
22. FD to Charles Sumner, 4/8/62, Charles Sumner Papers, Houghton Library, Harvard University; Furgurson, *Freedom Rising*, 171.
23. DM, 5/62.
24. DM, 5/62.
25. DM, 6/62.
26. *New York Times*, 5/6/62, in Edward A. Miller Jr., *Lincoln's Abolitionist General: The Biography of David Hunter* (Columbia: University of South Carolina Press, 1997), 101; Peter Sturtevant to Abraham Lincoln, 5/16/62, ALP.
27. Carl Schurz to Abraham Lincoln, 5/16/62, ALP.
28. CW, 5:222–23.
29. CW, 5:425, Don E. Fehrenbacher and Virginia Fehrenbacher, eds., *Recollected Words of Abraham Lincoln* (Stanford: Stanford University Press, 1996), 433; John Hope Franklin, *The Emancipation Proclamation* (Garden City, N.Y.: Doubleday, 1963), 36.
30. David Herbert Donald, *Charles Sumner and the Rights of Man* (New York: Alfred A. Knopf, 1970), 60; William K. Klingaman, *Abraham Lincoln and the Road to Emancipation, 1861–1865* (New York: Viking, 2001), 75.
31. Klingaman, *Abraham Lincoln and the Road to Emancipation*, 139.

32. CW, 5:279.
33. DM, 8/62.
34. FDS, 196.
35. DM, 9/62.
36. Richard Carwardine, *Lincoln, Profile in Power* (London: Pearsons, 2003), 207.
37. Lerone Bennett Jr., *Forced Into Glory: Abraham Lincoln's White Dream* (Chicago: Johnson Publishing, 2000), 455.
38. CW, 5:371–75.
39. DM, 9/62.
40. Salmon Chase to FD, 5/4/50, Salmon Chase Papers, LC.
41. DM, 10/62.
42. Philip Foner, *The Life and Writings of Frederick Douglass*, 5 vols. (New York: International Publishers, 1950–1975), 2:443.
43. DM, 9/62.
44. CW, 5:389.
45. CW, 5:389.
46. Rosetta Douglass to FD, 8/31/62 and 10/9/62, LC.
47. Rosetta Douglass to FD, 8/31/62 and 10/9/62, LC.
48. Julia Griffiths Crofts to FD, 9/1/62, LC.
49. Ira Berlin, Barbara J. Fields, Steven F. Miller, Joseph P. Reidy, and Leslie S. Rowland, *Free at Last: A Documentary History of Slavery, Freedom, and the Civil War* (New York: New Press, 1992), 55.
50. Mark E. Neely Jr. *The Last Best Hope of Earth: Abraham Lincoln and Promise of America* (Cambridge: Harvard University Press, 1993), 117; Berlin et al., *Free at Last,* 67–68.
51. DM, 7/62.
52. CW, 5:53.
53. Fehrenbacher and Fehrenbacher, eds., *Recollected Words of Abraham Lincoln*, 28.

CHAPTER 8: ON THE WIRE

1. CW, 6:30.
2. FD to Gerrit Smith, 9/8/62, Gerrit Smith Papers, Syracuse University.
3. FDA, 790.
4. FDA, 792.
5. Allen Guelzo, *Lincoln's Emancipation Proclamation: The End of Slavery in America* (New York: Simon & Schuster, 2004), 159; Howard Jones, *Abraham Lincoln and a New Birth of Freedom: The Union and Slavery in the Diplomacy of the Civil War* (Lincoln: University of Nebraska Press, 1999), 152; William K. Klingaman, *Abraham Lincoln and the Road to Emancipation, 1861–1865* (New York: Viking, 2001), 238.
6. Dean B. Mahin, *One War at a Time: The International Dimensions of the American Civil War* (Washington, D.C.: Brassey's, 1999), 24, 25, 30–31.
7. *London Spectator*, 10/11/62, XXXV, 1125–26; Jones, *Abraham Lincoln and a New Birth of Freedom*, 116; Janet Brunswick to FD, 11/20/62, LC.
8. Christoph Lohmann, ed., *Radical Passion* (New York: Peter Lang, 2000), 256; Mary Carpenter to FD, 12/5/62, LC.

9. DM, 10/62.
10. Henry Richardson to FD, 12/4/62, LC; *The Independent,* 10/20/62.
11. David Donald, *Lincoln Reconsidered* (New York: Alfred A. Knopf, 1956), 107.
12. Michael Burlingame, *The Inner World of Abraham Lincoln* (Urbana: University of Illinois Press, 1994), 105.
13. DM, 10/62.
14. DM, 10/62; Jolu Hope Franklin, *The Emancipation Proclamation* (Garden City, N.Y.: Doubleday, 1963), 67; Guelzo, *Lincoln's Emancipation Proclamation,* 159.
15. DM, 11/62; John Jones to FD, 12/1/62, LC; FD to Theodore Tilton, 11/22/62, Frederick Douglass Papers, Rochester University.
16. All annual message quotes, LLA, vol. 2, 393–415.
17. Michael Vorenberg, "Abraham Lincoln and the Politics of Black Colonization," *Journal of the Abraham Lincoln Association* 14, Summer 1993, 23.
18. George W. Julian, *Political Recollections* (Chicago: McClurg, 1884), 61; CW, 5:434.
19. Rosetta Douglass to FD, 12/28/62.
20. DM, 1/63.
21. FDA, 790.
22. FDP, 3:546–48.
23. FDA, 790–1.
24. FDA, 791; DM, 3/63.
25. DM, 3/63.
26. DM, 3/63; FDA, 791–2; FDP, 3:546–48.

CHAPTER 9: "GIVE THEM A CHANCE"

1. Philip S. Foner, *The Life and Writings of Frederick Douglass* (New York: International, 1950–1955), 3:204.
2. FD to Theodore Tilton, 10/21/62, Frederick Douglass Papers, New York Historical Society; FD to S.J. May, 1/28/63, Thomson-Kenney Collection, Connecticut State Library, Hartford, Connecticut.
3. DM, 3/63; FDP, 549–69.
4. Julia Griffiths Crofts to FD, 12/5/62, LC.
5. H. Ford Douglas to FD, 1/8/63, in DM, 2/63.
6. Dudley T. Cornish, *The Sable Arm: Black Troops in the Union Army, 1861–1865* (Lawrence: University of Kansas Press, 1956), 42; William K. Klingaman, *Abraham Lincoln and the Road to Emancipation* (New York: Viking, 2001), 160; Andre Trudeau, *Like Men of War: Black Troops in the Civil War, 1862–1865* (New York: Little, Brown, 1998), 18; Ruth Rosenberg-Naparsteck, "A Growing Agitation: Rochester Before, During and After the Civil War," *Rochester History* XLVI (January and April 1984): 29.
7. CW, 5:423; AL to Nathaniel Banks, 3/29/63, ALP; AL to Andrew Johnson, 3/26/63, ALP.
8. FDP, 3:567.
9. Charles Heller, *Portrait of an Abolitionist: A Biography of George Luther Stearns* (Westport: Greenwood Press, 1996*),* 143.
10. Ibid., 145.

11. Ibid., 139.
12. Ibid., 146.
13. Louis F. Emilio, *History of the Fifty-Fourth Regiment of the Massachusetts Volunteer Infantry, 1863–1865* (Boston: 1894), 12.
14. Benjamin Quarles, *Frederick Douglass* (New York: Da Capo Press, rpr. 1997), 205; FD to William C. Whiting, 4/17/63, Amistad Research Center, New Orleans.
15. DM, 2/63; DM, 6/63.
16. FD to William C. Whiting, 4/17/63, Amistad Research Center, New Orleans.
17. Martha Greene to FD, 7/7/64, LC.
18. Henry O. Waggoner to FD, 8/27/66; William S. McFeely, *Frederick Douglass* (New York: W. W. Norton, 1991), 224.
19. *National Anti-Slavery Standard*, 9/6/62.
20. Lewis Douglass to Amelia Loguen, 6/14/62, 8/12/62, Howard University.
21. DM, 3/63.
22. DM, 7/63; DM, 4/63.
23. DM, 3/63; David W. Blight, *Frederick Douglass's Civil War: Keeping Faith in Jubilee* (Baton Rouge: Louisiana State University Press, 1989), 159.
24. DM, 3/63; FD to Gerrit Smith, 3/6/63, Gerrit Smith Papers, Syracuse University.
25. George Stearns to FD, 3/24/63, LC; FD to Gerrit Smith, 6/19/63, Gerrit Smith Papers, Syracuse University.
26. DM, 3/63; FD to Gerrit Smith, 6/19/63, Gerrit Smith Papers, Syracuse University.
27. DM, 3/63; FD to Gerrit Smith, 3/6/63, 6/19/63, Gerrit Smith Papers, Syracuse University.
28. Rosine Draz to FD, 3/16/63, 5/12/63, Julia Griffiths Crofts to FD, 4/3/63, LC.
29. George Evans to FD, 6/6/63, LC.
30. Peter Burchard, *One Gallant Rush* (New York: St. Martin's Press, 1965), 91–92.
31. FD to Gerrit Smith, 6/19/63, Gerrit Smith Papers, Syracuse University; McFeely, *Frederick Douglass,* 225; Cornish, *The Sable Arm*, 148; *Boston Transcript*, 5/28/63; *Liberator*, 6/5/63; Emilio, *A History of the Fifty-Fourth Regiment*, 31–33, Maria Diedrich, *Love Across Color Lines: Ottilie Assing & Frederick Douglass* (New York: Hill & Wang, 1999), 247.
32. *Liberator*, 6/5/63.
33. FD to Gerrit Smith, 6/19/63, Gerrit Smith Papers, Syracuse University; Emilio, *A History of the Fifty-Fourth Regiment*, 33.
34. Burchard, *One Gallant Rush*, 136.
35. Lewis Douglass to Amelia Loguen, 7/20/63, LC; Emilio, *A History of the Fifty-Fourth Regiment*, 68–83.
36. DM, 8/63; Trudeau, *Like Men of War*, 85; Lewis Douglass to Amelia Loguen, 7/20/63, LC.
37. Lewis Douglass to Amelia Loguen, 7/20/63, LC.
38. DM, 8/63.
39. FDA, 781.
40. Heller, *Portrait of an Abolitionist*, 155.
41. Rosine Draz to FD, 7/12/63; Mary Carpenter to FD, 7/10/63, LC.
42. Joseph T. Glatthaar, *Forged in Battle: The Civil War Alliance of Black Soldiers and White Officers* (New York: Free Press, 1989), 124–29; Ira Berlin, ed., *Freedom:*

*Volume 1, Series II: The Black Military Experience: A Documentary History of Emanci-
pation, 1861–1867 (Freedom: A Documentary History of Emancipation)* (Cambridge:
Cambridge University Press, 1983), 518.

43. FDP, 590–98.

44. FDA, 793–94.

45. FDS, 537.

46. George Winston Smith and Charles Judah, *Life in the North During the Civil
War: A Source History* (Albuquerque: University of New Mexico Press, 1966),
143.

47. Charles Douglass to FD, 7/6/63, LC.

48. DM, 2/63.

49. Emilio, *A History of the Fifty-Fourth Regiment*, 179; James McPherson, *The Negro's
Civil War: How American Negroes Felt and Acted During the War for the Union* (New
York: Vintage Books, 1965), 200; Corporal James Henry Gooding to AL, 9/28/63,
in Berlin, ed., *Freedom: Volume 1, Series II: The Black Military Experience*, 385–86.

50. Blight, *Frederick Douglass's Civil War*, 164.

51. Edwin Redkey, *A Grand Army of Black Men: Letters from African-American Soldiers
in the Union Army, 1861–1865* (Cambridge: Cambridge University Press, 1992),
229–30.

52. Trudeau, *Like Men of War*, 257; Glatthaar, *Forged in Battle*, 35, 118; Redkey,
A Grand Army of Black Men, 211.

53. Trudeau, *Like Men of War*, 76; Berlin, ed., *Freedom: Volume 1, Series II: The Black
Military Experience*, 589.

54. Trudeau, *Like Men of War*, 246.

55. Ira Berlin et al., *Free at Last: A Documentary History of Slavery, Freedom, and the
Civil War* (New York: New Press, 1992), 450–51.

56. *Liberator*, 5/22/63.

57. DM, 8/63.

58. DM, 8/63.

CHAPTER 10: FIRST MEETING

1. Jerrold M. Packard, *The Lincolns in the White House: Four Years That Shattered a
Family* (New York: St. Martin's Press, 2005), 7–10, 162; Margaret Leech, *Reveille
in Washington: 1860–1865* (New York: Harper & Brothers, 1941), 10.

2. William K. Klingaman, *Abraham Lincoln and the Road to Emancipation*, 1861–
1865 (New York: Viking, 2001), 212; Ernest B. Furgurson, *Freedom Rising: Washington in the Civil War* (New York: Alfred A. Knopf, 2004), 193.

3. Daniel Mark Epstein, *Lincoln and Whitman: Parallel Lives in Civil War Washington*
(New York: Random House, 2004), 98–99; Matthew Pinsker, *Lincoln's Sanctuary:
Abraham Lincoln and the Soldiers' Home* (Oxford: Oxford University Press, 2003),
109; Klingaman, *Abraham Lincoln and the Road to Emancipation*, 267; Leech,
Reveille in Washington, 261.

4. Ronald C. White Jr., *Lincoln's Greatest Speech: The Second Inaugural* (New York:
Simon & Schuster, 2002), 26; Klingaman, *Abraham Lincoln and the Road to Emancipation*, 267.

5. Furgurson, *Freedom Rising*, 12; Leech, *Reveille in Washington*, 236, 251; Benjamin Quarles, *Lincoln and the Negro* (Oxford: Oxford University Press, 1962), 79.

6. *Daily National Republican*, 8/10/63; Furgurson, *Freedom Rising*, 332.

7. FD to George L. Stearns, 8/12/63, Abraham Barder Papers, Pennsylvania Historical Society; George Stearns to FD, 8/8/63, LC.

8. *National Anti-Slavery Standard*, 9/6/62; Michael Vorenberg, "Abraham Lincoln and the Politics of Black Colonization," *Journal of the Abraham Lincoln Association* 14, Summer 1993, 35–36.

9. Douglass's third autobiography mentions the Stanton meeting second, but the account he laid out in a letter to Stearns a few days after the meetings puts the Stanton meeting first. FD to George L. Stearns, 8/12/63, Abraham Barder Papers, Pennsylvania Historical Society.

10. FDP, 5:340.

11. FDA, 787; Benjamin Thomas and Harold M. Hyman, *Stanton: The Life and Times of Lincoln's Secretary of War* (New York: Alfred A. Knopf, 1962), 161–63.

12. FDA, 787; Thomas and Hyman, *Stanton*, 163, 166; Klingaman, *Abraham Lincoln and the Road to Emancipation*, 97.

13. David H. Donald, *Lincoln Reconsidered* (New York: Alfred A. Knopf, 1956), 71.

14. CW, 6:357.

15. FD to George L. Stearns, 8/12/63, Abraham Barder Papers, Pennsylvania Historical Society.

16. FDA, 787.

17. FD to George L. Stearns, 8/12/63, Abraham Barder Papers, Pennsylvania Historical Society. In Douglass's autobiography he writes of the commission as his idea, but the account from the time period says otherwise. Since the autobiography was written decades later, we believe his private letter to Stearns is more trustworthy.

18. FDA, 787.

19. Joseph T. Glatthaar, *Forged in Battle: The Civil War Alliance of Black Soldiers and White Officers* (New York: Free Press, 1989), 37; Dudley T. Cornish, *The Sable Arm: Black Troops in the Union Army, 1861–1865* (Lawrence: University of Kansas Press, 1956), 113–14, 123–26; Louis S. Gerteis, *From Contraband to Freedman: Federal Policy Toward Southern Blacks, 1861–1865* (Westport, Conn.: Greenwood Press, 1973), 120; AL to Edwin Stanton, 7/21/63, ALP.

20. Glatthaar, *Forged in Battle*, 69; Mary Frances Berry, *Military Necessity and Civil Rights Policy: Black Citizenship and the Constitution, 1861–1868* (Port Washington: Kennikat Press, 1977), 62.

21. Ira Berlin et al., *Free at Last:* 113; Brig. Genl. Thomas Ewing to Lt. Col. C.W. Marsh, 8/3/63, in Ira Berlin, ed., *Freedom: Volume 1, Series II: The Black Military Experience:* 229.

22. Affidavit of a Kentucky Black Soldier's Widow, 3/25/65, in Berlin, ed., *Freedom: Volume 1, Series II: The Black Military Experience*, 269.

23. Michael Burlingame, ed., *Lincoln Observed: Civil War Dispatches of Noah Brooks* (Baltimore: Johns Hopkins University Press, 1998), 80–84; FDP, 3: 606.

24. Brooks, *Lincoln Observed*, 84–86; Benjamin Thomas, *Abraham Lincoln* (New York: Alfred A. Knopf, 1952), 456.

25. FDP, 3:606; FDP, 5:539; FDA, 785.
26. FDP, 3:606.
27. AL to Mary Todd Lincoln, 8/8/1863, ALP.
28. FDA, 785; Benjamin Thomas, *Abraham Lincoln*, 457; FDP, 5:539; Brooks, *Lincoln Observed*, 84–86; Victoria Radford, *Meeting Mr. Lincoln: Firsthand Recollections of Abraham Lincoln by People, Great and Small, Who Met the President* (Chicago: Ivan R. Dee, 1998), 98.
29. FDA, 785; FDP, 3:606; FDP, 5:341; John C. Waugh, *Reelecting Lincoln: The Battle for the 1864 Presidency* (New York: Crown, 1997), 77–78; Harold Holzer, ed., *Lincoln As I Knew Him*: 119–20; Don E. Fehrenbacher and Virginia Fehrenbacher, eds., *Recollected Words of Abraham Lincoln* (Stanford: Stanford University Press, 1996), 507.
30. FDA, 785; FDA, 809; P.M. Zall, ed., *Abe Lincoln Laughing: Humorous Anecdotes from Original Sources by and about Abraham Lincoln* (Knoxville: University of Tennessee Press, 1995), 21.
31. FDA, 809; FDP, 5:538.
32. Allen Thorndike Rice, *Reminiscences of Abraham Lincoln by Distinguished Men of His Time* (New York: North American Review, 1888), 186; FDA, 785–86; FD to George L. Stearns, 8/12/63, Abraham Barder Papers, Pennsylvania Historical Society; FDP, 5:539–40.
33. FDP, 5:539–40; FDP, 5:539.
34. FD to George L. Stearns, 8/12/63, Abraham Barder Papers, Pennsylvania Historical Society.
35. FDP, 5:539–42.
36. FDP, 5:539–42; FDA, 787.
37. FDP, 3:607–8.
38. FD to George L. Stearns, 8/12/63, Abraham Barder Papers, Pennsylvania Historical Society.
39. Quarles, *Lincoln and the Negro*, 168.

CHAPTER 11: "CLENCHED TEETH AND STEADY EYE"

1. Charles Sumner to AL, 8/7/63, ALP.
2. CW, 6:410–11.
3. FD to George L. Stearns, 8/12/63, Abraham Barder Papers, Pennsylvania Historical Society; FDA, 785–86; FDP, 3:608, 5:540–41.
4. Abraham Lincoln to Ulysses S. Grant, 8/9/63, ALP.
5. Ulysses S. Grant to Abraham Lincoln, Sunday, 8/23/63, ALP.
6. Mark E. Neely Jr., *The Last Best Hope of Earth: Abraham Lincoln and the Promise of America* (Cambridge: Harvard University Press, 1993), 120; Zachariah Chandler to Lyman Trumbull, 8/6/83, in Trumbull Papers, Library of Congress.
7. Paul M. Angle, *Here I Have Lived: A History of Lincoln's Springfield* (New Brunswick: Rutgers University Press, 1950), 96; Ronald C. White Jr., *The Eloquent President: A Portrait of Lincoln Through His Words* (New York: Random House, 2005), 193–98.
8. White, *The Eloquent President*, 193–98, 216.

9. DM, 8/63.

10. C.W. Foster to Brigadier General Daniel H. Rucher, U.S. Vol. Depot Quarter Master, Washington, D.C., LC; C.W. Foster to FD, 8/13/63, LC.

11. FD to E.M. Stanton, 8/17/63, National Archives, RG94, Washington, D.C.

12. FD to Thomas Webster, 8/18/63, Gratz Collection, Historical Society of Pennsylvania.

13. C.W. Foster to FD, 8/21/63, LC.

14. FD to Thomas Webster, 8/18/63, Gratz Collection, Historical Society of Pennsylvania.

15. Christoph Lohmann, ed., *Radical Passion: Ottilie Assing's Reports from America and Letters to Frederick Douglass* (New York: Peter Lang, 2000), 270.

16. FDA, 788.

17. Julia Griffiths Crofts to FD, 12/10/63, LC; FDA, 788; David W. Blight, *Frederick Douglass's Civil War: Keeping Faith in Jubilee* (Baton Rouge: Louisiana State University Press, 1989), 172.

18. Benjamin Quarles, *Frederick Douglass* (New York: DaCapo Press, 1997), 213; Blight, *Frederick Douglass's Civil War*, 172.

19. FDA, 773.

20. Julia Griffiths Crofts to FD, 12/10/63, 8/19/64, LC.

21. Charles Douglass to FD, 9/18/63, LC; FD to Gerrit Smith, 10/10/63, Gerrit Smith Papers, Syracuse University.

22. Charles Douglass to FD, 9/18/63, LC; FD to Gerrit Smith, 10/10/63, Gerrit Smith Papers, Syracuse University; Julia Griffiths Crofts to FD, 12/10/65, LC.

23. FD to "My dear friend," 11/21/63, Frederick Douglass Papers, Yale University.

24. FD to Gerrit Smith, 10/18/63, GSP.

25. FD to "My dear friend," 11/21/63, Frederick Douglass Papers, Yale University.

26. Charles Douglass to FD, 9/18/63, LC; FD to "My dear friend," 11/21/63, Frederick Douglass Papers, Yale University.

27. Charles Douglass to FD, 9/8/63, LC.

28. Ira Berlin, ed., *Freedom: Volume 1, Series II: The Black Military Experience, A Documentary History of Emancipation, 1861–1867* (Cambridge: Cambridge University Press, 1989), 633–36.

29. Charles Douglass to FD, 9/8/63, LC.

30. Julia Griffiths Crofts to FD, 12/10/65, LC.

31. Rosine Draz to FD, 8/17/63, 10/1/63, LC.

32. CW, 7:83–84.

CHAPTER 12: "AN ABOLITION WAR"

1. FDP, 3:3.

2. FDP, 3:3–24.

3. CW, 7:49; FDP, 4:12.

4. CW, 7:50.

5. FDP, 4:xix.

6. War of the Rebellion Official Records, Series II, Vol. VI.

7. Edwin M. Stanton to AL, 4/2/64, LC; Benjamin Quarles, *Lincoln and the Negro* (Oxford: Oxford University Press, 1962), 186.

8. Andrew Ward, *River Run Red: The Fort Pillow Massacre in the American Civil War* (New York: Viking, 2005), 200, 220, 225, 269.

9. Dudley Taylor Cornish, *The Sable Arm: Black Troops in the Union Army, 1861–1865* (Lawrence: University of Kansas Press, 1956), 176–77; Ward, *River Run Red,* 327.

10. Quarles, *Lincoln and the Negro,* 174; *Liberator,* 4/29/64.

11. CW, 7:301–3.

12. Abraham Lincoln to Cabinet, 5/3/64, ALP.

13. Ronald C. White Jr., *Lincoln's Greatest Speech: The Second Inaugural* (New York: Simon & Schuster, 2002), 174–77; AL to Charles Sumner, 5/19/64, CW, suppl.: 243.

14. Trudeau, *Like Men of War: Black Troops In the Civil War, 1862–1865* (New York: Little, Brown, 1998), 207–8; William D. Stoddard, *Inside the White House in War Times: Memories and Reports of Lincoln's Secretary* (Lincoln: University of Nebraska Press, 1980), 173.

15. Ronald C. White Jr., *The Eloquent President: A Portrait of Lincoln Through His Words* (New York: Random House, 2005), 261.

16. CW, 7:281–83.

17. FDP, 4:19.

18. Charles Douglass to FD, 5/31/64, LC.

19. Charles Douglass to FD, 5/31/64, LC.

20. *National Anti-Slavery Standard,* 7/2/64.

21. Pension file, Charles R. Douglass (Laura A.), I, 5 Mass. Cav. And F, 54 Mass. Inf., WC 898,477, Record Group 15 (Records of the Veterans Administration), National Archives Building, Washington, D.C.

CHAPTER 13: REVOLUTIONARY DIALOGUE

1. Blake McKelvey, *Rochester, The Flower City: 1855–1890* (Cambridge: Harvard University Press, 1949), 67.

2. *New York Times,* 5/22/64.

3. Don E. Fehrenbacher and Virginia Fehrenbacher, eds., *Recollected Words of Abraham Lincoln* (Stanford: Stanford University Press, 1996), 486.

4. Benjamin Quarles, *Lincoln and the Negro* (Oxford: Oxford University Press, 1962), 226–27.

5. AL to Michael Hahn, 3/13/64, ALP.

6. *Liberator,* 2/10/65.

7. AL to Nathaniel P. Banks, 8/5/63, ALP.

8. John Eaton, *Grant, Lincoln and the Freedmen* (New York: Longmans, Green, 1907), 2, 19.

9. Eaton, *Grant, Lincoln and the Freedmen,* 90.

10. *Rochester Union and Advertiser,* 9/5/64.

11. FD to English Correspondent, *Liberator,* 9/16/64.

12. Eaton, *Grant, Lincoln and the Freedmen,* 174–75.

13. AL to Nathaniel P. Banks, 8/9/64.

14. *In Memoriam Frederick Douglass* (Philadelphia: John C. Yorston, 1897), 70–71.

15. FDA, 795.

16. Noah Brooks, *Mr. Lincoln's Washington: Selections from the Writings of Noah Brooks, Civil Correspondent*, ed. P. J. Staudenraus (South Brunswick, N.J.: T. Yoseloff, 1967), 7.

17. John C. Waugh, *Reelecting Lincoln: The Battle of the 1864 Presidency* (New York: Crown, 1997), 262; Thurlow Weed to William H. Seward, August 22, 1864, ALP; Henry J. Raymond to AL, August 22, 1864, ALP.

18. David Goodman Croly and George Wakeman, *Miscegenation: The Theory of the Blending of the Races, Applied to the White Man and Negro*. 1864 (Upper Saddle River, N.J.: Literature House/Gregg Press, rpr. 1970), 1–2, 8–9.

19. Tyler Dennett, ed., *Lincoln and the Civil War in the Diaries and Letters of John Hay* (New York: Dodd, Mead, 1939), 203; CW, 7:145.

20. Edwin M. Stanton to AL, 4/2/64, ALP; Fehrenbacher and Fehrenbacher, eds., *Recollected Words of Abraham Lincoln*, 187; DM, 8/63, Dudley Taylor Cornish, *The Sable Arm: Black Troops in the Union Army, 1861–1865* (Lawrence: University of Kansas Press, 1956), 258–59; William K. Klingaman, *Abraham Lincoln and the Road to Emancipation, 1861–1865* (New York: Viking, 2001), 256.

21. Quarles, *Lincoln and the Negro*, 198.

22. William P. Dole to AL, 8/18/64, ALP.

23. CW, 7:506; Ida Tarbell, *The Life of Abraham Lincoln*, 2 vols. (New York: Lincoln Memorial Association, 1900), 2:201–3.

24. *Daily National Intelligencer*, 8/19/64; *Daily National Republican,* 8/19/64; *Daily Morning Chronicle*, 8/19/64.

25. *Dictionary of Wisconsin Biography* (Madison: State Historical Society of Wisconsin, 1960).

26. CW, 7:508.

27. FD to Theodore Tilton, 10/15//64, Buffalo and Erie County Public Library; FDP, 4:542.

28. Harold Holzer, *Lincoln As I Knew Him: Gossip, Tributes, and Revelations From His Best Friends and Worst Enemies* (Chapel Hill: Algonquin Books, 1999), 193; Rufus Rockwell Wilson, ed., *Lincoln Among His Friends: A Sheaf of Intimate Memories* (Caldwell, Id.: Caxton Printers, 1942), 179; Wilson, *Lincoln Among His Friends*, 360.

29. Rosine Draz to FD, 5/30/64, 7/5/64, LC.

30. FDA, 796, *Daily National Intelligencer*, 8/19/64, CW, 7:451.

31. *Cincinnati Enquirer,* 7/25/64.

32. Charles Robinson to AL, 8/7/63, ALP.

33. FDA, 796.

34. CW, 7:500–1.

35. The primary account of this meeting comes from FD to Theodore Tilton, 10/15/64, Buffalo and Erie County Public Library. Douglass also left accounts in FDA, 796; FDP, 5:541; FDA, 797. Allen Thorndike Rice, *Reminiscences of Abraham Lincoln by Distinguished Men of His Time* (New York: North American Review, 1888), 320.

36. FDA, 716, 757–60.

37. J.G. Randall, *Lincoln: The Liberal Statesman* (New York: Dodd, Mead, 1947), 28; DM, 11/62.

38. Cornish, *The Sable Arm*, 158–60.

39. Augustus Montgomery to General William Rosecrans, 5/17/63, ALP.

CHAPTER 14: GOING HOME

1. FDA, 796.

2. FD to Theodore Tilton, 10/15/64, Buffalo and Erie County Public Library.

3. CW, 7:507.

4. Francine Curro Cary, *Urban Odyssey: A Multicultural History of Washington, D.C.* (Washington: Smithsonian Institution Press, 1996), 31; Andrew Boyd, *Boyd's Washington and Georgetown Directory* (Washington: Hudson Taylor, 1864); Andrew Hilyer, ed., *The Twentieth Century Union League Directory* (Washington: Union League, 1901).

5. John Eaton, *Grant, Lincoln and the Freedmen* (New York: Longmans, Green, 1907), 175.

6. FD to AL, 8/29/64.

7. CW, 7:514.

8. Lewis Douglass to FD, 8/22/64, LC.

9. File 620 (C.T.) 1879, entry 360, Letters Received, Colored Troops Division, Record Group 94, Records of the Adjutant General's Office, National Archives Building, Washington, D.C.

10. National Archives microfilm publication M817, Compiled Service Records of Volunteer Union Soldiers Who Served with the 5th Massachusetts Cavalry (Colored), roll 80, Record Group 94, Records of the Adjutant General's Office, National Archives Building, Washington, D.C.

11. Charles Douglass, 9/15/64, LC.

12. *Chicago Tribune*, 9/5/64.

13. *Official Proceedings of the Democratic National Convention Held in 1864 at Chicago* (Chicago: Times Steam Book and Job Printing House, 1864), 60–61.

14. Philip S. Foner, *Frederick Douglass* (New York: Citadel Press, 1964), 231.

15. Benjamin Quarles, *Lincoln and the Negro* (Oxford: Oxford University Press, 1962), 216.

16. FD to Theodore Tilton, 10/15/64, Buffalo and Erie County Public Library.

17. FD to William Lloyd Garrison, 9/17/64, LC.

18. Martin B. Pasternak, *Rise Now and Fly to Arms: The Life of Henry Highland Garnet* (New York: Garland Publishing, 1995), 4.

19. Pasternak, *Rise Now and Fly to Arms*, 117.

20. Pasternak, *Rise Now and Fly to Arms*, 118.

21. Larry E. Nelson, "Black Leaders and the Presidential Election of 1864," *Journal of Negro History* (January 1978): 53; Edwin Redkey, *A Grand Army of Black Men: Letters from African-American Soldiers in the Union Army, 1861–1865* (Cambridge: Cambridge University Press, 1992), 207.

22. *Proceedings of the National Convention of Colored Men, held in the city of Syracuse, N.Y., October 4, 5, 6, and 7, 1864; with the bill of wrongs and rights, and the address*

to the American people (Boston: J. S. Rock and G. L. Ruffin, 1864), Library of Congress; Michael Vorenberg, *Final Freedom: The Civil War, the Abolition of Slavery, and the Thirteenth Amendment* (New York: Cambridge University Press, 2001), 158–59.

23. Redkey, *A Grand Army of Black Men*, 213.
24. FD to Theodore Tilton, 10/15/64, Buffalo and Erie County Public Library.
25. Quarles, *Lincoln and the Negro*, 217.
26. Michael Burlingame, ed., *Lincoln Observed: Civil War Dispatches of Noah Brooks* (Baltimore: Johns Hopkins University Press, 1998), 143–44.
27. Burlingame, *Lincoln Observed*, 141–42.
28. Christopher Phillips, *Freedom's Port: The African American Community of Baltimore, 1790–1860* (Urbana: University of Illinois Press, 1997), 131–40; Dickson J. Preston, *Young Frederick Douglass: The Maryland Years* (Baltimore: Johns Hopkins University Press, 1980), 97–98.
29. FDP, 4:38–40.
30. Preston, *Young Frederick Douglass*, 163–64; *New York Independent*, 3/2/65.
31. Preston, *Young Frederick Douglass*, 163–64.
32. FDP, 4:38–50.

CHAPTER 15: SACRED EFFORTS

1. Mary Carpenter to FD, 3/25/65, LC.
2. FDP, 4:59–60; FDP, 4:62.
3. FDP: 4:66–67.
4. Charles Douglass to FD, 2/19/65, LC.
5. Lewis H. Douglass et al. to Hon. E. M. Stanton (Jan. 1865), D-51 1865, Letters Received, ser. 360, Colored Troops Division, RG 94 (B-584); Charles Douglass to FD, 2/9/65, LC; Rosetta Douglass Sprague to FD, 2/21/65.
6. AL to Edward Bates, 6/24/64, ALP; Mary Frances Berry, *Military Necessity and Civil Rights Policy: Black Citizenship and the Constitution, 1861–1868* (Port Washington, N.Y.: Kennikat Press, 1977), 68–70.
7. James McPherson, *The Negro's Civil War: How American Negroes Felt and Acted During the War for the Union* (New York: Vintage Books, 1965), 202–3.
8. Frank A. Rollin, *Life and Public Services of Martin R. Delany* (New York: Arno Press, 1969), 172–76.
9. Ronald C. White Jr., *The Eloquent President: A Portrait of Lincoln Through His Words* (New York: Random House, 2005), 297.
10. Richard Striner, *Father Abraham: Lincoln's Relentless Struggle to End Slavery* (Oxford: Oxford University Press, 2006), 233.
11. Christoph Lohmann, ed., *Radical Passion: Ottilie Assing's Reports from America and Letters to Frederick Douglass* (New York: Peter Lang, 2000), 298–300.
12. Charles Douglass to FD, 2/9/65.
13. Rosine Draz to FD, 4/23/65, LC.
14. FDA, 800.
15. George Templeton Strong, *The Diary of George Templeton Strong: The Civil War, 1860–1865,* ed. Allan Nevins and Milton Halsey Thomas (New York: Macmillan,

1954), 500; Doris Kearns Goodwin, *Team of Rivals: The Political Genius of Abraham Lincoln* (New York: Simon & Schuster, 2005), 680.

16. Mary Merwin Phelps, *Kate Chase: Dominant Daughter: The Life Story of a Brilliant Woman and Her Famous Father* (New York: Thomas Y. Crowell, 1935), 133, 138, 167.

17. FDA, 800.

18. Michael Burlingame, ed., *Lincoln Observed: Civil War Dispatches of Noah Brooks* (Baltimore: Johns Hopkins University Press, 1998), 165; Margaret Leech, *Reveille in Washington: 1860–1865* (New York, Harper & Brothers, 1941), 366; Allen T. Rice, *Reminiscences of Abraham Lincoln by Distinguished Men of His Time* (New York: North American Review, 1888), 320; Ronald C. White Jr., *Lincoln's Greatest Speech: The Second Inaugural* (New York: Simon & Schuster, 2002), 32–33; FDA, 800; FDP, 5:542.

19. *London Times*, 3/20/65.

20. George Fort Milton, *The Age of Hate: Andrew Johnson and the Radicals* (New York: Coward-McCann, 1930), 147.

21. Rice, *Reminiscences of Abraham Lincoln*, 320–21.

22. FDA, 801; White Jr., *Lincoln's Greatest Speech*, 42.

23. Harold Holzer, *Lincoln at Cooper Union: The Speech That Made Abraham Lincoln President* (New York: Simon & Schuster, 2004), 111–114; *The New York Herald*, 3/6/65.

24. FDP, 5:343.

25. DM, 10/61.

26. CW, 8:333.

27. FDP, 5:544.

28. FDA, 803.

29. FDP, 5:544.

30. FDP: 5:544.

31. Rice, *Reminiscences of Abraham Lincoln*, 322; FDP: 5:544; Burlingame, *Lincoln Observed*, 169; FDA, 804.

32. FDP: 5:544.

33. FDA, 804.

34. Elizabeth Keckley, *Behind the Scenes: Thirty Years a Slave, and Four Years in the White House*, ed. Frances Smith Foster (Urbana: University of Illinois Press, 2001), 120.

35. White, *Lincoln's Greatest Speech*, 183.

36. AL to Thurlow Weed, 3/15/65; CW, 8:356.

CHAPTER 16: "IT MADE US KIN"

1. Blake McKelvey, *Rochester, The Flower City: 1855–1890* (Cambridge: Harvard University Press, 1949), 69–71; Blake McKelvey, *Rochester on the Genesee: The Growth of a City.* (Syracuse: Syracuse University Press, 1973), 85.

2. Benjamin Quarles, *Lincoln and the Negro* (Oxford: Oxford University Press, 1962), 236–37; Edwin Redkey, *A Grand Army of Black Men: Letters from African-American Soldiers in the Union Army, 1861–1865* (Cambridge: Cambridge University Press, 1992), 177.

3. FDP, 69–74.

4. McKelvey, *Rochester*, 71.

5. CW, 8:400–5.

6. Edward Steers Jr., *Blood on the Moon: The Assassination of Abraham Lincoln* (Lexington: University of Kentucky Press, 2001), 91.

7. Michael Burlingame, ed., *Lincoln Observed: Civil War Dispatches of Noah Brooks* (Baltimore: Johns Hopkins University Press, 1998), 192; Rosine Draz to FD, 4/27/65, LC; Julia Griffiths Crofts to FD, 4/28/65, LC.

8. Redkey, *A Grand Army of Black Men*, 200.

9. FDP, 4:76–79.

10. FDA, 809–10.

EPILOGUE: AMERICA'S STEPCHILDREN

1. Benjamin Quarles, *Lincoln and the Negro* (Oxford: Oxford University Press, 1962), 247; FD to Mary Todd Lincoln, 8/17/65, Frederick Douglass Papers, Yale University.

2. Elizabeth Keckley, *Behind the Scenes: Thirty Years a Slave, and Four Years in the White House*, ed. Frances Smith Foster (Urbana: University of Illinois Press, 2001), 227, 248, 254.

3. Benjamin Quarles, *Frederick Douglass* (New York: Da Capo Press, rpr. 1997), 226.

4. Philip S. Foner, *The Life and Writings of Frederick Douglass* (New York: International, 1950–1955), 4:182–93.

5. *New York Tribune*, 2/12/66; Maria Diedrich, *Love Across Color Lines: Ottilie Assing & Frederick Douglass* (New York: Hill & Wang, 1999), 270.

6. FDA, 820–22.

7. Nathan Irvin Huggins, *Slave and Citizen: The Life of Frederick Douglass* (Boston: Little, Brown, 1980), 126.

8. *Rochester Union and Advertiser*, 1/8/66.

9. Mary Frances Berry, *Military Necessity and Civil Rights Policy: Black Citizenship and the Constitution, 1861–1868* (Port Washington, N.Y.: Kennikat Press, 1977), 84.

10. James McPherson, *Abraham Lincoln and the Second American Revolution* (New York: Oxford University Press, 1990), 16–19, 24.

11. Quarles, *Lincoln and the Negro*, 7.

12. Quarles, *Lincoln and the Negro*, 3.

13. *Oration of Frederick Douglass Delivered on the Occasion of the Unveiling of the Freedman's Monument in Memory of Abraham Lincoln, in Lincoln Park, Washington, D.C., April 14th, 1876; with an Appendix* (Washington, D.C., 1876), 1–15 (rpr. New York, 1940).

14. W. E. B. Du Bois: *Writings* (New York: Library of America, 1986), 1196.

15. Kenneth O'Reilly, *Nixon's Piano* (New York: Free Press, 1995), 66.

16. Ibid., 89.

17. James Washington, ed., *A Testament of Hope: Essential Writings of Martin Luther King, Jr.* (San Francisco: Harper & Row, 1986), 217.

18. Waldo E. Martin Jr., *The Mind of Frederick Douglass* (Chapel Hill: University of North Carolina Press, 1985), 276.

19. Ibid., 277.
20. FDS, 485.

APPENDIX: AFTERMATH—THE DOUGLASS FAMILY

1. Rosetta Douglass Sprague to Frederick Douglass, 9/17/76, LC; William S. McFeely, *Frederick Douglass* (New York: W. W. Norton, 1991), 288; Lara Becker Lui, "Douglass Kin Graves Found," *Rochester Democrat and Chronicle*, 5/2/2003.
2. *National Anti-Slavery Standard*, 8/19/65.
3. Lewis Douglass to FD, 6/9/65, Howard University; *National Anti-Slavery Standard*, 12/7/65.
4. Rosine Draz to FD, 7/18/65, LC; FD to James M. McKim, 4/29/65, Cornell University Anti-Slavery Papers.
5. Waldo E. Martin, *The Mind of Frederick Douglass* (Chapel Hill: University of North Carolina Press, 1985), 251.
6. W. E. B. Du Bois, *The Souls of Black Folk*, in *Three Negro Classics* (New York: Avon Books, 1999), 215.

Bibliography

PUBLISHED WORKS

Anderson, Dwight G. *Abraham Lincoln: The Quest for Immortality*. New York: Knopf, 1982.

Angle, Paul M. *Here I Have Lived: A History of Lincoln's Springfield*. New Brunswick, N.J.: Rutgers University Press, 1950.

Angle, Paul M., ed. *Herndon's Life of Lincoln*. New York: Albert and Charles Boni, 1930.

Angle, Paul M. *The Lincoln Reader*. New Brunswick, N.J.: Rutgers University Press, 1947.

Aptheker, Herbert. *Abolitionism: A Revolutionary Movement*. Boston: Twayne Publishers, 1989.

Basler, Roy P., ed. *The Collected Works of Abraham Lincoln*. 8 vols. New Brunswick, N.J.: Rutgers University Press, 1953.

Belz, Herman. *A New Birth of Freedom: The Republican Party and Freedmen's Rights, 1861 to 1866*. Westport, Conn.: Greenwood, 1976.

Bennett, Lerone Jr. *Forced into Glory: Abraham Lincoln's White Dream*. Chicago: Johnson Publishing, 2000.

Bercovitch, Sacvan. *The American Jeremiad*. Madison: University of Wisconsin Press, 1978.

Berlin, Ira, ed. *Freedom: The Black Military Experience, A Documentary History of Emancipation, 1861–1867*. Vol. 1, series II. Cambridge: Cambridge University Press, 1983.

Berlin, Ira, Barbara J. Fields, Steven F. Miller, Joseph P. Reidy, and Leslie S. Rowland. *Free at Last: A Documentary History of Slavery, Freedom, and the Civil War*. New York: New Press, 1992.

Berry, Mary Frances. *Military Necessity and Civil Rights Policy: Black Citizenship and the Constitution, 1861–1868*. Port Washington, N.Y.: Kennikat Press, 1977.

Beverage, Albert. *Abraham Lincoln*. 2 vols. Boston: Houghton Mifflin, 1928.

Blassingame, John W., and John McKivigan, eds. *The Frederick Douglass Papers*. 5 vols. New Haven: Yale University Press, 1979.

Blight, David W. *Beyond the Battlefield.* Amherst: University of Massachusetts Press, 2002.

Blight, David W. *Frederick Douglass and Abraham Lincoln: A Relationship in Language, Politics and Memory.* Milwaukee: Marquette University Press, 2001.

Blight, David W. *Frederick Douglass's Civil War: Keeping Faith in Jubilee.* Baton Rouge: Louisiana State University Press, 1989.

Blight, David W., ed. *Narrative of the Life of Frederick Douglass.* Boston: Bedford Press, 1993.

Blight, David W. *Race and Reunion.* Cambridge: Harvard University Press, 2002.

Boritt, Gabor. *Lincoln and the Economics of the American Dream.* Urbana: University of Illinois Press, 1994.

Boritt, Gabor. *The Lincoln Enigma: The Changing Faces of an American Icon.* New York: Oxford University Press, 2001.

Boritt, Gabor, ed. *Why the Civil War Came.* New York: Oxford University Press, 1996.

Boyd, Andrew. *Boyd's Washington and Georgetown Directory.* Washington, D.C.: Hudson Taylor, 1864.

Boyd, Willis D. "James Redpath and American Negro Colonization in Haiti, 1860–1862." *Americas* XII (October 1955), 169–82.

Braden, Waldo. *Abraham Lincoln, Public Speaker.* Baton Rouge: Louisiana State University Press, 1988.

Breiseth, Christopher. "Lincoln and Douglass: Another Debate." *Illinois State Historical Society Journal* 68 (1975), 9–26.

Brooks, Noah. *Mr. Lincoln's Washington: Selections from the Writings of Noah Brooks, Civil Correspondent.* P. J. Staudenraus, ed. South Brunswick, N.J.: T. Yoseloff, 1967.

Burchard, Peter. *One Gallant Rush.* New York: St. Martin's Press, 1965.

Burlingame, Michael. *The Inner World of Abraham Lincoln.* Urbana: University of Illinois Press, 1994.

Burlingame Michael, ed. *Lincoln Observed: Civil War Dispatches of Noah Brooks.* Baltimore: Johns Hopkins University Press, 1998.

Burlingame, Michael, and John R. Turner Ettlinger, eds. *Inside Lincoln's White House: The Complete Civil War Diary of John Hay.* Carbondale: Southern Illinois University Press, 1997.

Burns, Edward McNall. *The American Idea of Mission.* New Brunswick, N.J.: Rutgers University Press, 1957.

Carpenter, Francis B. *Six Months at the White House.* New York: Hurd & Houghton, 1866.

Carwardine, Richard. *Lincoln, Profile in Power.* London: Pearson, 2003.

Cary, Francine Curro, *Urban Odyssey: A Multicultural History of Washington, D.C.* Washington, D.C.: Smithsonian Institution Press, 1996.

Chaffin, Tom. *Pathfinder: John Charles Frémont and the Course of American Empire.* New York: Hill & Wang, 2002.

Chesnutt, Charles Waddell. *Frederick Douglass.* Mineola, N.Y.: Dover Publications, 2002.

Colaiaco, James A. *Frederick Douglass and the Fourth of July.* New York: Palgrave Macmillan, 2006.

Conway, Moncure Daniel. *Autobiography, Memories and Experiences.* New York: Houghton Mifflin, 1904.

Cornish, Dudley Taylor. *The Sable Arm: Black Troops in the Union Army, 1861–1865.* Lawrence: University of Kansas Press, 1956.

Cox, LaWanda. *Lincoln and Black Freedom: A Study in Presidential Leadership.* Columbia: University of South Carolina Press, 1982.

Croly, David Goodman, and George Wakeman. *Miscegenation: The Theory of the Blending of the Races, Applied to the White Man and Negro.* 1864. Upper Saddle River, N.J.: Literature House/Gregg Press, rpr. 1970.

Current, Richard N. *The Lincoln Nobody Knows.* New York: Hill & Wang, 1958, rpr. 1963.

Current, Richard N. *Speaking of Abraham Lincoln.* Urbana: University of Illinois Press, 1983.

Davis, Allison. *Leadership, Love, and Aggression.* San Diego: Harcourt Brace Jovanovich, 1983.

Davis, Reginald F. *Frederick Douglass: A Precursor of Liberation Theology.* Macon, Ga.: Mercer University Press, 2005.

Dennett, Tyler, ed. *Lincoln and the Civil War in the Diaries and Letters of John Hay.* New York: Dodd, Mead, 1939.

Dictionary of Wisconsin Biography. Madison: State Historical Society of Wisconsin, 1960.

Diedrich, Maria. *Love Across Color Lines: Ottilie Assing & Frederick Douglass.* New York: Hill & Wang, 1999.

Donald, David Herbert. *Charles Sumner and the Rights of Man.* New York: Alfred A. Knopf, 1970.

Donald, David Herbert. *Lincoln.* New York: Simon & Schuster, 1995.

Donald, David Herbert. *Lincoln Reconsidered.* New York: Alfred A. Knopf, 1956.

Douglass, Frederick. *Autobiographies: Narrative of the Life, My Bondage and My Freedom, Life and Times.* 1845, 1855, 1893. New York: Library of America, rpr. 1994.

Du Bois, W. E. B. *Writings.* New York: Library of America, 1986.

Eaton, John. *Grant, Lincoln and the Freedmen.* New York: Longmans, Green, 1907.

Emilio, Louis F. *History of the Fifty-Fourth Regiment of the Massachusetts Volunteer Infantry, 1863–1865.* Boston: 1894.

Epstein, Daniel Mark. *Lincoln and Whitman: Parallel Lives in Civil War Washington.* New York: Random House, 2004.

Fehrenbacher, Don E. *Lincoln.* 2 vols. New York: Library of America, 1989.

Fehrenbacher, Don E. *Lincoln in Text and Context.* Palo Alto, Calif.: Stanford University Press, 1987.

Fehrenbacher, Don E. *Prelude to Greatness.* Palo Alto, Calif.: Stanford University Press, 1962.

Fehrenbacher, Don E., and Virginia Fehrenbacher, eds. *Recollected Words of Abraham Lincoln.* Palo Alto, Calif.: Stanford University Press, 1996.

Foner, Eric. *Free Soil, Free Labor, Free Men: The Ideology of the Republican Party Before the Civil War.* New York: Oxford University Press, 1970.

Foner, Eric, and Olivia Mahoney. *A House Divided: America in the Age of Lincoln.* New York: W. W. Norton, 1990.

Foner, Philip S. *Frederick Douglass: A Biography.* New York: Citadel Press, 1964.

Foner, Philip S., ed. *Frederick Douglass: Selected Speeches and Writings.* Chicago: Lawrence Hill Books, 1999.

Foner, Philip S. *The Life and Writings of Frederick Douglass.* 4 vols. New York: International, 1950–1955.

Fornieri, Joseph R. *Abraham Lincoln's Political Faith.* DeKalb: Northern Illinois University Press, 2003.

Franklin, John Hope. *The Emancipation Proclamation.* Garden City, N.Y.: Doubleday, 1963.

Frederickson, George. "A Man but Not a Brother: Abraham Lincoln and Racial Equality." *Journal of Southern History* (1975).

Furgurson, Ernest B. *Freedom Rising: Washington in the Civil War.* New York: Alfred A. Knopf, 2004.

Gerteis, Louis S. *From Contraband to Freedman: Federal Policy Toward Southern Blacks, 1861–1865.* Westport, Conn.: Greenwood Press, 1973.

Gienapp, William E. *Abraham Lincoln and Civil War America: A Biography.* Oxford: Oxford University Press, 2002.

Glatthaar, Joseph T. *Forged in Battle: The Civil War Alliance of Black Soldiers and White Officers.* New York: Free Press, 1989.

Goldstein, Leslie Friedman. "Violence as an Instrument for Social Change: The Views of Frederick Douglass (1817–1895)." *Journal of Negro History* 61, no. 1 (Jan. 1976), pp. 61–72.

Goodwin, Doris Kearns. *Team of Rivals: The Political Genius of Abraham Lincoln.* New York: Simon & Schuster, 2005.

Gregory, James M. *Frederick Douglass, the Orator.* New York: Apollo Editions, 1971.

Guelzo, Allen. *Abraham Lincoln: Redeemer President.* Grand Rapids, Mich.: Eerdmans, 1999.

Guelzo, Allen. *Lincoln's Emancipation Proclamation: The End of Slavery in America.* New York: Simon & Schuster, 2004.

Hanmer-Croughton, Amy. "Anti-Slavery Days in Rochester." *Publications of the Rochester Historical Society* XVI (1936).

Harris, William C. *Lincoln's Last Months.* Cambridge, Mass.: Belknap Press of Harvard University Press, 2004.

Harris, William C. *With Charity for All: Lincoln and the Restoration of the Union.* Lexington: University Press of Kentucky, 1997.

Heller, Charles. *Portrait of an Abolitionist: A Biography of George Luther Stearns.* Westport, Conn.: Greenwood Press, l996.

Herndon, William Henry, and Jesse W. Weik. *Herndon's Lincoln: The True Story of a Great Life.* 2 vols. New York: D. Appleton, l892.

Hertz, Emanuel. *The Hidden Lincoln.* New York: Viking, 1938.

Hilyer, Andrew, ed. *The Twentieth Century Union League Directory.* Washington, D.C.: Union League, 1901.

Holzer, Harold, ed., *Lincoln as I Knew Him: Gossip, Tributes, and Revelations from His Best Friends and Worst Enemies.* Chapel Hill, N.C.: Algonquin Books, 1999.

Holzer, Harold. *Lincoln at Cooper Union: The Speech That Made Abraham Lincoln President.* New York: Simon & Schuster, 2004.

Holzer, Harold. *Lincoln Seen and Heard.* Lawrence: University Press of Kansas, 2000.

Howard-Pitney, David. *The Afro-American Jeremiad: Appeals for Justice in America.* Philadelphia: Temple University Press, 1990.

Hubbard, Charles M. *Lincoln and His Contemporaries*. Macon, Ga.: Mercer University Press, 1999.

Huggins, Nathan Irvin. *Slave and Citizen: The Life of Frederick Douglass*. Boston: Little, Brown, 1980.

In Memoriam Frederick Douglass. Philadelphia: John C. Yorston, 1897.

Jaffa, Harry V. *A New Birth of Freedom: Abraham Lincoln and the Coming of the Civil War*. Lanham, Md.: Rowman & Littlefield, 2000.

Jaffa, Harry V. *Crisis of the House Divided: An Interpretation of the Lincoln-Douglas Debates*. Chicago: University of Chicago Press, 1959.

Johannsen, Robert W., ed. *The Lincoln-Douglas Debates*, 1858. New York: Oxford University Press, 1965.

Johannsen, Robert W. *Lincoln, the South and Slavery: The Political Dimension*. Baton Rouge: Louisiana State University Press, 1991.

Johannsen, Robert W. *Stephen A. Douglas*. Urbana: University of Illinois Press, 1997.

Johnson, Michael P., ed. *Abraham Lincoln, Slavery, and the Civil War: Selected Writings and Speeches*. Boston: Bedford-St. Martin's, 2001.

Jones, Howard. *Abraham Lincoln and a New Birth of Freedom: The Union and Slavery in the Diplomacy of the Civil War*. Lincoln: University of Nebraska Press, 1999.

Julian, George W. *Political Recollections*. Chicago: McClurg, 1884.

Kachun, Mitch. *Festivals of Freedom: Memory and Meaning in African American Emancipation Celebrations, 1808–1915*. Amherst: University of Massachusetts Press, 2003.

Keckley, Elizabeth. *Behind the Scenes: Thirty Years a Slave, and Four Years in the White House*, ed. Frances Smith Foster. Urbana: University of Illinois Press, 2001.

Klingaman, William K. *Abraham Lincoln and the Road to Emancipation, 1861–1865*. New York: Viking, 2001.

Kunhardt Jr., Phillip, Phillip Kunhardt III, and Peter Kunhardt. *Lincoln*. New York: Alfred A. Knopf, 1992.

Lamon, Ward Hill. *The Life of Abraham Lincoln: From His Birth to His Inauguration as President*. Lincoln: University of Nebraska Press, rpr. 1999.

Lampe, George P. *Frederick Douglass: Freedom's Voice, 1818–1845*. East Lansing: Michigan State University Press, 1998.

Lawson, Bill E., and Frank M. Kirkland, eds. *Frederick Douglass: A Critical Reader*. Malden, Mass.: Blackwell, 1999.

Leech, Margaret. *Reveille in Washington: 1860–1865*. New York: Harper & Brothers, 1941.

Levine, Robert S. *Martin Delany, Frederick Douglass, and the Politics of Representative Identity*. Chapel Hill: University of North Carolina Press, 1997.

Lind, Michael. *What Lincoln Believed: The Values and Convictions of America's Greatest President*. New York: Doubleday, 2005.

Lohmann, Christoph, ed. *Radical Passion: Ottilie Assing's Reports from America and Letters to Frederick Douglass*. New York: Peter Lang, 2000.

Long, David. *Black Writers and the American Civil War*. Secaucus, N.J.: Blue and Gray Press, 1998.

Long, David. *The Jewell of Liberty*. New York: Da Capo Press, 1997.

Mabee, Carleton. *Black Freedom: The Nonviolent Abolitionists from 1830 Through the Civil War*. London: Collier-Macmillan, 1970.

Mahin, Dean B. *One War at a Time: The International Dimensions of the American Civil War.* Washington, D.C.: Brassey's, 1999.

Martin, Waldo E., Jr. *The Mind of Frederick Douglass.* Chapel Hill: University of North Carolina Press, 1985.

McFeely, William S. *Frederick Douglass.* New York: W. W. Norton, 1991.

McGuire, Horace. "Two Episodes of Anti-Slavery History," read before Rochester Historical Society, 10/27/1916.

McKelvey, Blake. "Lights and Shadows in Local Negro History." *Rochester History* XXI, 4 (Oct. 1959).

McKelvey, Blake. *Rochester, the Flower City: 1855–1890.* Cambridge, Mass.: Harvard University Press, 1949.

McKelvey, Blake. *Rochester on the Genesee: The Growth of a City.* Syracuse: Syracuse University Press, 1973.

McPherson, James. *Abraham Lincoln and the Second American Revolution.* New York: Oxford University Press, 1990.

McPherson, James. *Drawn with the Sword.* New York: Oxford University Press, 1996.

McPherson, James. *The Negro's Civil War: How American Negroes Felt and Acted During the War for the Union.* New York: Vintage Books, 1965.

McPherson, James M., ed. *"We Cannot Escape History": Lincoln and the Last Best Hope of Earth.* Urbana: University of Illinois Press, 1995.

Mellon, James. *The Face of Lincoln.* New York: Bonanza Books, 1979.

Miers, Earl S., ed. *Lincoln Day by Day: A Chronology, 1809–1865.* Washington, D.C.: Lincoln Sesquicentennial Commission, 1960.

Miller, Douglas T. *Frederick Douglass and the Fight for Freedom.* New York: Facts on File, 1988.

Miller, Edward A., Jr. *Lincoln's Abolitionist General: The Biography of David Hunter.* Columbia: University of South Carolina Press, 1997.

Miller, William Lee. *Lincoln's Virtues: An Ethical Biography.* New York: Alfred A. Knopf, 2002.

Milton, George Fort. *The Age of Hate: Andrew Johnson and the Radicals.* New York: Coward-McCann, 1930.

Moses, Wilson Jeremiah. *Creative Conflict in African American Thought: Frederick Douglass, Alexander Crummell, Booker T. Washington, W. E. B. Du Bois, and Marcus Garvey.* Cambridge: Cambridge University Press, 2004.

Neely, Mark E., Jr. "Abraham Lincoln and Black Colonization, Benjamin Butler's Spurious Testimony." *Civil War History* XXV (Jan. 1979), 77–83.

Neely, Mark E., Jr. *The Abraham Lincoln Encyclopedia.* New York: Da Capo Press, 1982.

Neely, Mark E., Jr. *The Last Best Hope of Earth: Abraham Lincoln and the Promise of America.* Cambridge, Mass.: Harvard University Press, 1993.

Nelson, Larry E. "Black Leaders and the Presidential Election of 1864." *Journal of Negro History* (Jan. 1978), 42–58.

Nevins, Allan. *The Emergence of Lincoln.* New York: Charles Scribner's Sons, 1950.

Nicolay, John G., and John Hay. *Abraham Lincoln: A History.* 10 vols. New York: Century, 1890.

Nicolay, John G., and John Hay. *Complete Works of Abraham Lincoln.* 2 vols. New York: Century, 1894.

Oates, Stephen B. *The Man Behind the Myth.* New York: Harper & Row, 1984.

Oates, Stephen B. *With Malice Toward None: The Life of Abraham Lincoln.* New York: Harper & Row, rpr. 1994.

Official Proceedings of the Democratic National Convention Held in 1864 at Chicago. Chicago: Times Steam Book and Job Printing House, 1864.

Oration of Frederick Douglass Delivered on the Occasion of the Unveiling of the Freedman's Monument in Memory of Abraham Lincoln, in Lincoln Park, Washington, D.C., April 14th, 1876; with an Appendix. Washington, D.C.: 1876.

Packard, Jerrold M. *The Lincolns in the White House: Four Years That Shattered a Family.* New York: St. Martin's Press, 2005.

Palmer, Erwin. "A Partnership in the Abolition Movement." *University of Rochester Library Bulletin* 26 (1970–71), 1–19.

Paludan, Phillip Shaw. *The Presidency of Abraham Lincoln.* Lawrence: University of Kansas Press, 1994.

Pasternak, Martin B. *Rise Now and Fly to Arms: The Life of Henry Highland Garnet.* New York: Garland Publishing, 1995.

Payne, Daniel Alexander. *Recollections of Seventy Years.* Nashville: A. M. E. Sunday School Union, 1888.

Peterson, Merrill. *Lincoln in American Memory.* New York: Oxford University Press, 1994.

Phelps, Mary Merwin. *Kate Chase: Dominant Daughter: The Life Story of a Brilliant Woman and Her Famous Father.* New York: Thomas Y. Crowell, 1935.

Phillips, Christopher. *Freedom's Port: The African American Community of Baltimore, 1790–1860.* Urbana: University of Illinois Press, 1997.

Pinsker, Matthew. *Lincoln's Sanctuary: Abraham Lincoln and the Soldiers' Home.* Oxford: Oxford University Press, 2003.

Preston, Dickson J. *Young Frederick Douglass: The Maryland Years.* Baltimore: Johns Hopkins University Press, 1980.

Proceedings of the National Convention of Colored Men, held in the city of Syracuse, N.Y., October 4, 5, 6, and 7, 1864; with the bill of wrongs and rights, and the address to the American people. Boston: J. S. Rock and G. L. Ruffin, 1864.

Quarles, Benjamin. *Frederick Douglass.* New York: Da Capo Press, rpr. 1997.

Quarles, Benjamin, ed. *Frederick Douglass: Great Lives Observed.* Englewood Cliffs, N.J.: Prentice-Hall, 1968.

Quarles, Benjamin. *Lincoln and the Negro.* Oxford: Oxford University Press, 1962.

Radford, Victoria. *Meeting Mr. Lincoln: Firsthand Recollections of Abraham Lincoln by People, Great and Small, Who Met the President.* Chicago: Ivan R. Dee, 1998.

Randall, J. G. *Lincoln: The Liberal Statesman.* New York: Dodd, Mead, 1947.

Redkey, Edwin. *A Grand Army of Black Men: Letters from African-American Soldiers in the Union Army, 1861–1865.* Cambridge: Cambridge University Press, 1992.

Rice, Allen Thorndike. *Reminiscences of Abraham Lincoln by Distinguished Men of His Time.* New York: North American Review, 1888.

Robinson, Armstead L. *Bitter Fruits of Bondage: The Demise of Slavery and the Collapse of the Confederacy, 1861–1865.* Charlottesville: University of Virginia Press, 2005.

Rogers, William B. *"We Are All Together Now": Frederick Douglass, William Lloyd Garrison, and the Prophetic Tradition.* New York: Garland Publishing, 1995.

Rosenberg-Naparsteck, Ruth. "A Growing Agitation: Rochester Before, During and After the Civil War." *Rochester History* XLVI (Jan.–Apr., 1984), 2–39.

Rozett, John M. "Racism and Republican Emergence in Illinois, 1848–1860: A Re-Evaluation of Republican Negrophobia." *Civil War History* 22 (June 1976), 101–15.

Scheips, Paul J. "Lincoln and the Chiriquí Colonization Project." *Journal of Negro History* 37, no. 4 (Oct. 1952), 418–53.

Schwartz, Barry. *Abraham Lincoln and the Forge of National Memory*. Chicago: University of Chicago Press, 2000.

Simon, James. *Lincoln and Chief Justice Taney*. New York: Simon & Schuster, 2006.

Smith, George Winston, and Charles Judah. *Life in the North During the Civil War: A Source History*. Albuquerque: University of New Mexico Press, 1966.

Sprague, Rosetta Douglass. "Anna Murray Douglass: My Mother As I Recall Her." Delivered before the Anna Murray Douglass Union W.C.T.U., May 10, 1900, rpr. Washington, D.C., 1923.

Stamp, Kenneth, ed. *The Causes of the Civil War*. New York: Simon & Schuster, 1986.

Stauffer, John. *The Black Hearts of Men: Radical Abolitionists and the Transformation of Race*. Cambridge, Mass.: Harvard University Press, 2002.

Steers, Edward, Jr. *Blood on the Moon: The Assassination of Abraham Lincoln*. Lexington: University Press of Kentucky, 2001.

Stoddard, William O. *Inside the White House in War Times: Memories and Reports of Lincoln's Secretary*. Lincoln: University of Nebraska Press, 1980.

Striner, Richard. *Father Abraham: Lincoln's Relentless Struggle to End Slavery*. Oxford: Oxford University Press, 2006.

Strong, George Templeton. *The Diary of George Templeton Strong: The Civil War, 1860–1865*. Allan Nevins and Milton Halsey Thomas, eds. New York: Macmillan, 1954.

Sundquist, Eric J. *Frederick Douglass: New Literary and Historical Essays*. Cambridge: Cambridge University Press, 1990.

Tackard, James. *Lincoln's Moral Vision*. Jackson: University Press of Mississippi, 2002.

Tarbell, Ida. *The Life of Abraham Lincoln*. 2 vols. New York: Lincoln Memorial Association, 1900.

Thomas, Benjamin. *Abraham Lincoln*. New York: Alfred A. Knopf, 1952.

Thomas, Benjamin, and Harold M. Hyman. *Stanton: The Life and Times of Lincoln's Secretary of War*. New York: Alfred A. Knopf, 1962.

Toplin, Robert, ed. *Ken Burns's The Civil War*. New York: Oxford University Press, 1996.

Trefousse, Hans L. *Lincoln's Decision for Emancipation*. Philadelphia: Lippincott, 1975.

Trefousse, Hans L. *The Radical Republicans: Lincoln's Vanguard for Racial Justice*. New York: Alfred A. Knopf, 1969.

Trudeau, Andre. *Like Men of War: Black Troops in the Civil War, 1862–1865*. New York: Little, Brown, 1998.

Vaughan, Alden T., ed. *The Puritan Tradition in America, 1620–1730* (rev. ed.). Hanover, N.H.: University Press of New England, 1972.

Vorenberg, Michael. "Abraham Lincoln and the Politics of Black Colonization," *Journal of the Abraham Lincoln Association* 14 (Summer 1993), 23–45.

Vorenberg, Michael. *Final Freedom: The Civil War, the Abolition of Slavery, and the Thirteenth Amendment*. New York: Cambridge University Press, 2001.

Voss, Frederick S. *Majestic in His Wrath: A Pictorial Life of Frederick Douglass*. Washington, D.C.: Smithsonian Institution Press, 1995.

Walker, Peter. *Moral Choices: Memory, Desire, and Imagination in Nineteenth Century American Abolition.* Baton Rouge: Louisiana State University Press, 1978.

Ward, Andrew. *River Run Red: The Fort Pillow Massacre in the American Civil War.* New York: Viking, 2005.

Washington, Booker T. *Frederick Douglass.* Philadelphia: George W. Jacobs, 1906.

Washington, James, ed. *A Testament of Hope: Essential Writings of Martin Luther King, Jr.* San Francisco: Harper & Row, 1986.

Waugh, John C. *Reelecting Lincoln: The Battle for the 1864 Presidency.* New York: Crown, 1997.

White, Ronald C., Jr. *The Eloquent President: A Portrait of Lincoln Through His Words.* New York: Random House, 2005.

White, Ronald C., Jr. *Lincoln's Greatest Speech: The Second Inaugural.* New York: Simon & Schuster, 2002.

Wilson, Douglas, and Rodney O. Davis, eds. *Herndon's Informants.* Urbana: University of Illinois Press, 1998.

Williams, T. Harry. *Lincoln and the Radicals.* Madison: University of Wisconsin Press, 1941.

Wills, Garry. *Lincoln at Gettysburg: The Words That Remade America.* New York: Simon & Schuster, 1992.

Wilson, Rufus Rockwell, ed. *Lincoln Among His Friends: A Sheaf of Intimate Memories.* Caldwell, Id.: Caxton Printers, 1942.

Wilson, Rufus Rockwell, ed. *Lincoln in Caricature.* New York: Horizon Press, 1953.

Wright, John S. *Lincoln and the Politics of Slavery.* Reno: University of Nevada Press, 1970.

Wu, Jin-Ping. *Frederick Douglass and the Black Liberation Movement: The North Star of American Blacks.* New York: Garland, 2000.

Zall, Paul. M., ed. *Abe Lincoln Laughing: Humorous Anecdotes from Original Sources by and about Abraham Lincoln.* Knoxville: University of Tennessee Press, 1995.

Zall, Paul. M., ed. *Lincoln on Lincoln.* Lexington: University of Kentucky Press, 1999.

Note: The publication of James Oakes's *The Radical and the Republican* (New York: Norton, 2007) was too late for the book to be consulted in the writing of *Douglass and Lincoln,* but we note it as a useful reference for readers.

NEWSPAPERS AND PERIODICALS

Belvidere Standard
Boston Daily Journal
Chicago Tribune
Cincinnati Enquirer
Daily Morning Chronicle
Daily National Intelligencer
Daily National Republican
Dixon Republican and Telegraph
Douglass Monthly
Frederick Douglass' Paper
Freeport Journal

Galesburg Democrat
Illinois Daily Journal
The Independent
The Liberator
London Inquirer
London Spectator
Mendota Press Observer
National Anti-Slavery Standard
New National Era
New York Herald
New York Times
New York Tribune
The North Star
Peoria Daily Transcript
Rochester Democrat and American
Rochester Democrat and Chronicle
Rochester Union and Advertiser
Syracuse Daily Courier and Union
Syracuse Journal

MANUSCRIPT COLLECTIONS

Abraham Lincoln Presidential Library, Springfield, Illinois
Amistad Research Center, New Orleans, Louisiana
Boston Public Library
    William Lloyd Garrison Papers
Buffalo and Erie County Public Library
Connecticut State Library, Hartford, Connecticut
    Thomson-Kenney Collection
Cornell University
    Anti-Slavery Papers
Houghton Library, Harvard University
    Charles Sumner Papers
Library of Congress, Washington, D.C.
    Abraham Lincoln Papers
    Frederick Douglass Papers
    Lyman Trumbull Papers
    Salmon Chase Papers
Lincoln Museum, Fort Wayne, Indiana
Maryland Historical Society
    Maryland Colonization Society Papers
Moorland-Spingarn Research Center, Howard University, Washington, D.C.
    Frederick Douglass Collection
National Archives Building, Washington, D.C.
    Records of the Adjutant General's Office
    Records of the Veterans Administration

New-York Historical Society
    Frederick Douglass Papers
Pennsylvania Historical Society, Philadelphia, Pennsylvania
    Gratz Collection
    Abraham Barder Papers
Syracuse University Library, Syracuse, New York
    Gerrit Smith Papers
University of Rochester
    Amy Post Papers
Yale University
    Frederick Douglass Papers

Index

Note: Page numbers in *italics* refer to illustrations.

A Note on the Authors

Paul Kendrick and Stephen Kendrick are coauthors of *Sarah's Long Walk: The Free Blacks of Boston and How Their Struggle for Equality Changed America*, named one of the five best history books of 2005 by the *Christian Science Monitor*. Paul is an assistant director of the Harlem Children's Zone in New York City and was previously a Presidential Administrative Fellow at the George Washington University. Stephen is senior minister of First Church in Boston and the author of *Holy Clues: The Gospel According to Sherlock Holmes* and *Night Watch*, a novel.